IMAGES
of America

Historic Homes of Northeast Tennessee

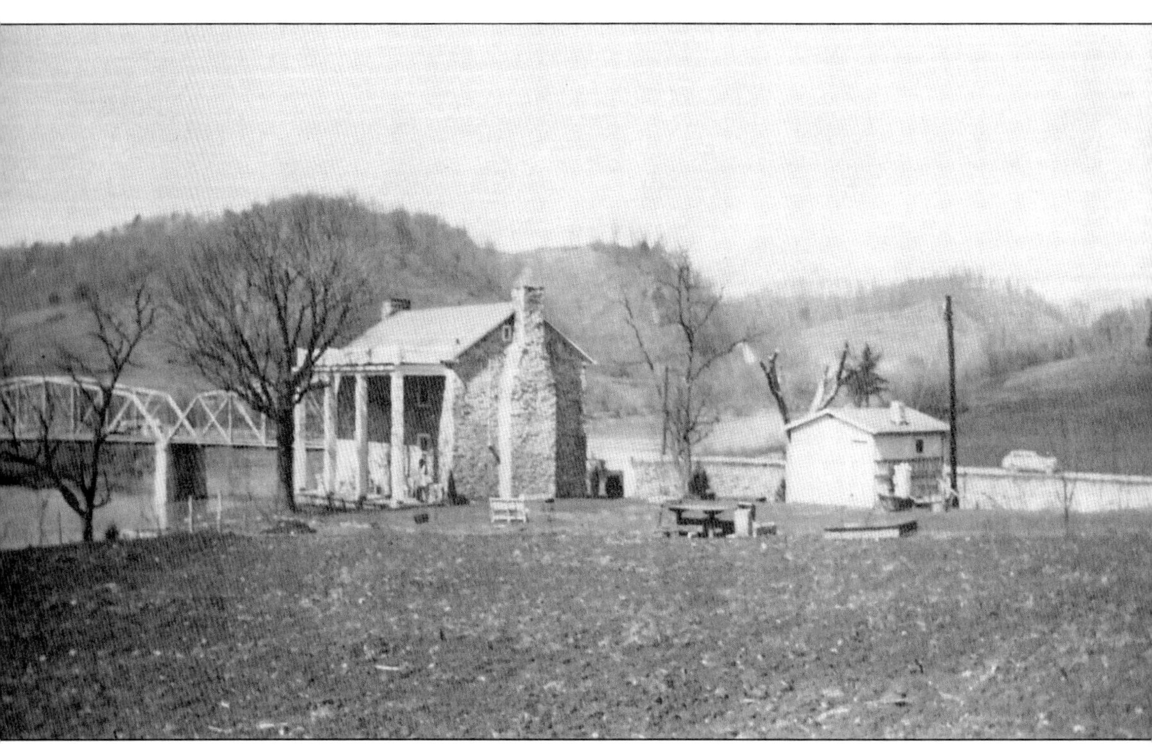

Wills Stone House. A number of stone houses were built in Northeast Tennessee during the late 18th and early 19th centuries. The Wills-Dickey House was constructed of cut stone along the North Fork Holston River in the Carter's Valley community of Sullivan County. It was built about 1790 by Jacob and Mary Wills. (Courtesy of the City of Kingsport Archives.)

On the Cover: Christopher Taylor House: Taken prior to the 1930s, this photograph of the Christopher Taylor House was made decades before the structure was relocated to downtown Jonesborough. It was built during the late 18th century just outside of town. Andrew Jackson lived at the house before he was elected president. The home was moved to Main Street in 1974. (Courtesy of the Tennessee State Library and Archives.)

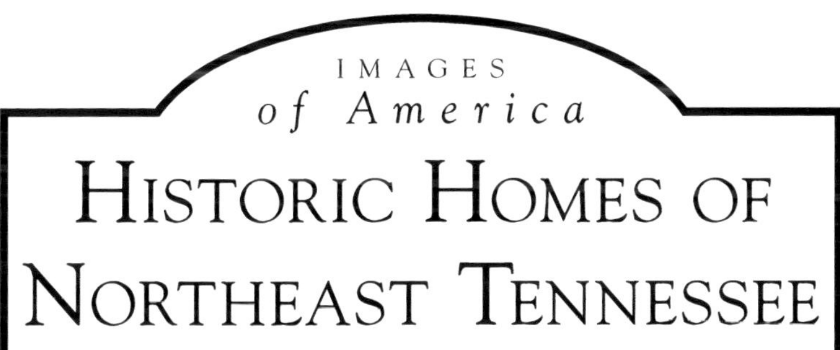

Robert Sorrell

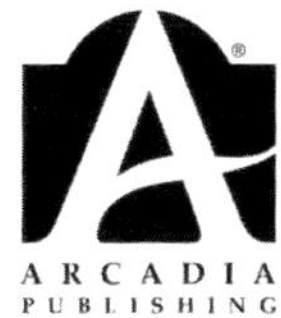

ISBN 978-1-4671-1707-4

Published by Arcadia Publishing
Charleston, South Carolina

Printed in the United States of America

Library of Congress Control Number: 2016930621

For all general information, please contact Arcadia Publishing:
Telephone 843-853-2070
Fax 843-853-0044
E-mail sales@arcadiapublishing.com
For customer service and orders:
Toll-Free 1-888-313-2665

Visit us on the Internet at www.arcadiapublishing.com

For my family and friends, who have supported me during this project

Contents

ACKNOWLEDGMENTS

This book would not have been possible without the extraordinary help from the outstanding people of Northeast Tennessee. First of all, I would like to thank my family and friends, who have supported me throughout this project.

I would also like to thank the many archivists, historians, and residents who call the region home. I want to thank the wonderful staffs at the City of Kingsport Archives, Archives of Appalachia, Milligan College, Tusculum College, the Bristol Historical Association, Rogersville Heritage Association, Rocky Mount Historical Association, Tipton-Haynes State Historic Site, Tennessee State Library and Archives, Tennessee Historical Commission, National Register of Historic Places, the Greeneville Greene County History Museum, and the Heritage Alliance of Jonesborough. I also want to thank the many individuals who helped me along the way, including Callie Ruble, Patrick Stern, Brenda Dodson, Patsy Green, Robert White III, Doug Ledbetter, Scott Bowers, Tom Vaughan, Elizabeth Smith, Kathy Serago, Mary Ann Hager, and Connie Landreth.

Introduction

Welcome to Northeast Tennessee, a region of quiet, charming communities and bustling urban centers, nestled in the foothills of the southern Appalachian Mountains. This is a guidebook to these communities, with particular interest in the historic homes that make up the urban and rural landscape.

Readers may be surprised by the homes featured within this book, showcasing an array of residences, some up to 300 years old. While many are simple, smaller residences, others are magnificent mansions and estates. This book is not prejudiced to one type of home. There are mansions, log cabins, urban row houses, apartment complexes, and homes of brick, stone, and wood. There are some homes with just one room and some with 20 to 30 rooms. There are some homes that welcome visitors with art, history, and brilliant architecture, and others are hidden away, tucked behind private fences and old trees.

The oldest homes in this book were built during the early days of Tennessee settlement, in the mid- to late 1700s. Colonists from the East Coast had begun settling west of the Appalachian Mountains, primarily along the Holston, Nolichucky, and Watauga Rivers.

In 1772, settlers along the Watauga River developed the Watauga Association, which is considered by historians to be the first constitutional government in North America, in present-day Elizabethton. A few homes and a fort were constructed.

The people living in Northeast Tennessee were violating British law, which prohibited colonists from settling west of the Appalachian Mountains. In 1775, the Watauga Association reorganized as the Washington District, as the colonies headed for war against the British government. During the Revolutionary War, a number of men from Tennessee and Virginia crossed the mountains to fight at Kings Mountain, South Carolina, which was a definitive American victory.

One of the early Watauga settlers, John Carter, and his son Landon Carter built a home about 1780. The Carter Mansion, which is considered to be the oldest frame home in the state of Tennessee, has been completely restored and is now part of Sycamore Shoals State Historic Area. Sabine Hill, another early Watauga settlement home, is also owned by the state. Historians and architects have restored the home to its heyday, when Gen. Nathaniel Taylor constructed the home in the early 1800s.

Another early settler, George Gillespie, contracted stonemason Seth Smith in 1792 to build a sturdy, fort-like home along Big Limestone Creek in Washington County, near the Nolichucky River. Smith designed and built a number of houses in present-day Greene and Washington Counties. Gillespie's home is an immaculate and imposing structure, built of locally procured stone. Like many homes in the region, Gillespie's house is listed in the National Register of Historic Places.

After the Revolutionary War and American independence, area residents were practically abandoned by North Carolina, which claimed the land west of the mountains. Residents created the state of Franklin in 1784 and sought official recognition. They used the name Franklin to honor Benjamin Franklin. The unofficial state lasted for about five years, before the area became known as the Southwest Territory.

Pres. George Washington appointed William Blount as territorial governor. Blount and his family regularly visited the home of the Cobbs in present-day Piney Flats. The house, now the site of the Rocky Mount State Historic Site, was constructed sometime between 1770 and 1772.

In 1796, Congress approved the admission of Tennessee as the 16th state of the Union. The borders were drawn by extending the northern and southern borders of North Carolina to the Mississippi River. A few towns in Northeast Tennessee had already begun to grow by the time the state was founded, including Greeneville, Jonesborough, and Rogersville. By the time the Civil War began in 1861, a number of homes had been built in the region.

Pres. Andrew Johnson lived in Greeneville. His homes now comprise the Andrew Johnson National Historic Site. There were also many Confederate supporters in the region. In many cases, neighbors, family members, business partners, and friends, supported differing sides. For example, Maj. Henderson Folsom fought for the Confederacy. He lived in a large home on present-day Elk Avenue in Elizabethton. His neighbor, Samuel P. Carter, who lived across the street in another large colonial home, fought for the Union. A number of battles were fought in the region during the war, including at Blountville, Limestone, and Blue Springs. Many homes still standing today in the region were used as military hospitals and headquarters for Union or Confederate armies.

After the war, the area saw growth with the development of the railroad. Agricultural enterprises flourished and industry developed throughout the rest of the 19th and early 20th centuries. Farming has always been one of the most important industries in the region, and a number of families have thrived in rural Northeast Tennessee.

The Earnest family was likely one of the wealthiest farming families. They lived along the Nolichucky River in the present-day Chuckey community of Greene County. Early settler Henry Earnest acquired the property in the 18th century. He quickly cultivated the land and built shelter for his family. The Earnest Farms Historic District now features the Mauris-Earnest Fort House, one of the oldest extant structures in the region. It was built around 1780 and was used by local settlers for protection from Indian attacks. The district also includes the main Earnest farmhouse, which was built in 1800 and expanded to its present design in the 1820s. The Earnest-Broyles House, an 1820s-era residence on Sandbar Road, and the Jim Earnest Home, an 1880s-era residence on Earnest Road, are also recognized in the district.

A number of century farms, or properties owned by one family for at least 100 years, can be found throughout Northeast Tennessee, including the Earnest farm, the Massengill farm in Sullivan County, and the Squibb farm in Washington County.

While farming has been the dominant industry in the region, a number of companies have also provided employment for people. The early 1900s brought many factories to Northeast Tennessee, including German-owned rayon factories in Elizabethton, the Eastman Kodak Company and Mead Corporation in Kingsport, and Blue Ridge Pottery in Erwin. Each new facility brought thousands of new residents to the area and large housing developments. Montrose Court Apartments and the Tree Streets neighborhood of Johnson City; the Shelby Street Row Houses, Borden neighborhood, and the Dobyns Addition in Kingsport; and Pottery Houses of Erwin were all the result of industrial growth in the region.

During the late 1800s and early 1900s, industry and community leaders like J. Fred Johnson, Perley Wilcox, and John B. Dennis of Kingsport; Samuel Cole Williams and Thaddeus Cox of Johnson City; and the Reynolds brothers of Bristol lived in large, luxurious residences.

The architecture of Northeast Tennessee is deeply rooted in the history of those who settled and developed the land. Residents built and moved into an array of home styles. Many of their homes are featured in this book. While landmark homes, such as the Johnson homes in Greeneville and Carter Mansion in Elizabethton, are included, there are also lesser-known residences like Long Shadows in Bluff City and Maymead in Mountain City. A number of homes that have been demolished or abandoned are also featured.

One

Bristol, Bluff City, and Piney Flats

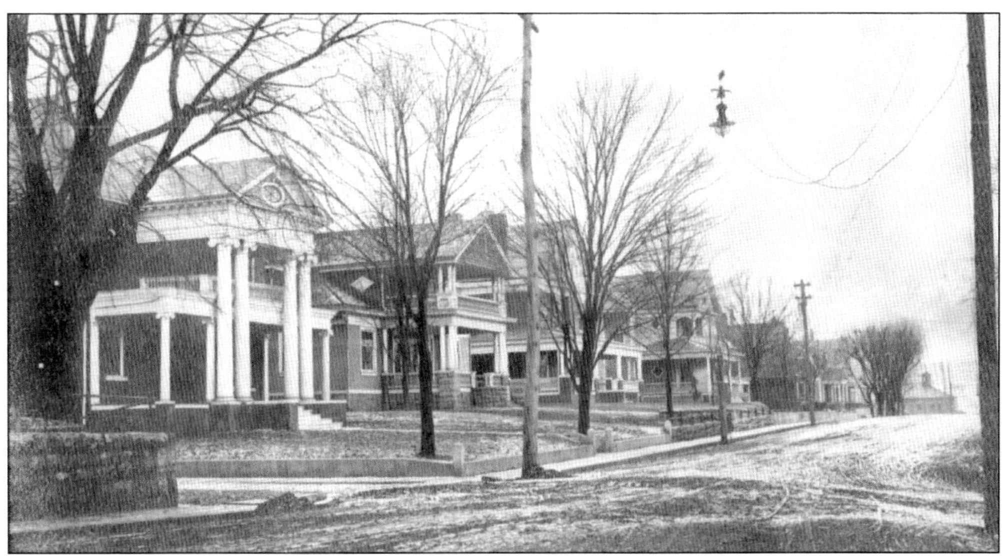

Holston Avenue. Some of Bristol's most beautiful homes were constructed along Holston Avenue. The avenue, now a nationally recognized historic district, is comprised of 132 buildings. Residences in the neighborhood date from 1900 to the 1960s. Bungalows and Colonial Revival styles predominate in the district, although there are examples of other styles, such as Tudor Revival and Queen Anne. (Courtesy of the Tennessee State Library and Archives.)

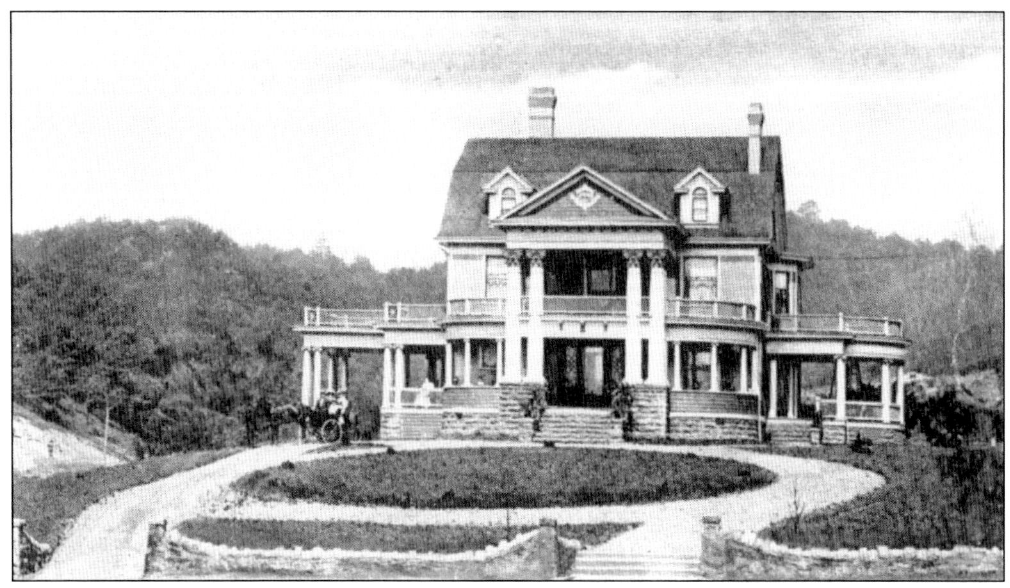

MASSENGILL MANSION. This stately mansion, which still stands at 920 Holston Avenue in Bristol, was built in 1910 for Dr. Samuel E. Massengill. The home's foundation was made of stone blocks that are believed to have weighed 2,000 pounds each. Massengill started a drug manufacturing company in Bristol. (Courtesy of George Stone.)

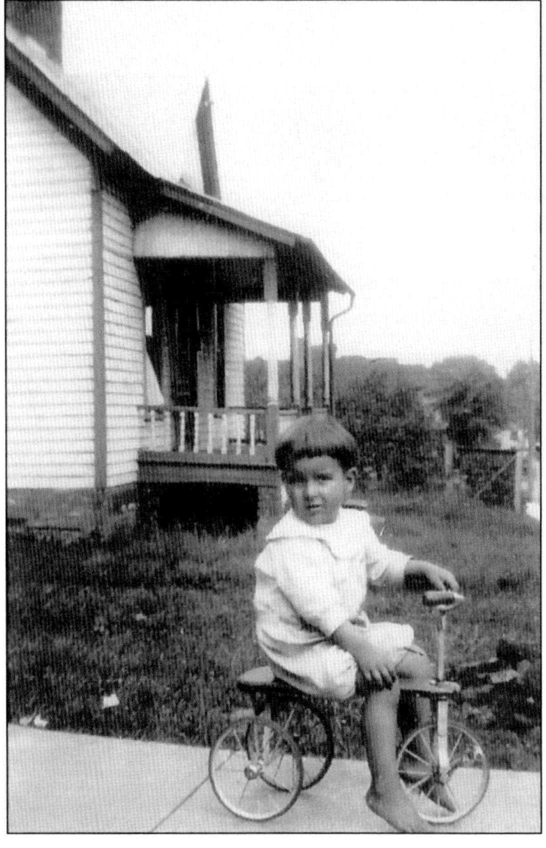

ERNIE FORD HOUSE. Country music legend Tennessee Ernie Ford, best known for the song "Sixteen Tons," was born in this Bristol home in 1919. The home, located on Anderson Street, has been restored by the historical association. It features two fireplaces, pine floors, white clapboard siding, and rooms that appear as they did at the time Ford lived here. Ford is pictured riding a tricycle. (Courtesy of the Bristol Historical Association.)

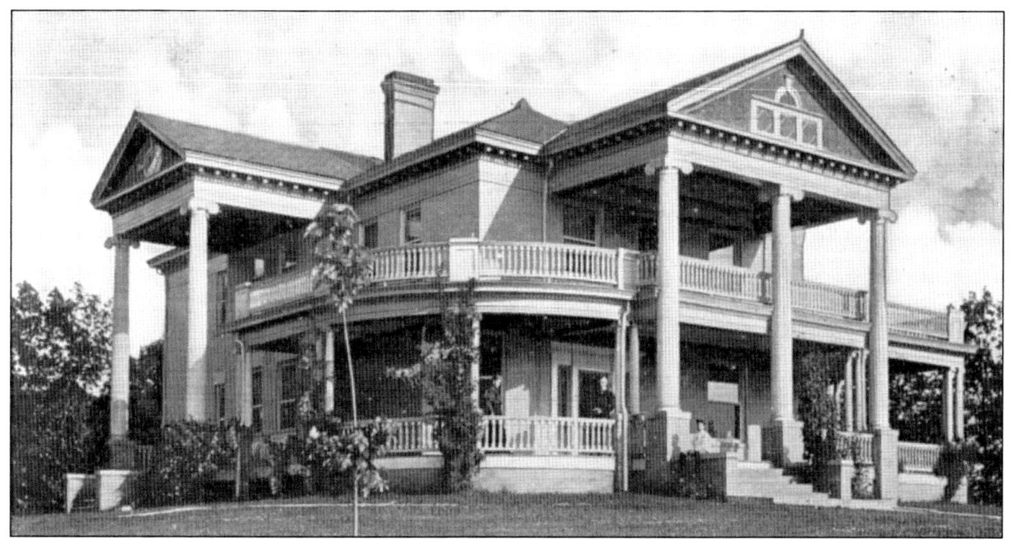

Fairmount. Col. J.M. Barker was an early developer in Bristol. His home in the Fairmount Historic District was built about 1904. It is at the site of the former Hotel Fairmount, which was built in 1889 but burned in 1901. Other developers of the hotel, brothers A.D. Reynolds and R.J. Reynolds, also built homes in the neighborhood, but both no longer exist. (Courtesy of George Stone.)

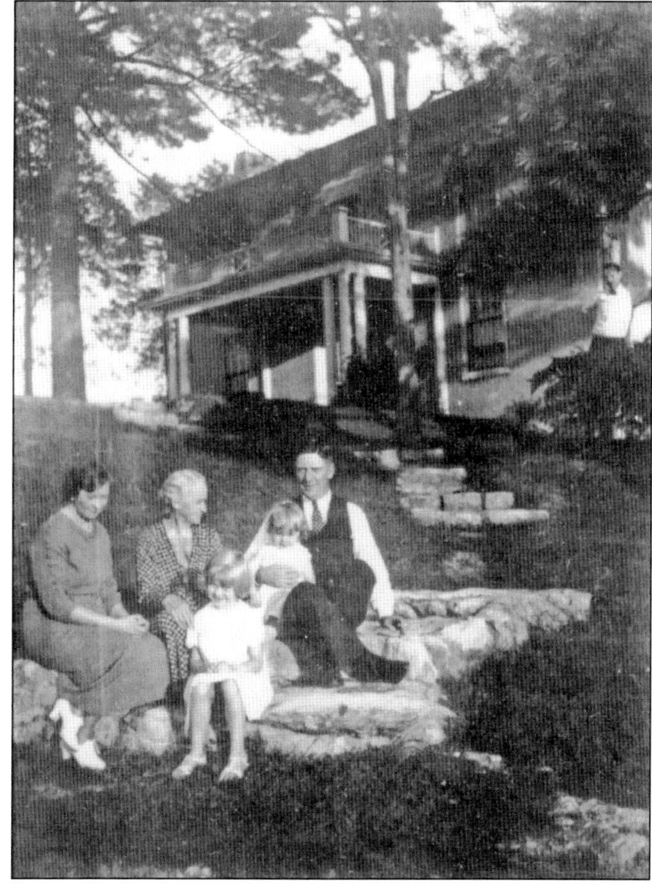

Hayter-Campbell Home. Likely built in the 1840s, this home was purchased by Abingdon tavern keeper John C. Hayter for his daughter Esther and her new husband, William, in 1851. The home was sold in 1903 to Judge Hal Haynes, and much of the land became the Haynesfield section of Bristol. Later owners included John York, Charles Lowry, and Robert F. White III. (Courtesy of Robert White.)

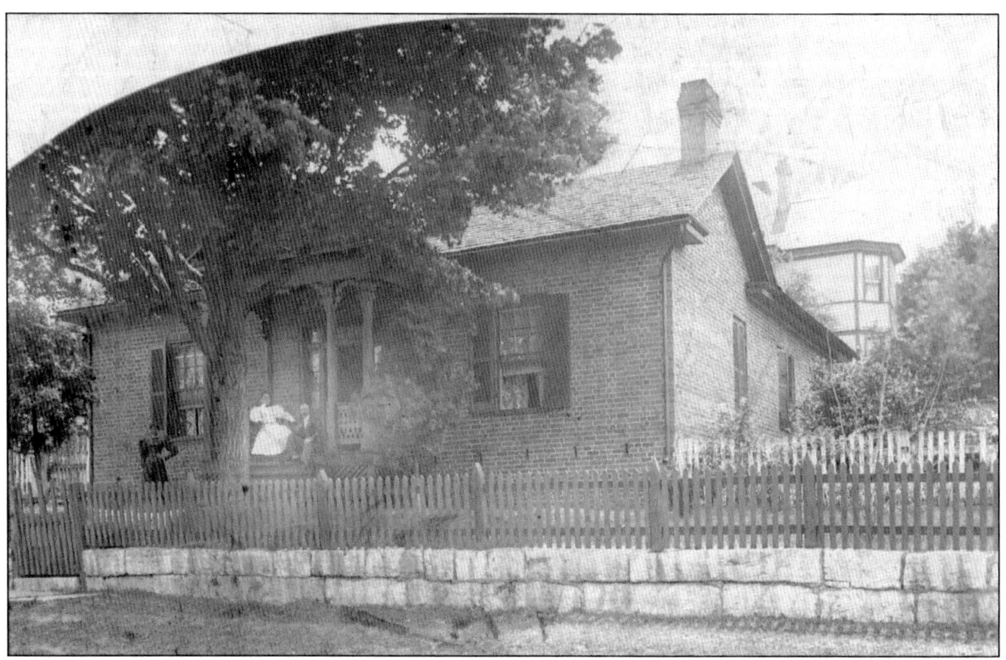

Crymble Home. Ellis K. Crymble's first home, located in Bristol, was built in the late 1800s. The family was related to Rev. James King, early owner of property that later became Bristol, through his youngest daughter, Charlotte "Chassie" King, who married Alfred Moore Carter of Carter County. (Courtesy of Robert White.)

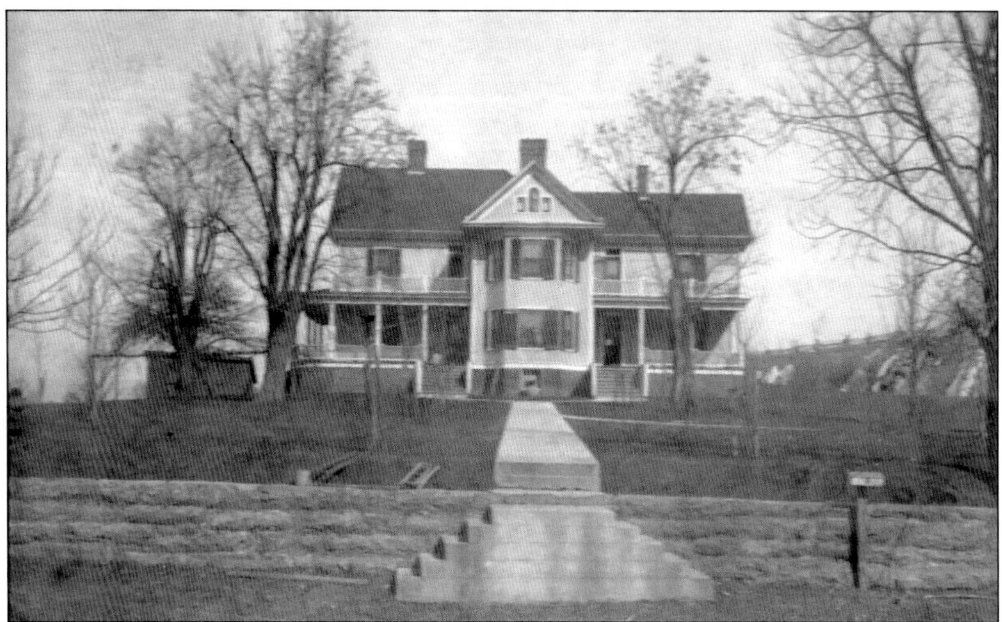

Smalling Home. Constructed in 1903 by Andy Smalling, this home is on the site of the home of his father-in-law, William Akard. Smalling was a relative of Rev. Andrew Shell of Piney Flats. He employed several hundred people on behalf of the Morton Lewis and Willy Lumber Company and had a variety of businesses in the region. His great-grandson's family most recently occupied the home. (Courtesy of Robert White.)

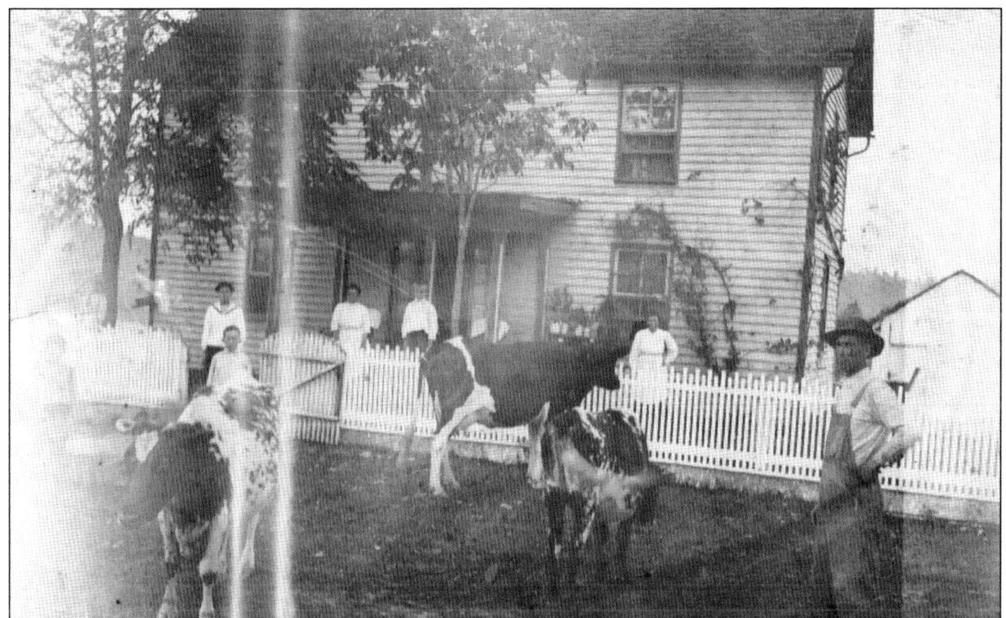

McGee House. The McGee House stands in the city of Bristol near Weaver Funeral Home. Two identical homes were built, with one used as a guesthouse. Charles James McGee was a Confederate veteran and would sell milk to the Caldwells, who lived in the home that now houses the funeral home. "Granny" McGee played an important role in the early Methodist Church in Bristol. (Courtesy of Robert White.)

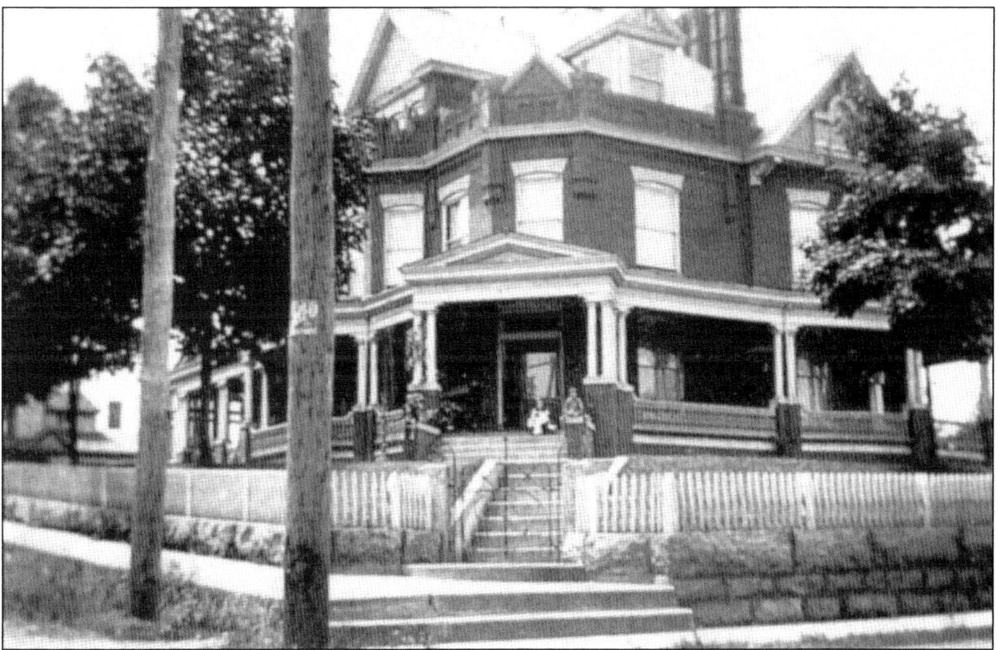

King House. The large Queen Anne home of Edward Washington King was built in 1902. The King family first purchased the property in 1814, but a house was not built on the land for nearly 100 years. According to local lore, the family did not want to construct a home above a cemetery. King was a prominent Bristol businessman. (Courtesy of Tim Buchanan.)

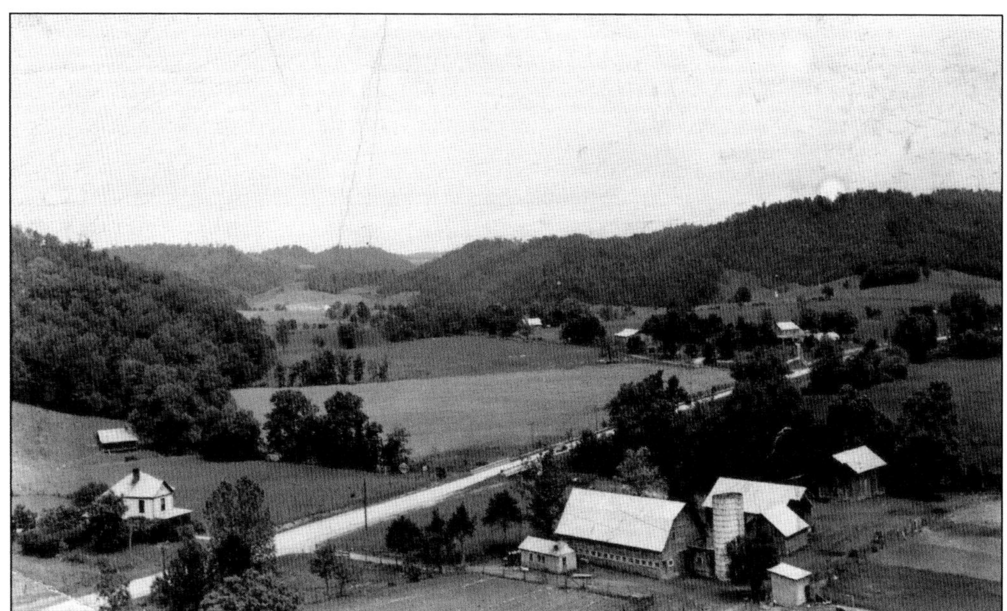

Earhart and Carter Homes. Bristol Motor Speedway was constructed just south of town in 1960 and held its first NASCAR race in 1961. The speedway was built among large dairy farms, including those owned by the Earhart and Carter families. The Earhart and Carter farms are pictured here before the speedway was constructed. (Courtesy of the Earhart family.)

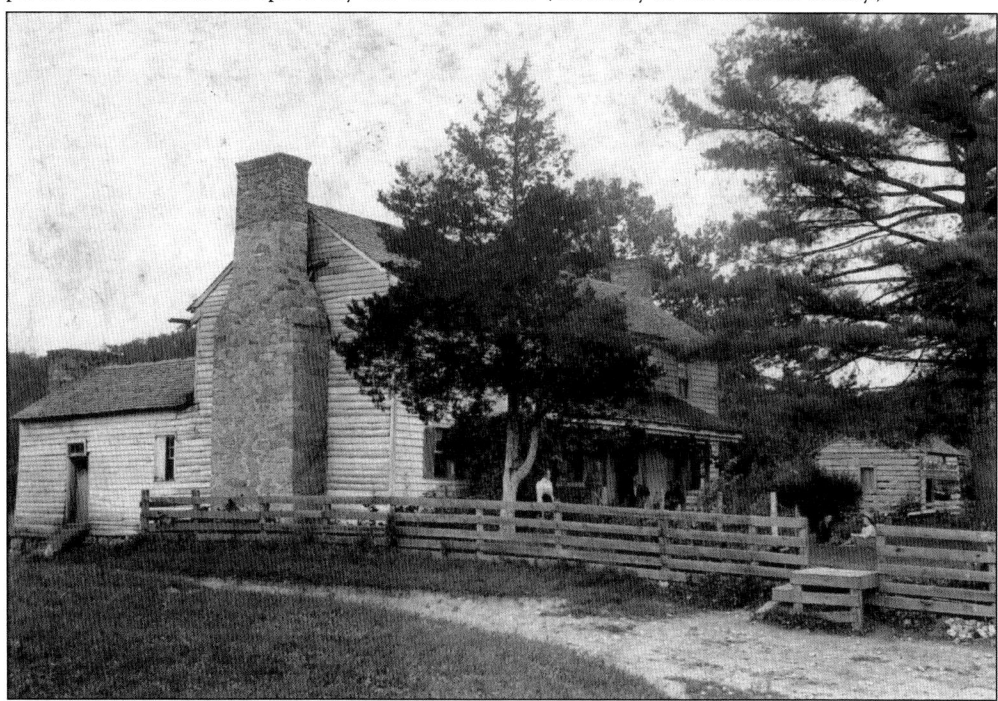

First Rhea-Earhart House. The Rhea family built their first home near Bristol about 1800. Family members constructed a large log house, located at present-day Bishop Drive near Bristol Motor Speedway. It burned on Thanksgiving Day in 1949, descendants recalled. (Courtesy of the Earhart family.)

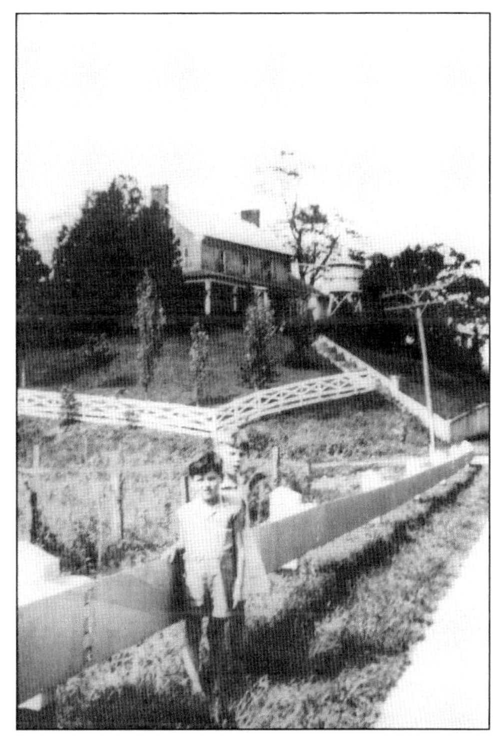

EARHART HOUSE. One of the oldest homes in Sullivan County, the Earhart House, also known as "the Elms," was built in 1806. It sits on a hill across Volunteer Parkway from Bristol Motor Speedway. The home, built by William Rhea, was constructed with handmade bricks. It was the childhood home of Charles and Robert Earhart, whose grandmother Margaret Rhea and her husband, John Taylor Earhart, purchased it from James Rhea, William Rhea's grandson, according to the family. The home remains in the Earhart family, who now operate a campground and parking areas for racefans. (Both, courtesy of the Earhart family.)

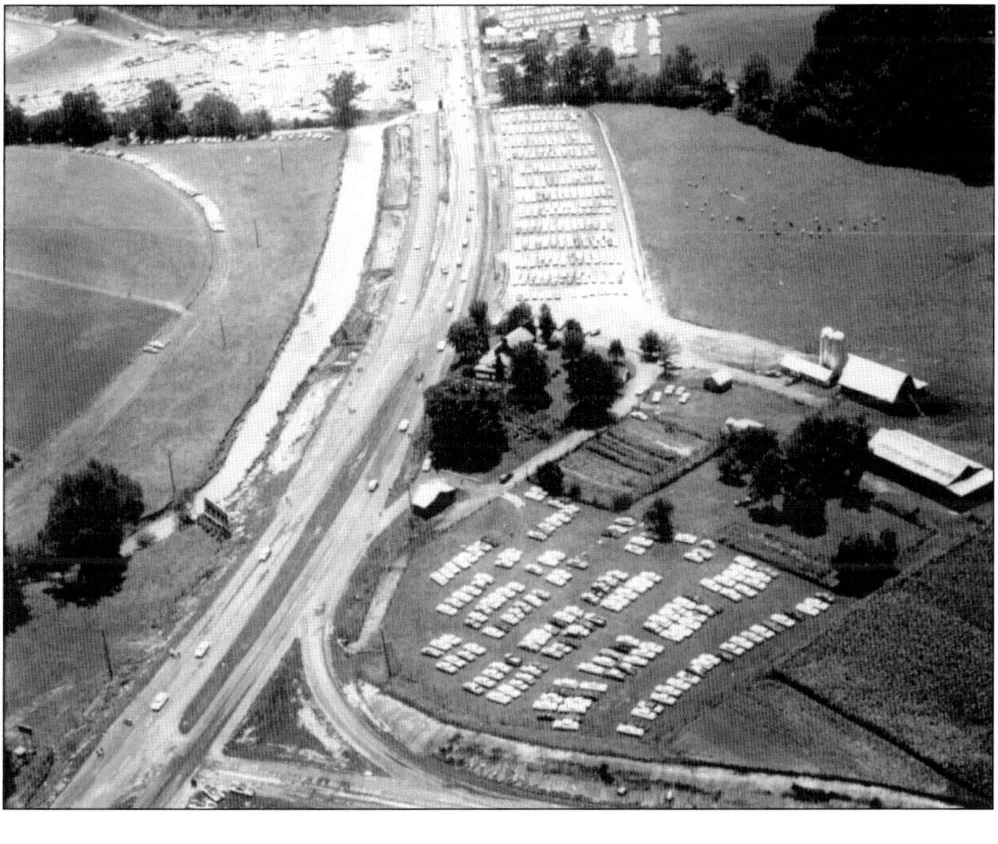

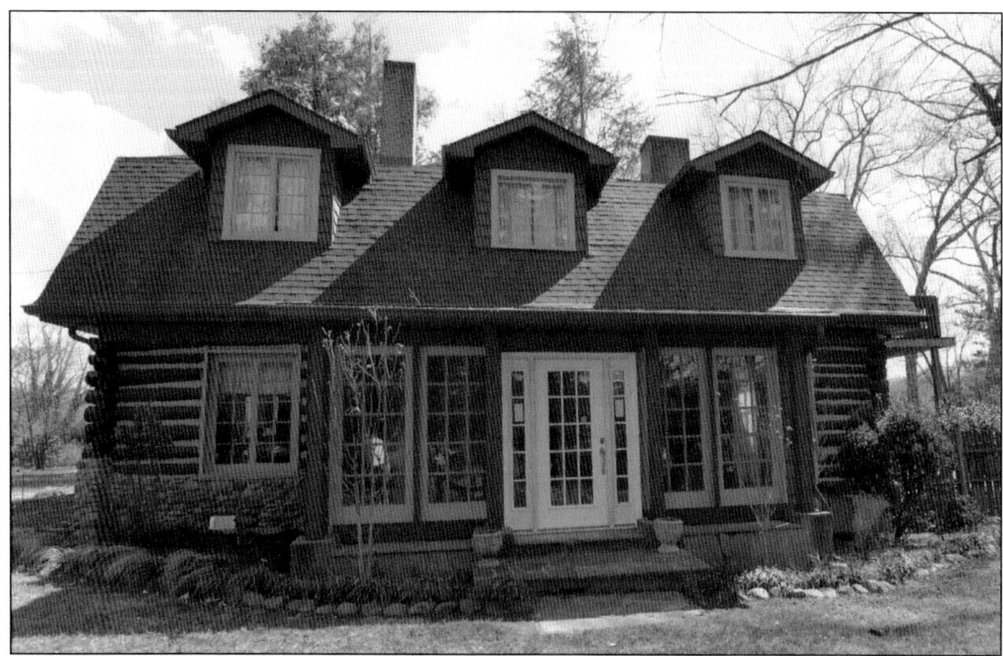

Tyler-Gragg House. The Tyler-Gragg House is located just off Volunteer Parkway in Bristol. Alonzo Jason Tyler, a lawyer and Tennessee state representative, had the home built in 1917. Tyler wanted the home to resemble a cottage he saw in the Rocky Mountains of Colorado, according to the local historical association. The Sellstrom and Gragg families later owned the home. (Courtesy of the *Bristol Herald Courier*.)

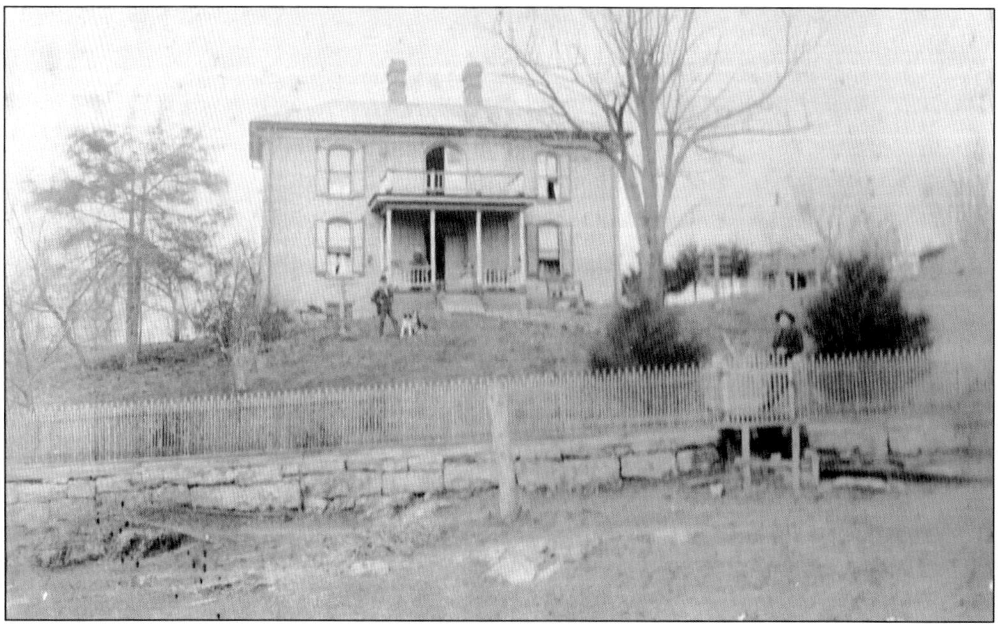

Carmack Home. Jacob Susong Carmack built his home in the Middlebrook neighborhood, east of Bristol, in 1884. Stones from a home's chimney that once stood on the property are still present. The Carmack Home has been recently owned by Ann Foley, the great-granddaughter of the builder. (Courtesy of Robert White.)

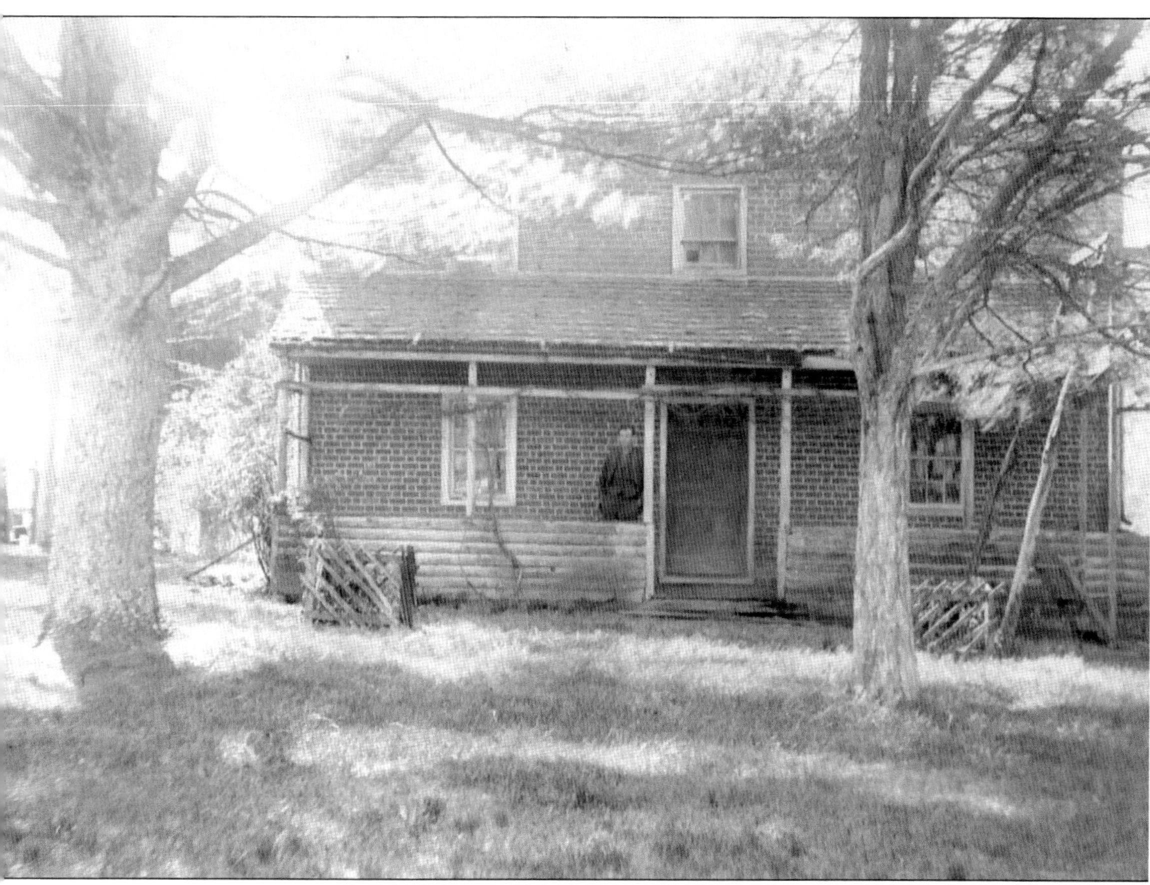

Painter Place. The historic Painter Place property was established in the late 18th century. The property, founded by pioneer David King, who was born in Dauphin County, Pennsylvania, uniquely sits on the border of Tennessee and Virginia, just east of Bristol. According to local historian Bud Phillips, about 1791, King built a two-pen log home with an open hall between them on the property. King called the home Cedar Hill because it had been covered with cedar trees when he first observed the land. His son David Orestus King later inherited property, tore down one of the pens, and added a two-story brick structure in 1845, Phillips said. The room in which he was born became the kitchen ell. King University most recently owned the home. The home is typically referred to as Painter Place, due to the Painter family, who once owned the property. (Courtesy of Robert White.)

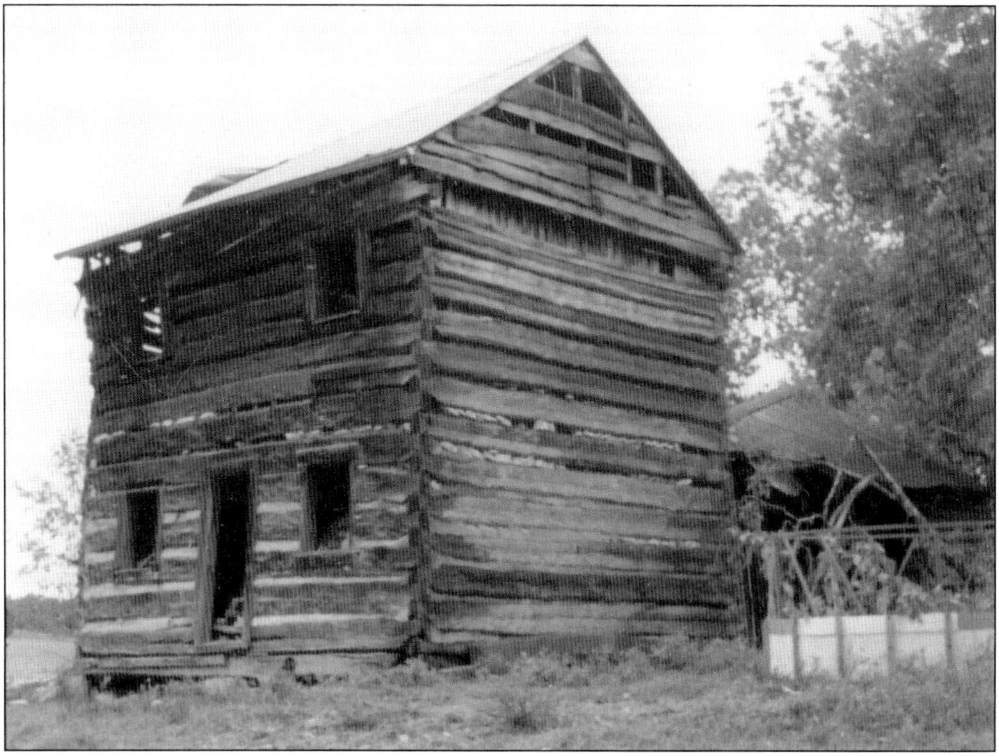

David Orestus King Home. David Orestus King was born at Painter Place in 1804. He married Mariamna McChesney in 1826. The couple built a log home near Painter Place in Sullivan County. This photograph shows the home before it was torn down sometime after 1996. Many of the logs were used to assemble another log home in the area. (Courtesy of Robert White.)

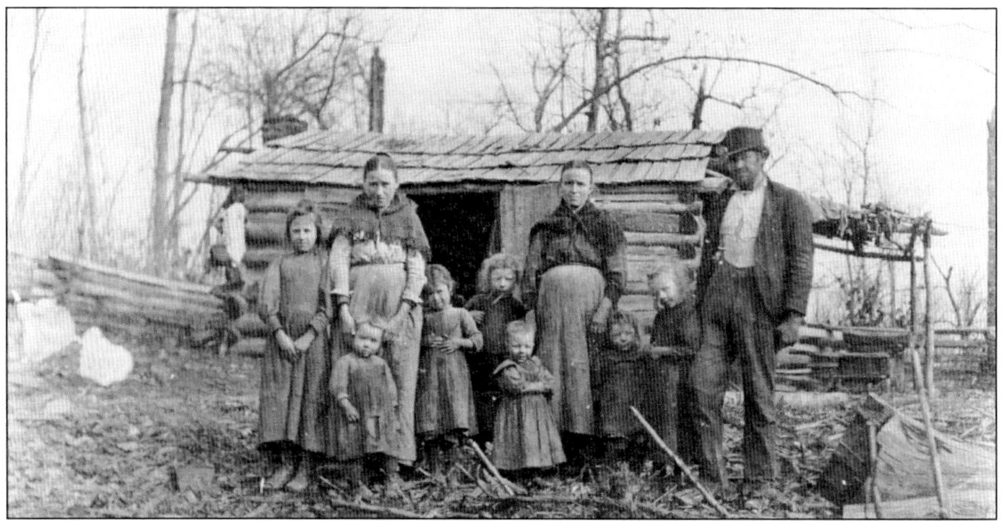

Sharps Creek and Holston Valley. A number of log homes once stood in the Sharps Creek and Holston Valley communities in present-day Sullivan County. Families farmed the fertile land that is now located near South Holston Lake. This unidentified photograph is believed to have been taken in the Sharps Creek community. (Courtesy of Robert White.)

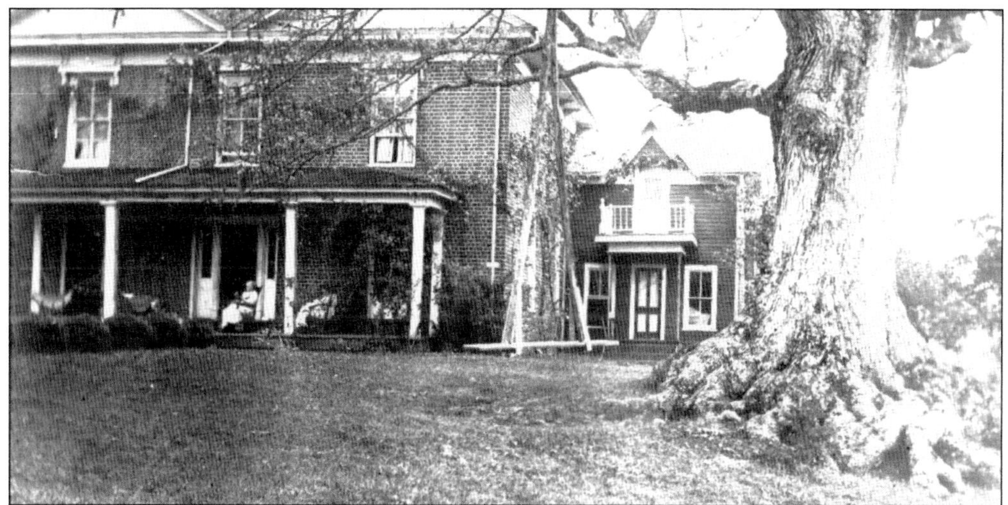

PEMBERTON MANSION. The Pemberton Farm in eastern Sullivan County was founded in the late 1700s. According to the National Register of Historic Places, the brick house standing today replaced a log house, which had been built by Col. John Pemberton around 1780. The log house stood until 1878 as the family of Thomas D. Pemberton Sr., builder of the brick house, was moving into their new home. A fire destroyed the log house, according to the Register. A log smokehouse and springhouse still stand. During the Revolutionary War, men mustered under a giant tree on the property before going to South Carolina to fight the British. The tree remained a vital part of the farm until it fell during a storm in 2002. (Above, courtesy of the Pemberton family; below, courtesy of the Tennessee State Library and Archives.)

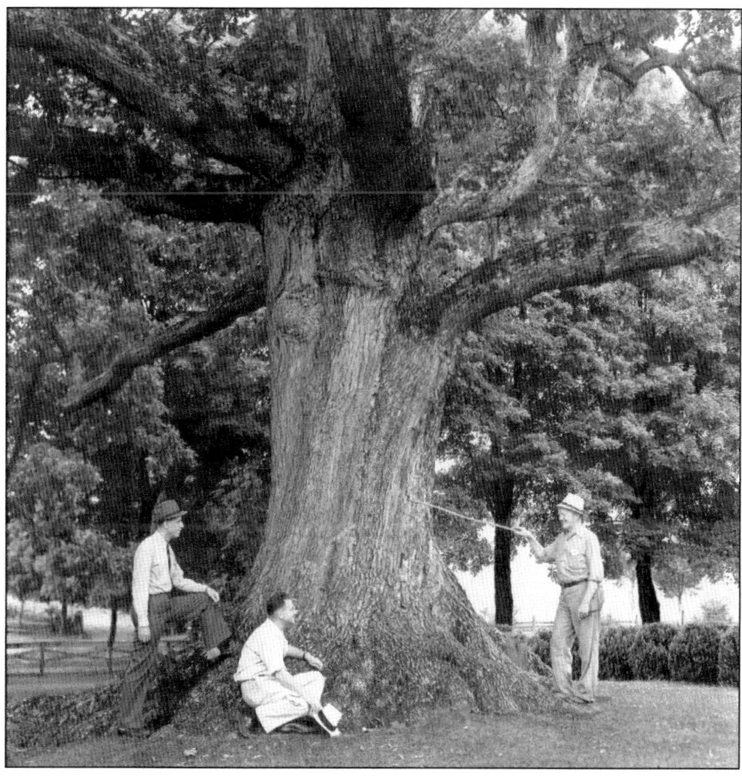

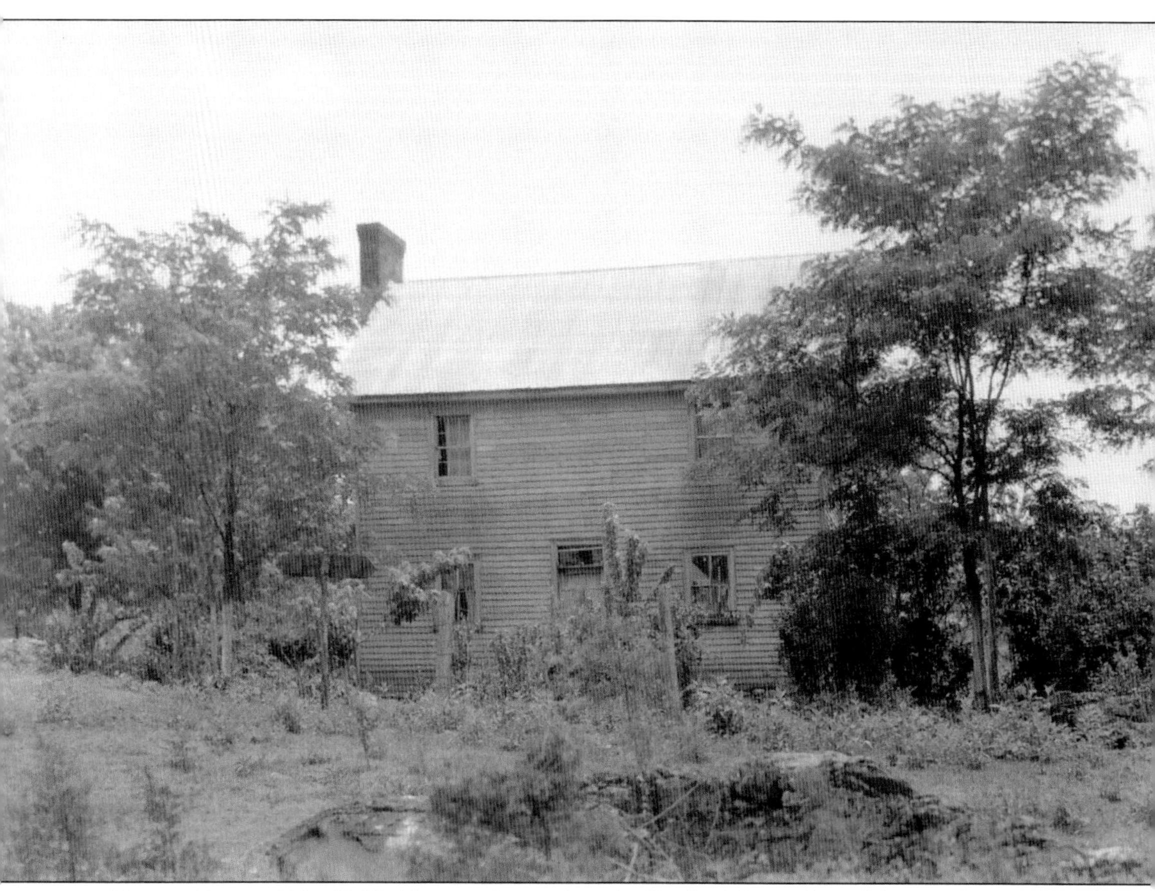

Rocky Mount. The Cobb House is located at the Rocky Mount State Historic Site, operated as a house museum by the state of Tennessee. William Cobb, a North Carolina native, moved here with his family around 1770. At that time, he built this two-story log home. During the Revolutionary War, Cobb supported the Overmountain Men and eventually joined them in their fight at Kings Mountain, South Carolina. After the war, Cobb supported William Blount, who was named governor of the Southwest Territory. Blount lived here with the Cobbs from 1790 to 1792, making Rocky Mount the capitol of the territory. The Cobbs moved to Knoxville in 1795, but the home stayed in the Cobb and Massengill families until the state purchased the property and opened it to the public in 1962. Through the years, the home has been clapboarded and tin-shingled but has always lacked running water. The clapboard siding has been removed, and the Cobb house now appears as it did when William Cobb was here. (Courtesy of the Rocky Mount Historical Association.)

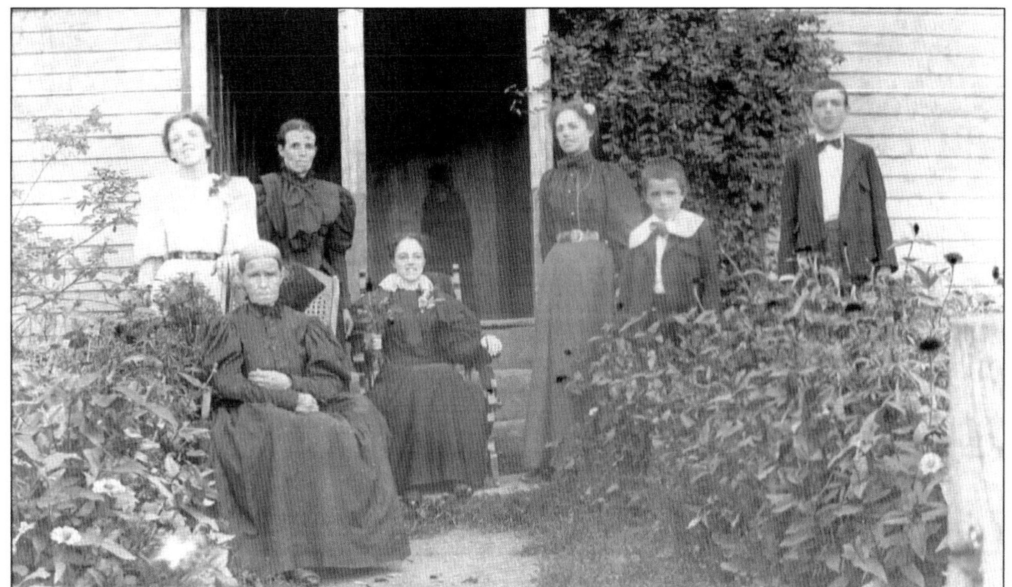

Rocky Mount State Historic Site. The Rocky Mount State Historic Site, located in the Piney Flats community of Sullivan County, opened to the public in 1962. The home had stayed in the Cobb and Massengill families until the state purchased the property. The photograph below was taken during the opening, when hundreds of area residents and officials visited the home. The historic site, which includes a large visitors center and museum, has been expanded to include a kitchen, springhouse, and slave cabin, barn, orchard, and gardens in an effort to enhance the living history atmosphere of the Cobb farm. The Massengill family is pictured in the above photograph, which was taken in 1892. (Both, courtesy of the Rocky Mount Historical Association.)

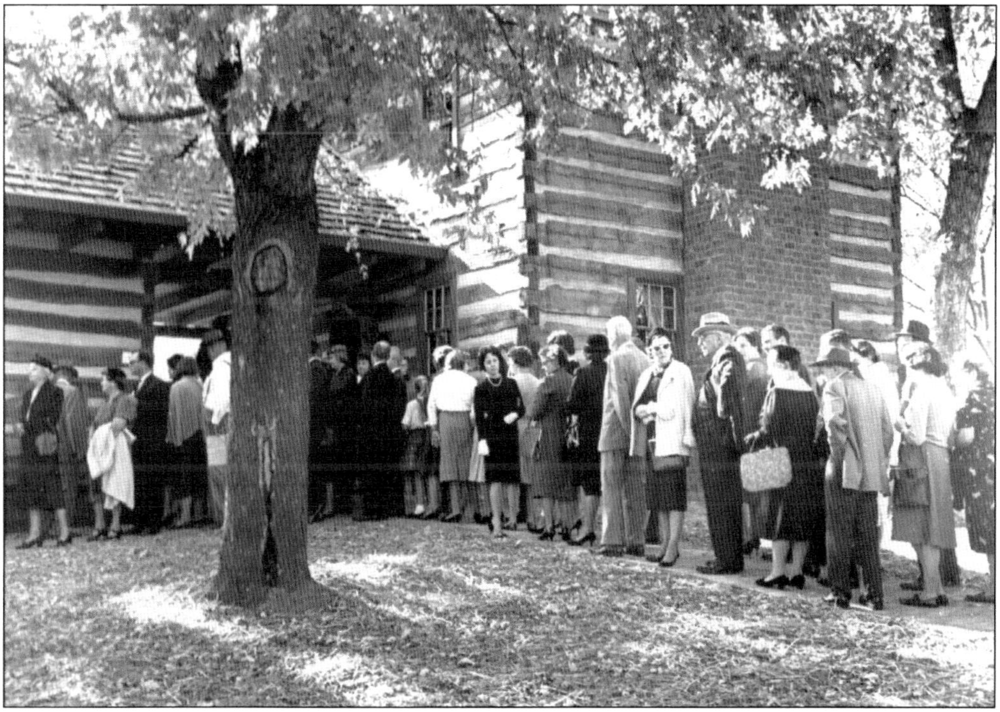

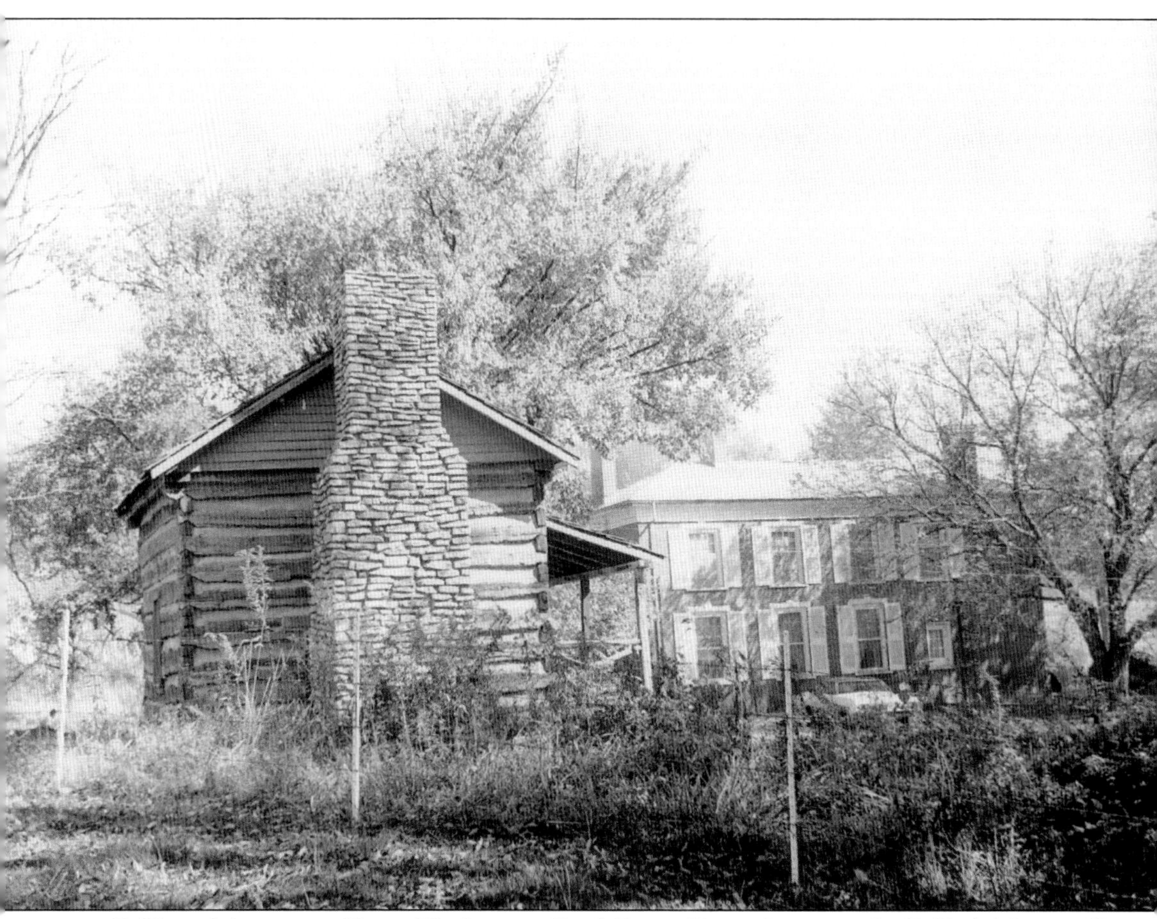

DeVault-Massengill Home. The historic Greek Revival home known as the DeVault-Massengill Home is the centerpiece of the old Massengill Farm. It is located along US Highway 11E in the Piney Flats community. Henry Massengill, who settled here about 1769, built a log house and a log slave cabin on the property. The DeVault family purchased the land in 1837, and Isaac DeVault built the large brick home in 1842. Constructed of hand-fired brick made on the premises, the main section of the house is three bays wide and one room deep, according to a listing in the National Register of Historic Places. A two-story ell (that is one bay wide and two rooms deep) extends from the northwest corner of the house. The DeVault family also built the nearby Valentine DeVault Mansion. In 1937, the DeVaults sold the farm and house back to the Massengill family, who live here today. The DeVault-Massengill Home and the slave cabin are pictured. (Courtesy of the City of Kingsport Archives.)

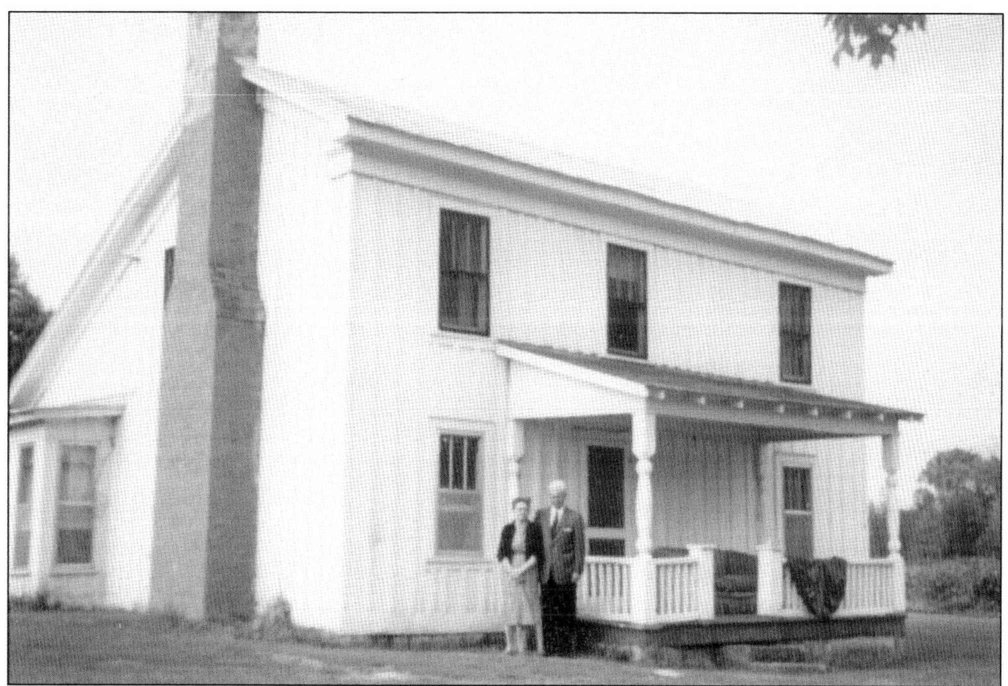

DAVID HUGHES HOUSE. David Hughes had a large land grant in the area. He built his home on present-day High Street at Huffman Hill Road. The oldest house in Piney Flats, it is a bungalow-style home that was built about 1800 but has been altered over the years. Hughes stored feathers in space that could be reached through a trapdoor in the floor. (Courtesy of Mary Ann Hager.)

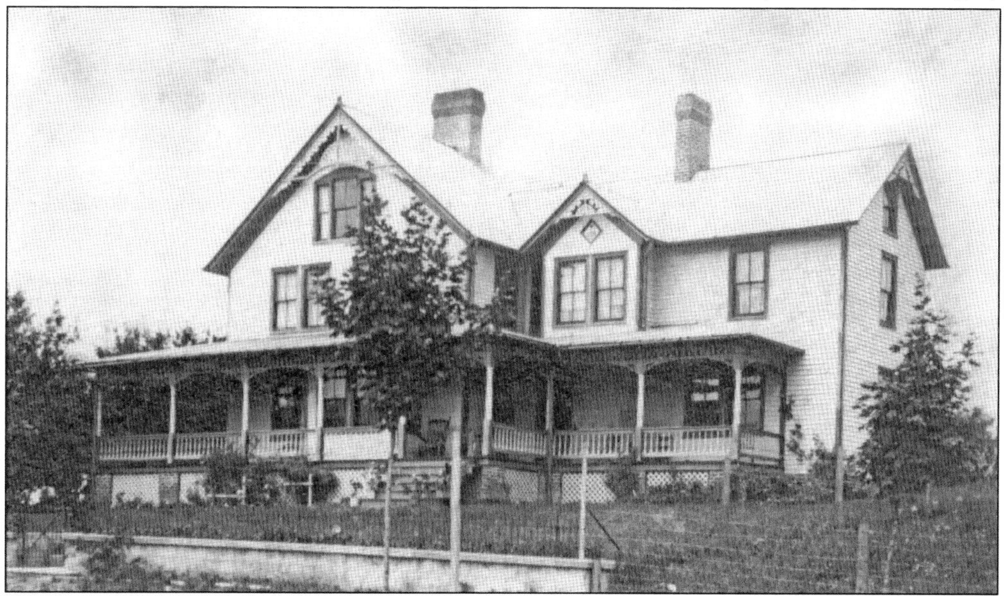

WOLFE HOUSE. John Bunyan Wolfe built a large home along Main Street in what is now the Piney Flats Historic District. Wolfe operated the Wolfe Brothers Furniture Factory, which still stands nearby. The business provided the Piney Flats community with a number of jobs. Wolfe also developed the village's first telephone system, which had a switchboard in his home. (Courtesy of Connie Landreth.)

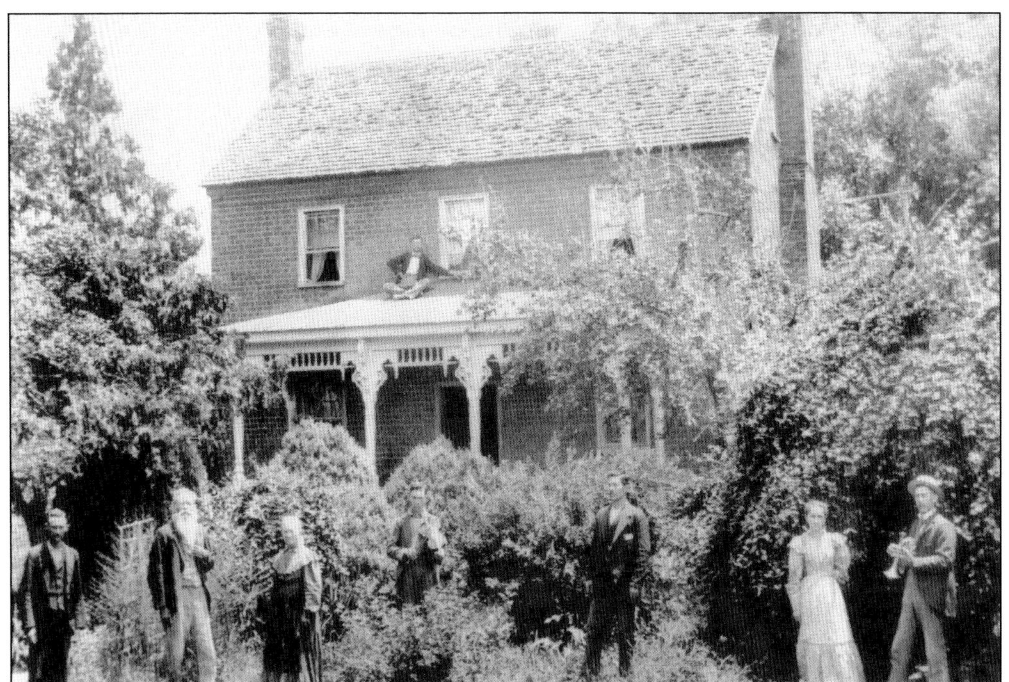

ANDREW SHELL HOUSE. The Andrew Shell House was a Federal-style farmhouse in Piney Flats, built in the early 1800s. It is one of a handful of homes in the district that are no longer standing. It was torn down in the 1920s. Family and friends, who are dressed up and holding musical instruments, are pictured at the home. (Courtesy of Mary Ann Hager.)

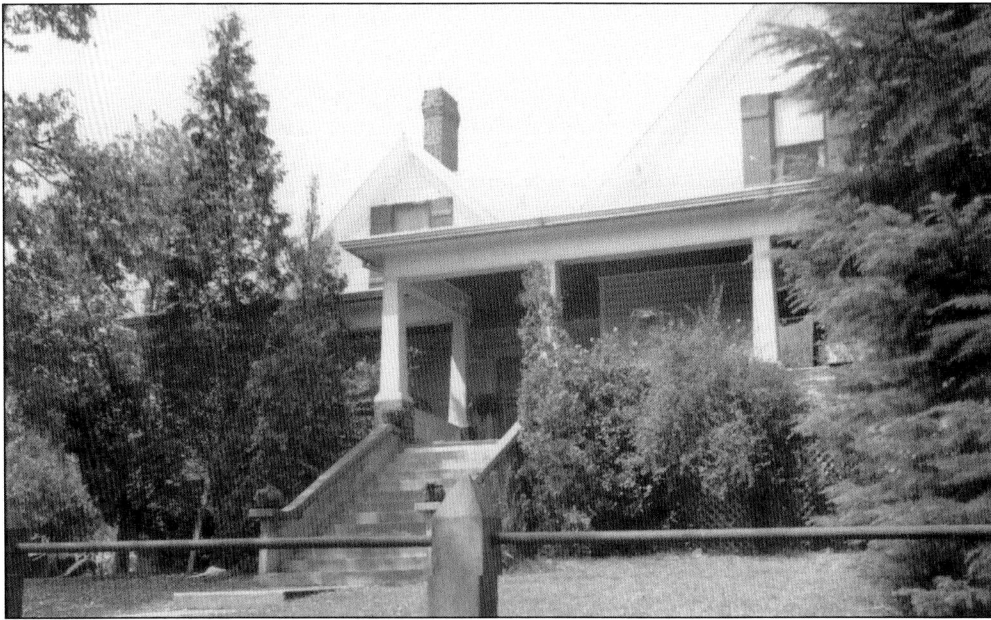

BOB SHELL HOUSE. The Bob Shell House, a Craftsman home, was built in 1908 along McKamey Street in the Piney Flats Historic District. Shell was the grandson of early Piney Flats founder Andrew Shell. The home still stands and is located near the family cemetery. (Courtesy of Mary Ann Hager.)

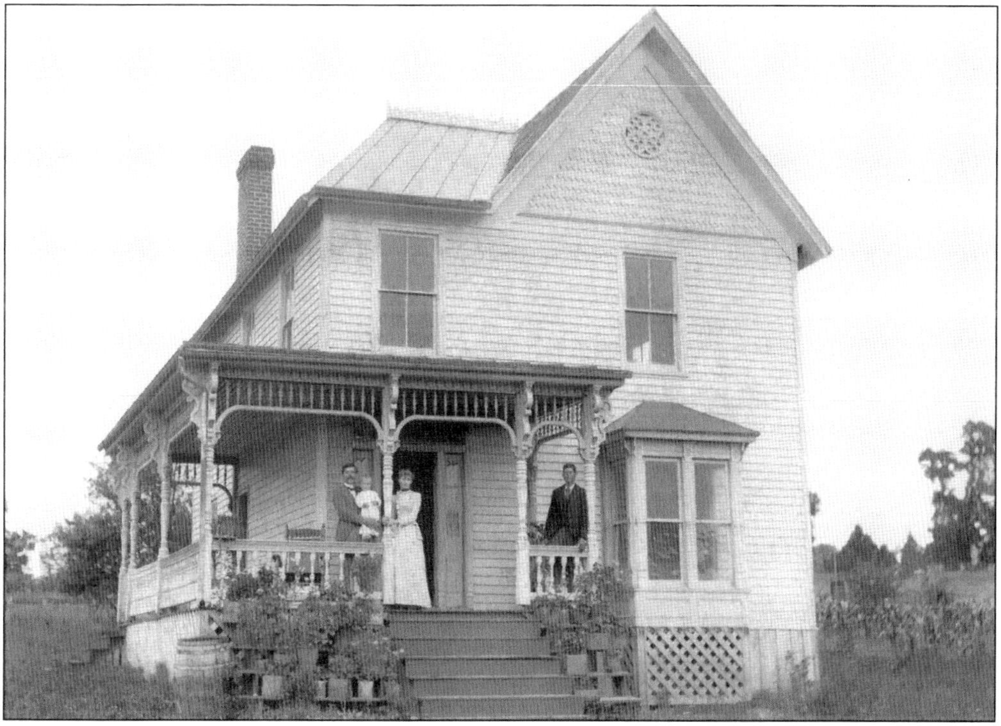

HUGHES HOUSE. Hiram Hughes built his home 1887 on Main Street in Piney Flats. The original portion of the house is pictured here. His son Ed Hughes, Ed's wife, Lula Hughes, and their infant son Guy Hughes are pictured here about 1891. Ed added a large west wing to the home. (Courtesy of Mary Ann Hager.)

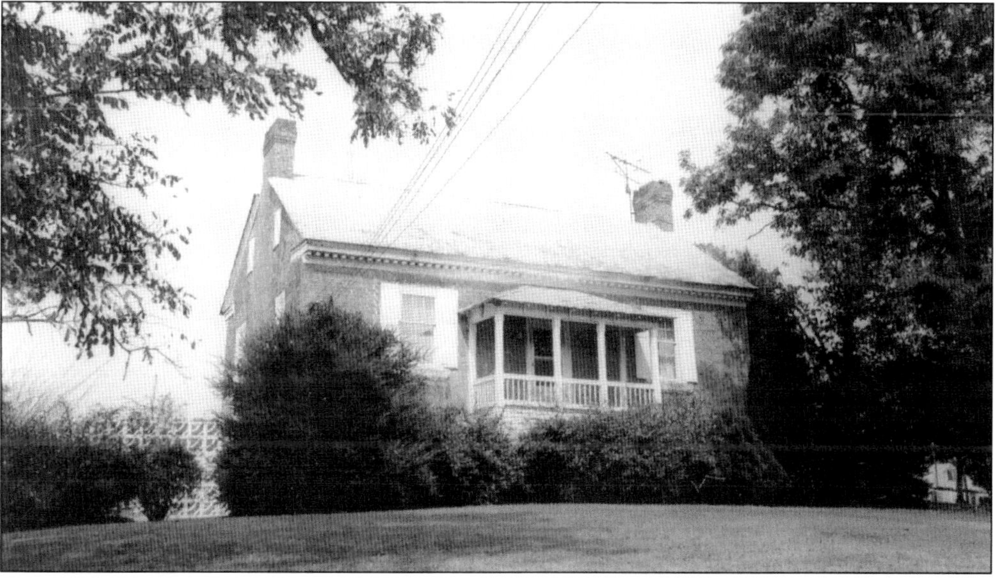

FINLAY ALISON HOME. Finlay Alison built a house, pictured here, along Pickens Bridge Road in Piney Flats between 1811 and 1813. The brick home features a wooden back addition. In 1833, Alison was found at the bottom of the stairs at the front of the home's veranda. He died from a fall. (Courtesy of the City of Kingsport Archives.)

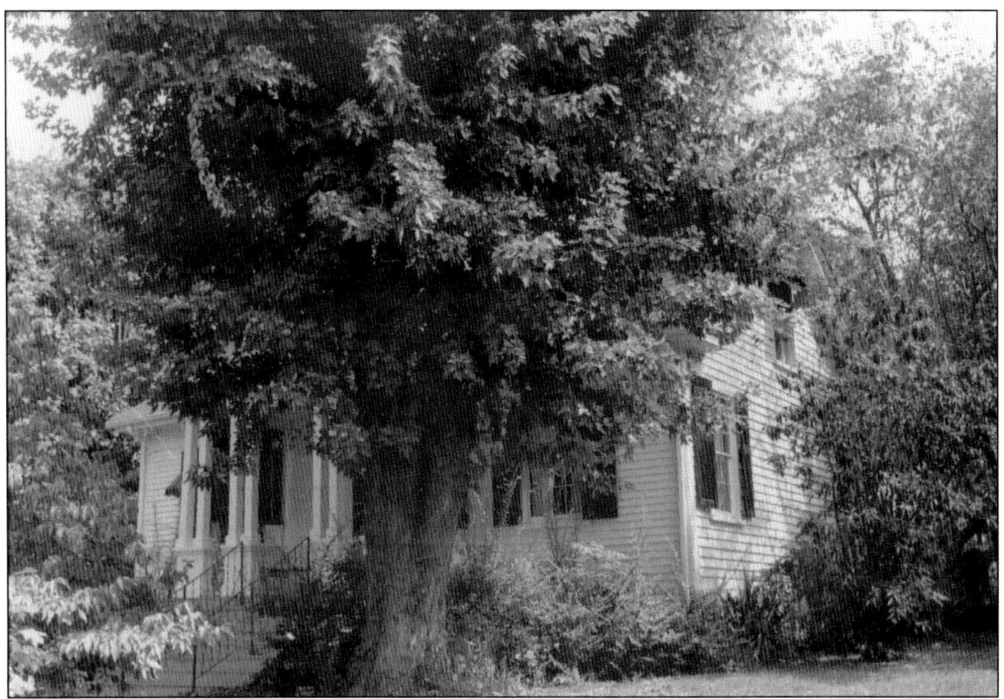

Gerstle House. The Gerstle House is a small Italianate cottage located along Main Street in Bluff City. Leopold Gerstle, a Bavarian Jew who manufactured medicine and operated a drugstore, moved here in the early 1880s. He moved to Chattanooga in 1889 and operated a business that eventually became the St. Joseph Company. (Courtesy of the City of Kingsport Archives.)

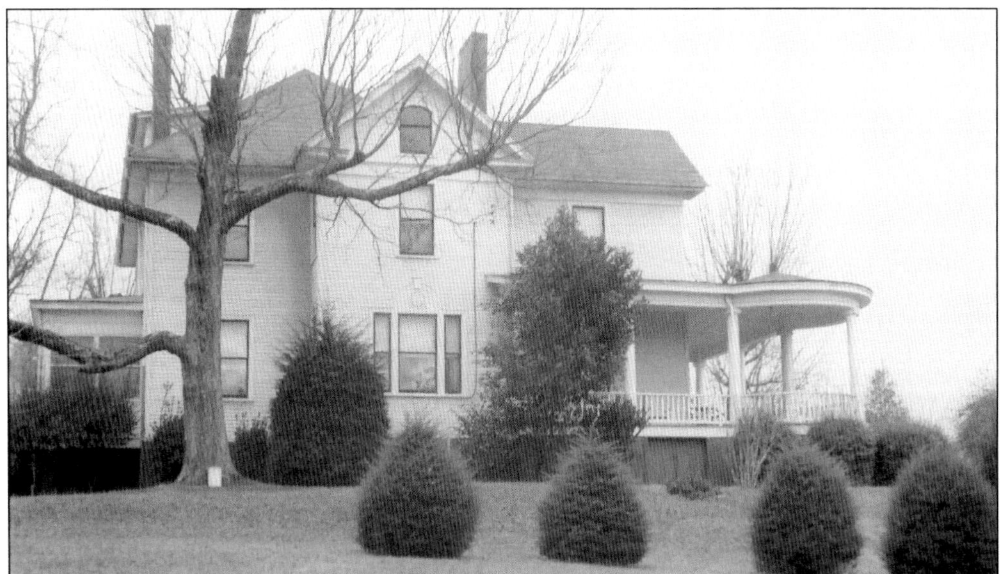

Long Shadows. Long Shadows, built in 1907, is a Victorian mansion in Bluff City. The 16-room home, with 10 fireplaces, was built by William Bruce Bachman. It is on the site of the 1867-era home of Mary Stover, Pres. Andrew Johnson's daughter. One of Stover's daughters married Bachman, who built Long Shadows after the original home burned. (Courtesy of the City of Kingsport Archives.)

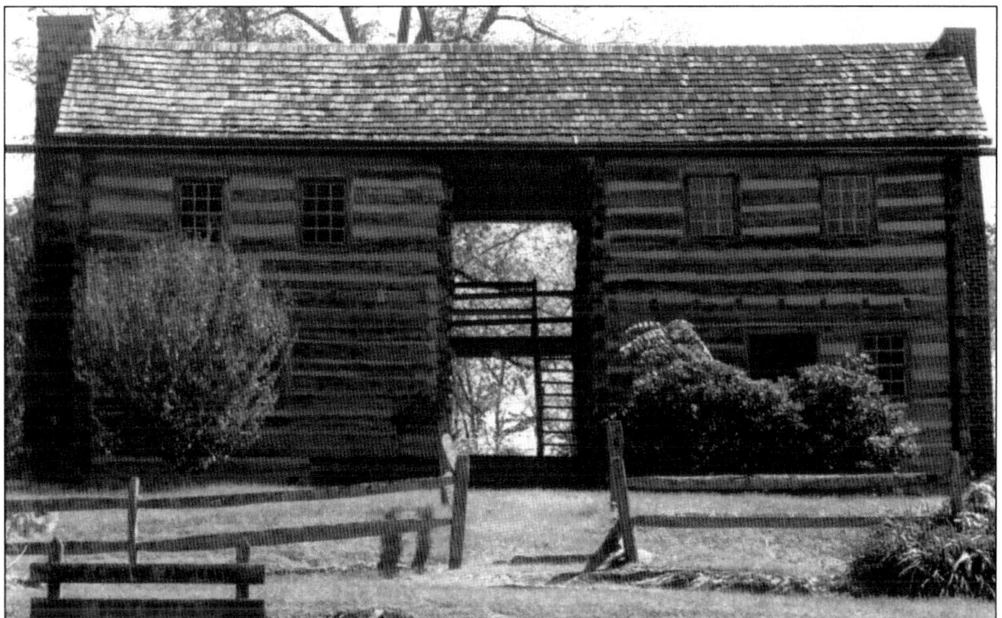

Cox Cabin. The Edward Cox Home is one of Sullivan County's oldest structures. The two-story log cabin was built in 1774 by Edward Cox, who served in the Revolutionary War. When he returned to Tennessee, Cox welcomed Methodist preachers to his home. The Holston Conference now owns the home, which features a dogtrot, or breezeway, in the center. (Author's collection.)

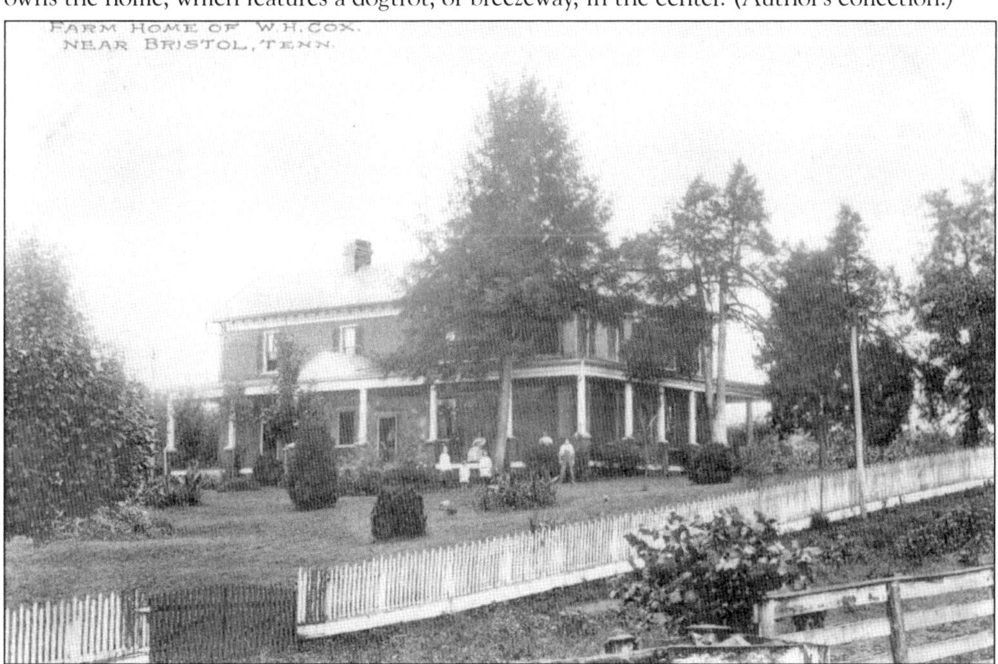

Cole-McClellan-Cox Mansion. Underneath the handsome Federal brick Cole-McClellan-Cox Mansion lies a log home built in 1784 by the Cole family. The home was enlarged by the McClellan family and later purchased by the Cox family. In 1918, Thomas Edison, Henry Ford, and Harvey Firestone reportedly visited just to get a glimpse of the spectacular home. (Courtesy of George Stone.)

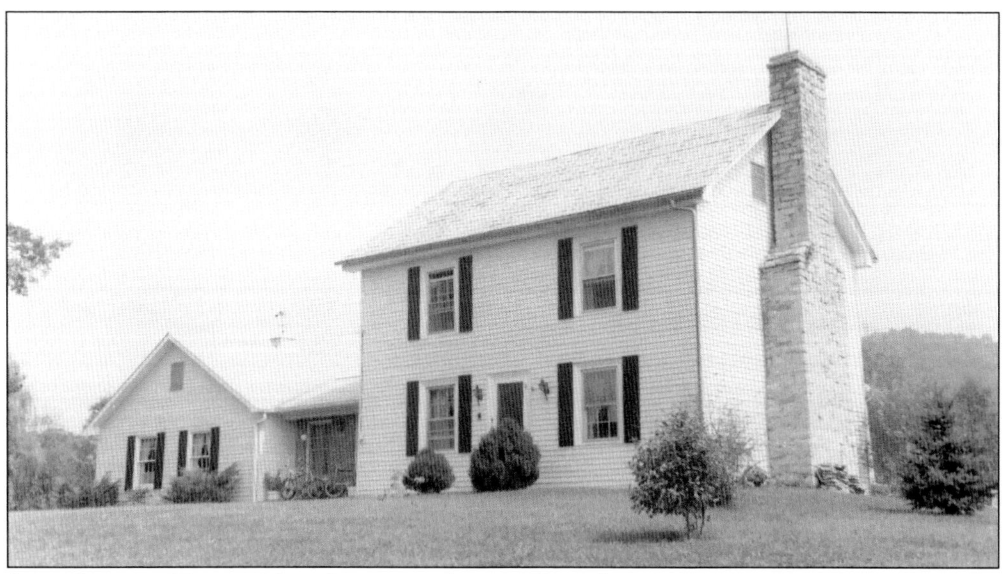

Steel-Seneker Houses. Three homes, southwest of Bristol, were once important rest stops on the old stagecoach line between Abingdon and Blountville. The Steel family built a log house here in 1777. The home, pictured above, is now covered in white aluminum siding. A brick residence, pictured below, located across the street from the Steel House, was built by John Steel in 1784. It is believed to be the second-oldest brick home in the county. In 1853, the Barker family bought the brick home. Union soldiers camped nearby during the war. By 1875, John Elias Lafayette Seneker purchased the structure, hence the name Steel-Barker-Seneker House. In 1870, James King Seneker built a large Greek Revival home nearby on State Route 126, overlooking the two older homes. (Above, courtesy of the City of Kingsport Archives; below, courtesy of Robert White.)

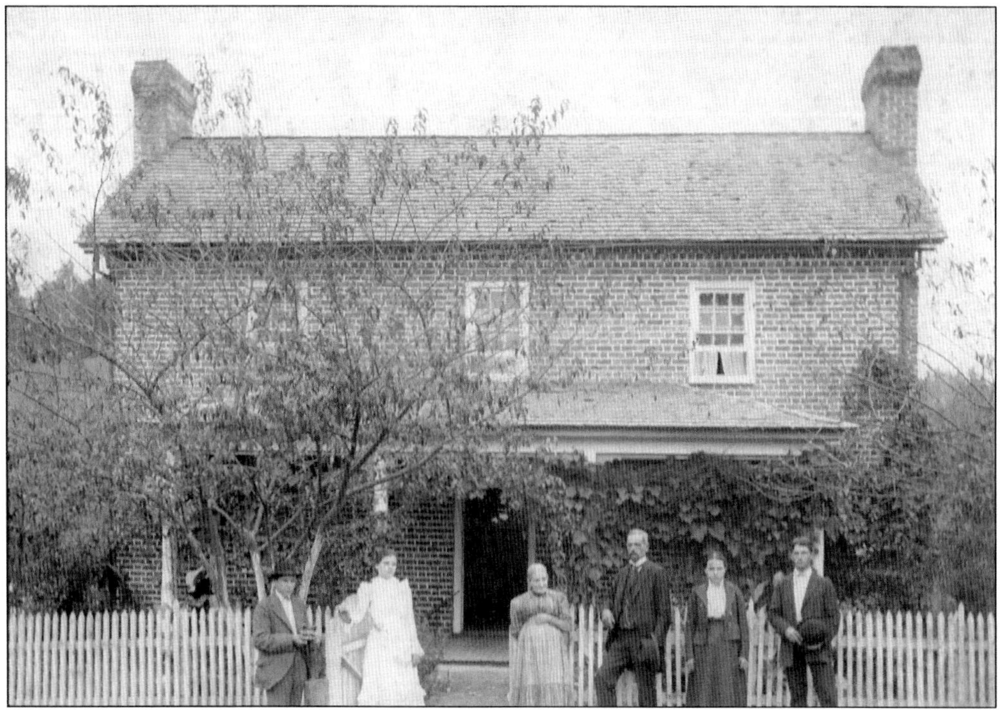

Two

Kingsport and Blountville

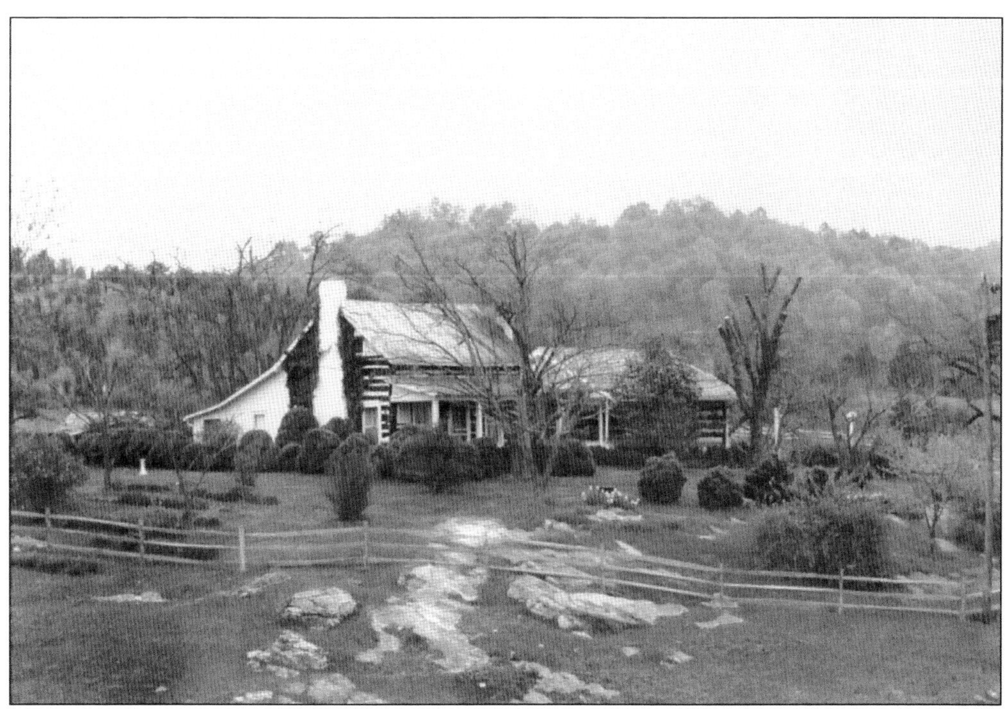

Rockledge. Rockledge suffered extensive damage during a fire in 2010. Built on a rock rise (hence the name Rockledge), it was constructed in 1806 by David Shaver, a powerful plantation owner. The property, featuring a large western portion and a smaller east wing, was a 300-acre farm. By 1835, John Welsh bought Rockledge, and L.M. Stuffle eventually purchased the home. (Courtesy of the City of Kingsport Archives.)

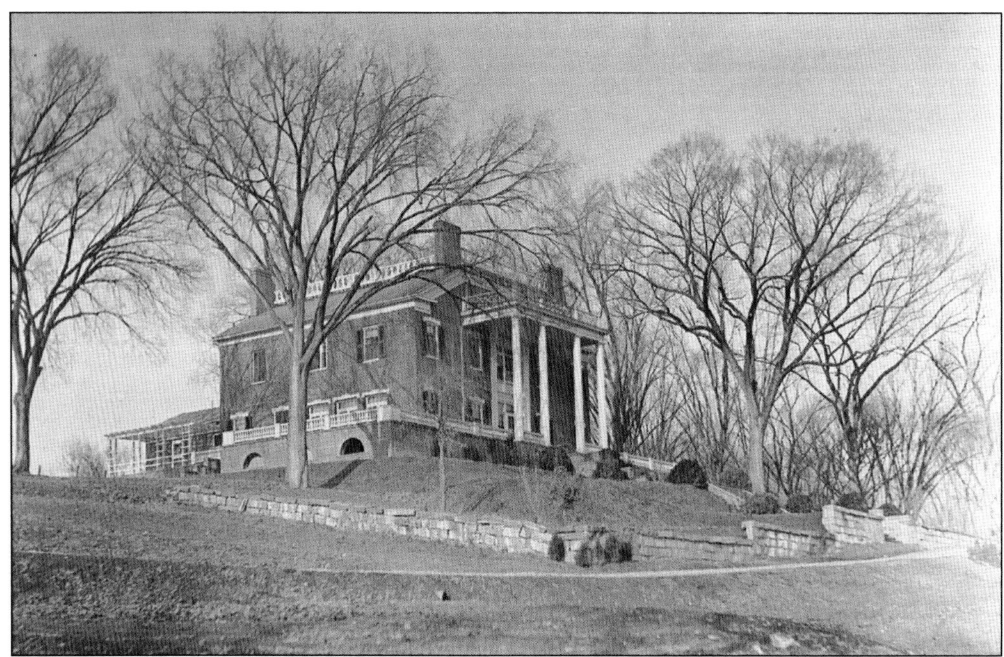

ROTHERWOOD MANSION. Rotherwood Mansion, a stately brick residence, was constructed in 1818 by Rev. Fredrick Ross. Overlooking the Holston River in Kingsport, Tennessee, the mansion at onetime consisted of two parallel wings. It has since undergone several changes, including the construction of a central hall between the wings. At least two prominent Kingsport officials, James W. Dobyns and John B. Dennis, have lived here. (Courtesy of the Tennessee State Library and Archives.)

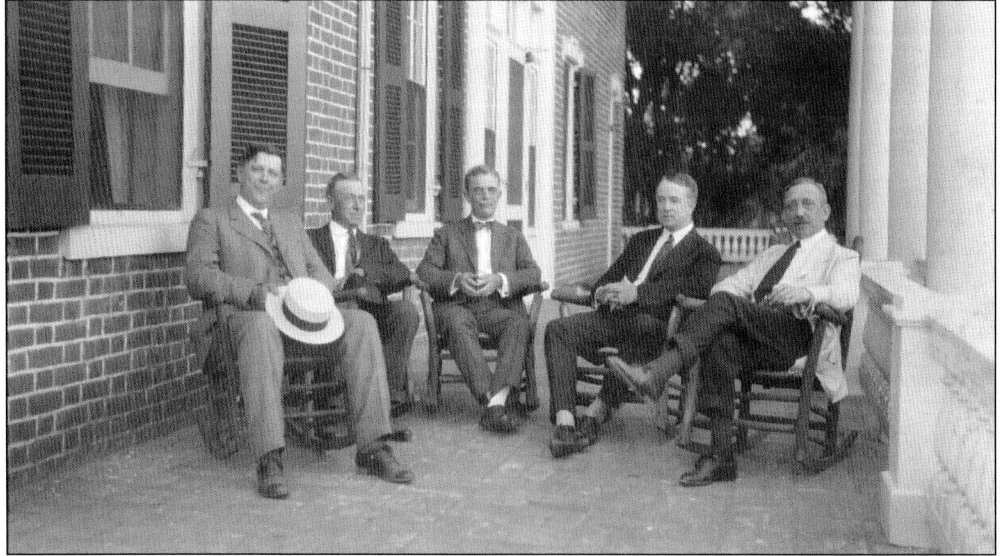

KINGSPORT'S LEADERS AT ROTHERWOOD. Kingsport businessman John B. Dennis (right) sits on the front porch of his home, Rotherwood Mansion, with other local leaders. Dennis regularly hosted business and political leaders at the home, built in 1818. The other men seen here are, from left to right, J. Fred Johnson, unidentified, and Eastman Kodak officials James Havens and Frank Lovejoy. (Courtesy of the City of Kingsport Archives.)

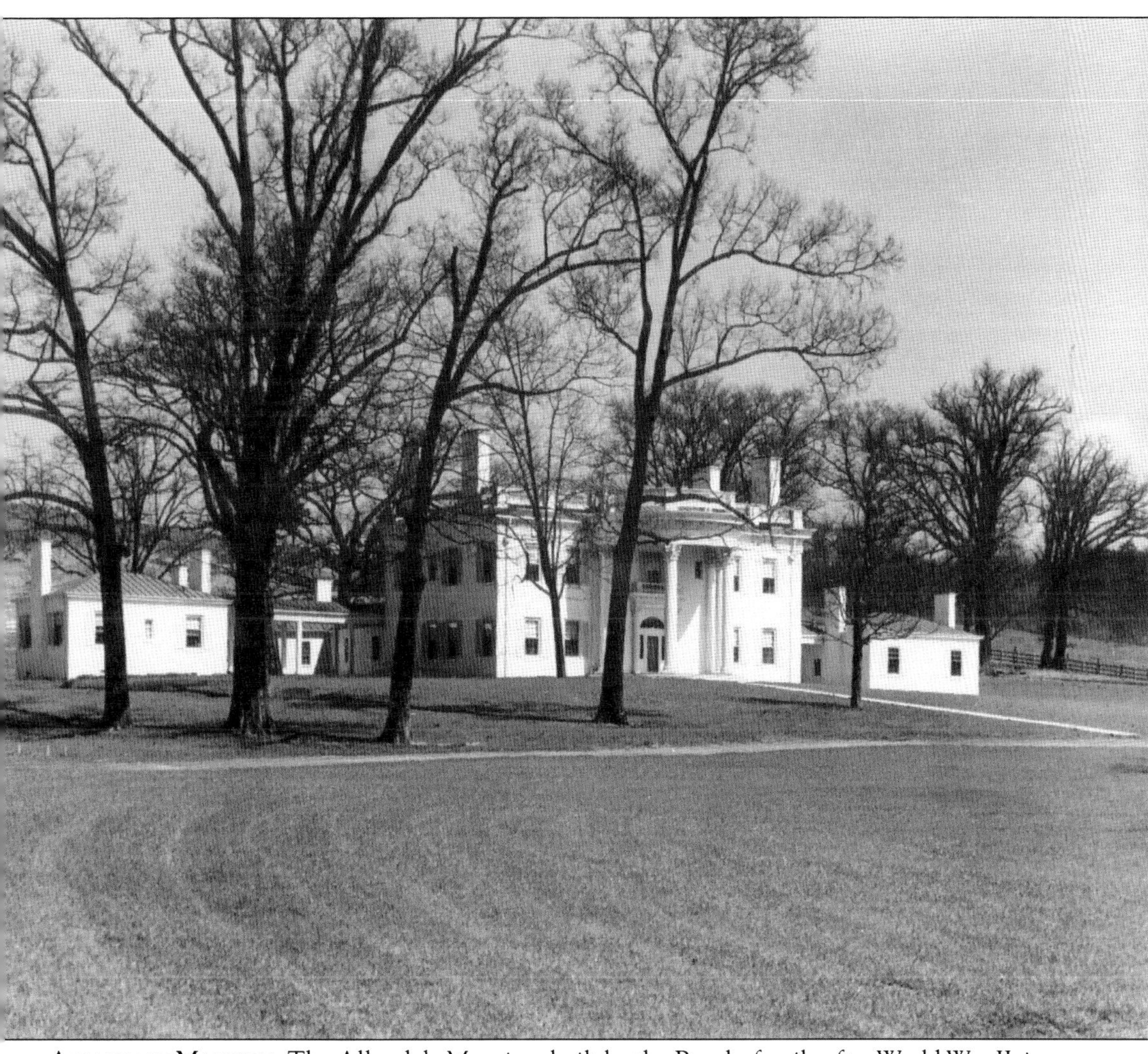

Allandale Mansion. The Allandale Mansion, built by the Brooks family after World War II, is one of Kingsport's most notable residences. Dubbed the White House of Kingsport, the mansion is a modern adaptation of an antebellum residence. In accordance with the style, all the main rooms lead off the central hallways. The Brookses worked with architect Allen Dryden Sr. During their initial consultation with Dryden, Ruth Haire Brooks expressed that she simply wanted "a farmhouse with a picket fence." When they began discussing the details, however, the architect realized the couple did not just want a simple cottage. The mansion features four chimneys, a hipped roof, and a grand wooden staircase. In addition, there are four hand-carved cypress columns on the front portico. The columns and the staircase were purchased from a mansion in Knoxville and transported by truck to Kingsport. (Courtesy of the Tennessee State Library and Archives.)

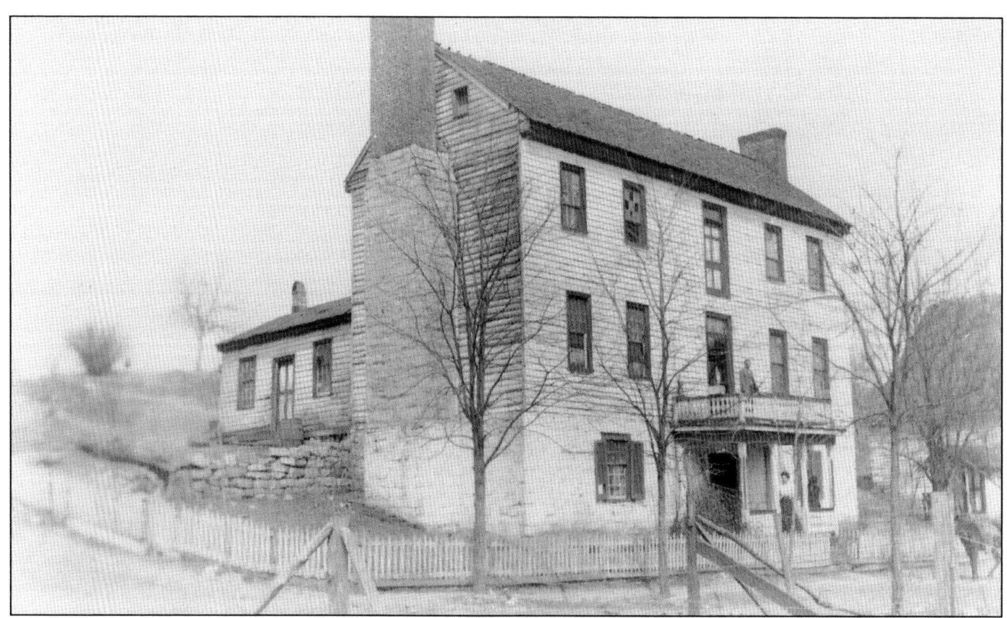

Netherland Inn. The Netherland Inn, now a house museum, was built in 1802 by William King, who also constructed a boatyard on the adjacent Holston River. The building was later sold to Richard Netherland, the building's namesake. It was a three-story structure along the old stagecoach road. It has also been used as a boardinghouse and private residence. The first floor was a tavern. The family lived on the second floor, and guests stayed on the third floor. The front of the inn, which faces the Holston River, is pictured above. The rear of the building is pictured in the photograph below. (Both, courtesy of the City of Kingsport Archives.)

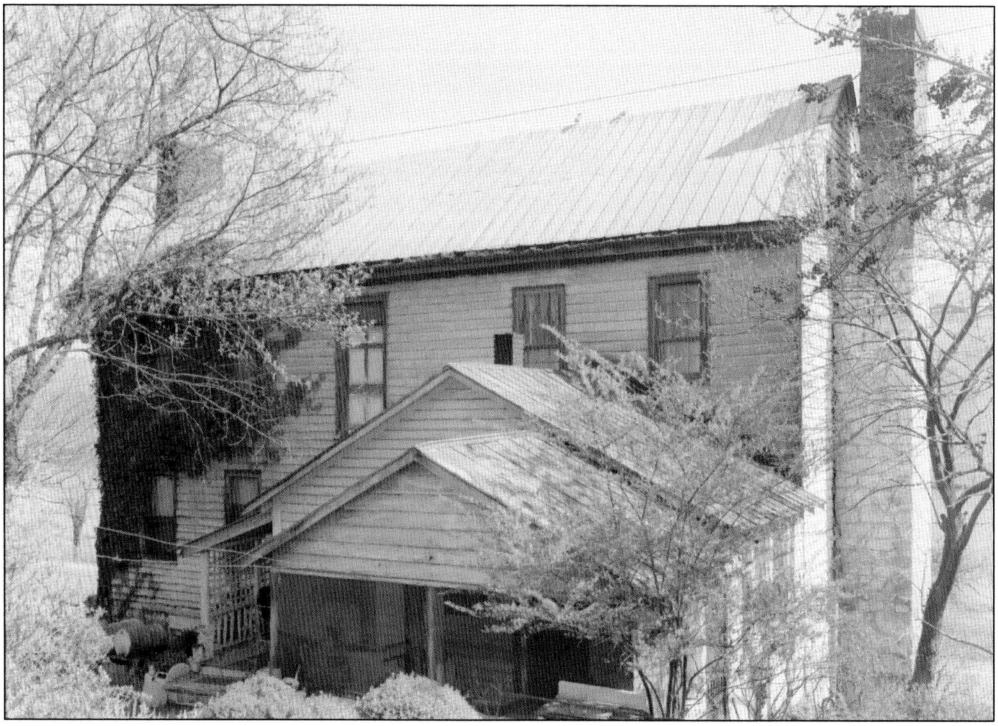

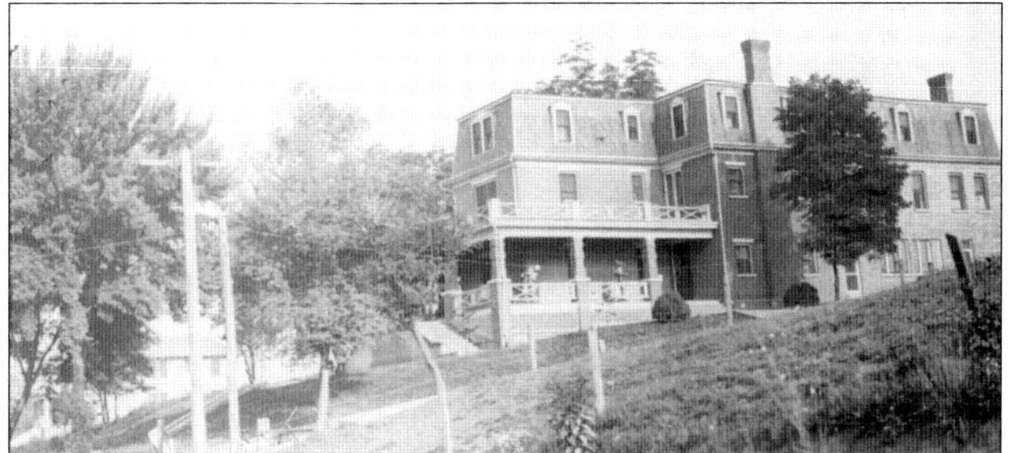

LYNN HOUSE. The Lynn House was built as a private residence about 1840 by John Lynn Jr., a prominent Kingsport merchant. The brick home was originally a two-story Federal structure. By 1915, the Roller family, who purchased the home in 1883, added a north and south wing and a third floor. It has served as a hospital, children's home, and apartment building. (Courtesy of the City of Kingsport Archives.)

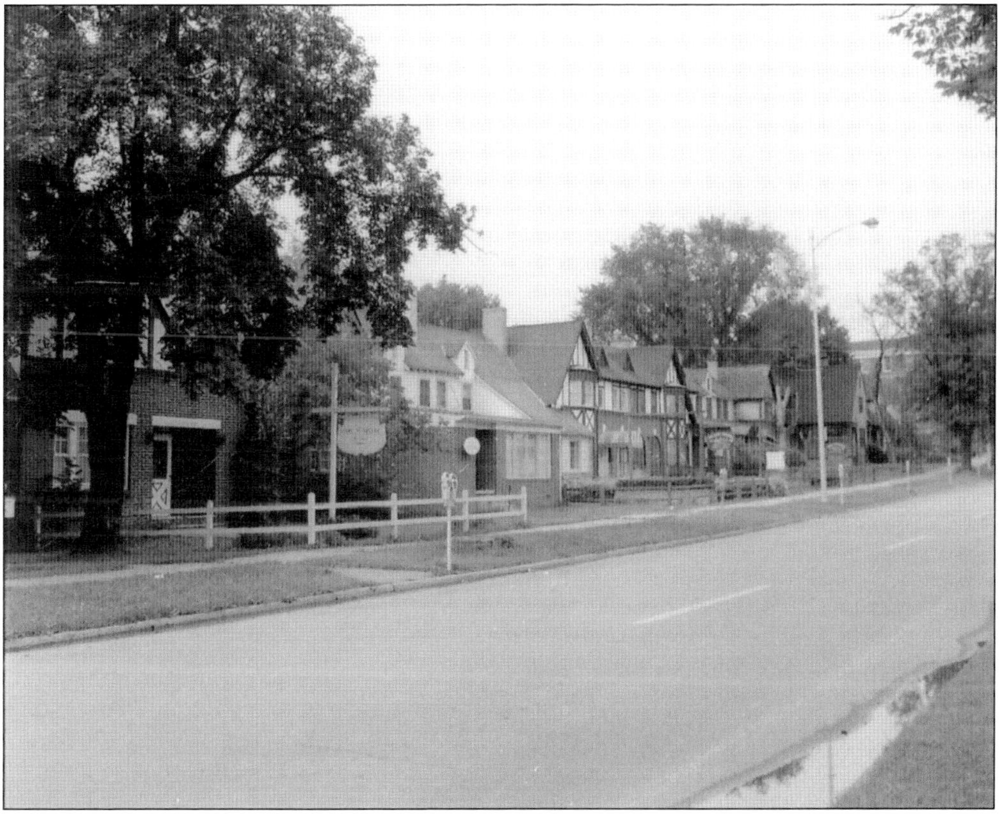

SHELBY STREET ROW HOUSES. The Tudor Revival row houses stretching along Shelby Street in Kingsport were built around 1916. Architect Clinton Mackenzie designed the brick and stucco buildings to house employees of Kingsport's improvement company. The row houses are adjacent to the Church Circle National Historic District. (Courtesy of the City of Kingsport Archives.)

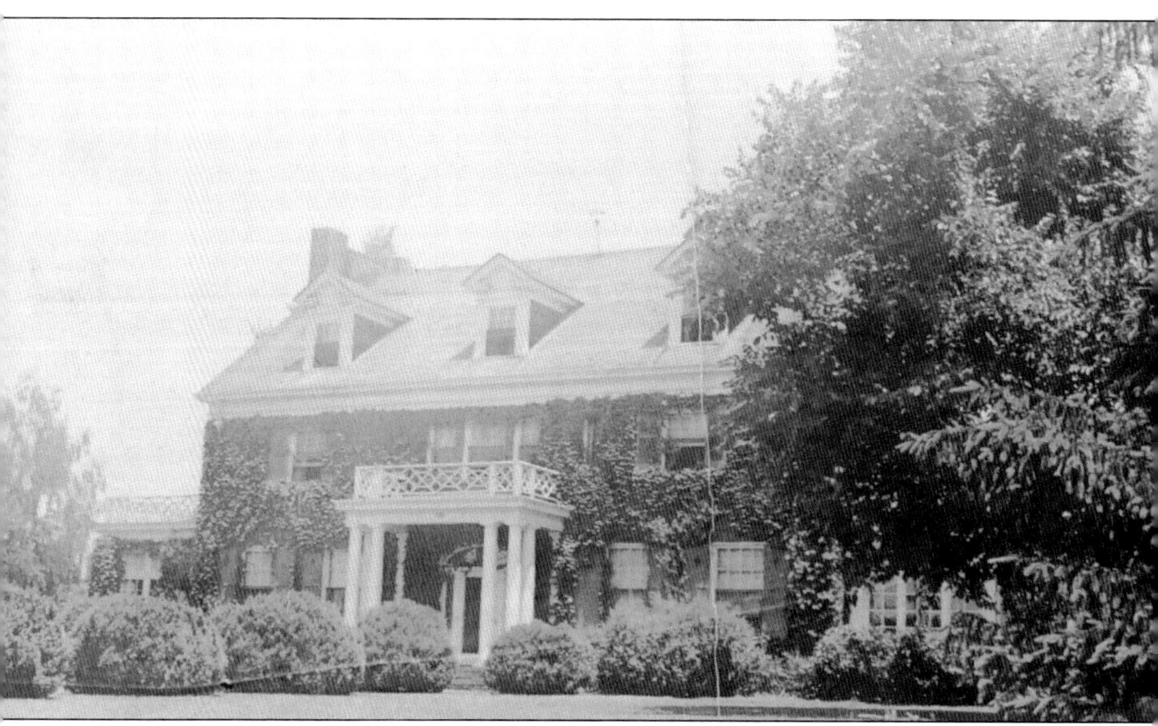

J. Fred Johnson Home. J. Fred Johnson, known as the "Father of Kingsport," lived in a large brick residence constructed in 1915 on Watauga Street. Johnson, who helped bring many businesses to Kingsport, including the Eastman Kodak Company, lived in the home until his death in 1944. The developer worked with John B. Dennis to create the Kingsport Improvement Company. Johnson's home, designed by architect Clinton Mackenzie, was the first to be built in Dobyns Addition, the first upper-class development in the city. A number of large residences were built on Watauga Street during the first few decades of the 20th century, including three now in the National Register of Historic Places. Johnson's home, which is listed in the Register, features two full stories and a third dormered story. The main entrance is framed by a columned portico. Boxwoods line the sidewalks. The property also includes a detached garage and a pool. (Courtesy of the City of Kingsport Archives.)

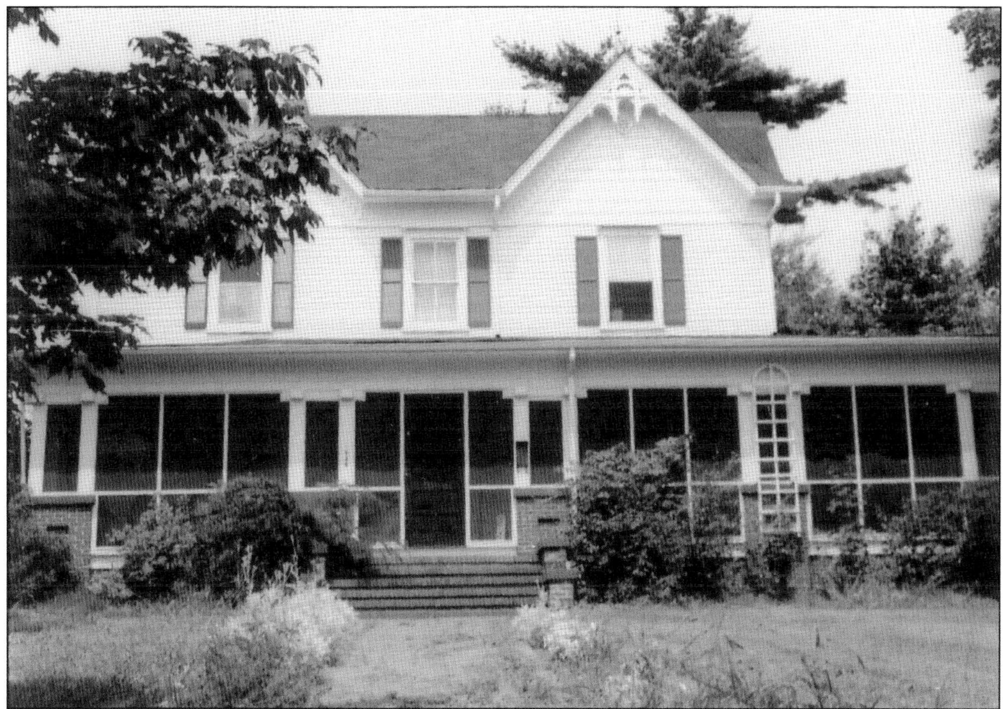

MARTIN-DOBYNS HOUSE. Former Kingsport mayor James Wiley Dobyns lived in this Folk Victorian home on Watauga Street in the early 20th century. The Dobyns family moved in 1915 from Rotherwood Mansion to the home built by Andrew F. Martin in 1884. The residence, a wood-frame structure, has an irregular floor plan on three floors. The porch was added in the 1930s. (Courtesy of the City of Kingsport Archives.)

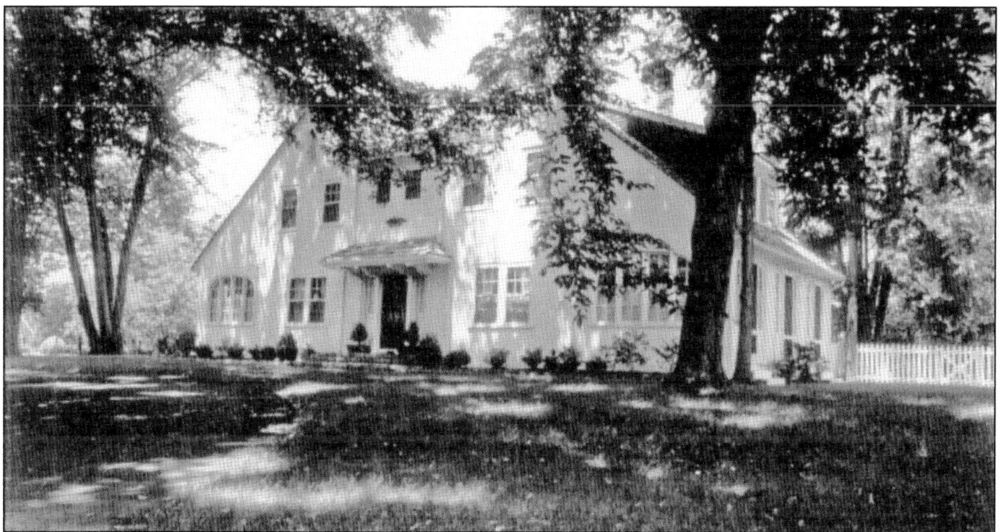

STONE-PENN HOUSE. The Stone-Penn House on Watauga Street in Kingsport was built in 1916 for Jerry Stone and his family by architect Clinton Mackenzie. Stone was president of the Tennessee Eastman Company. In 1922, George E. Penn bought the large English Cottage–style home with Craftsman and Colonial Revival features. Penn was a lawyer for the Clinchfield Railroad. (Courtesy of the Tennessee Historical Commission.)

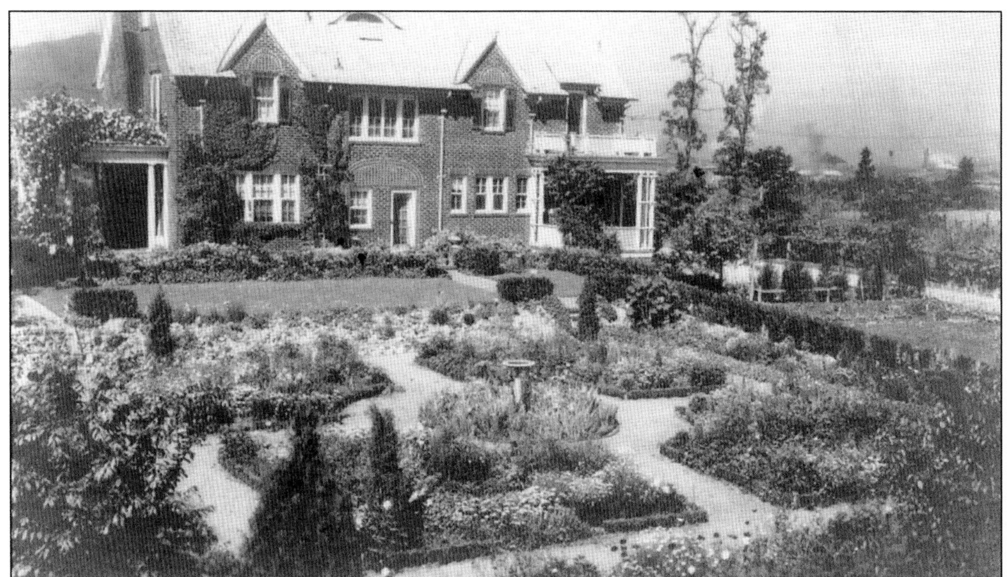

Mead Home. The Mead Corporation, which produced paper products, was one of the largest employers in the city in the early 20th century. C.B. Mead, who directed the Kingsport subsidiary, owned a large property with a brick residence on Watauga Street. His wife took care of beautiful gardens and landscaping behind the home, as pictured here. The home was built in the mid-1910s. (Courtesy of the City of Kingsport Archives.)

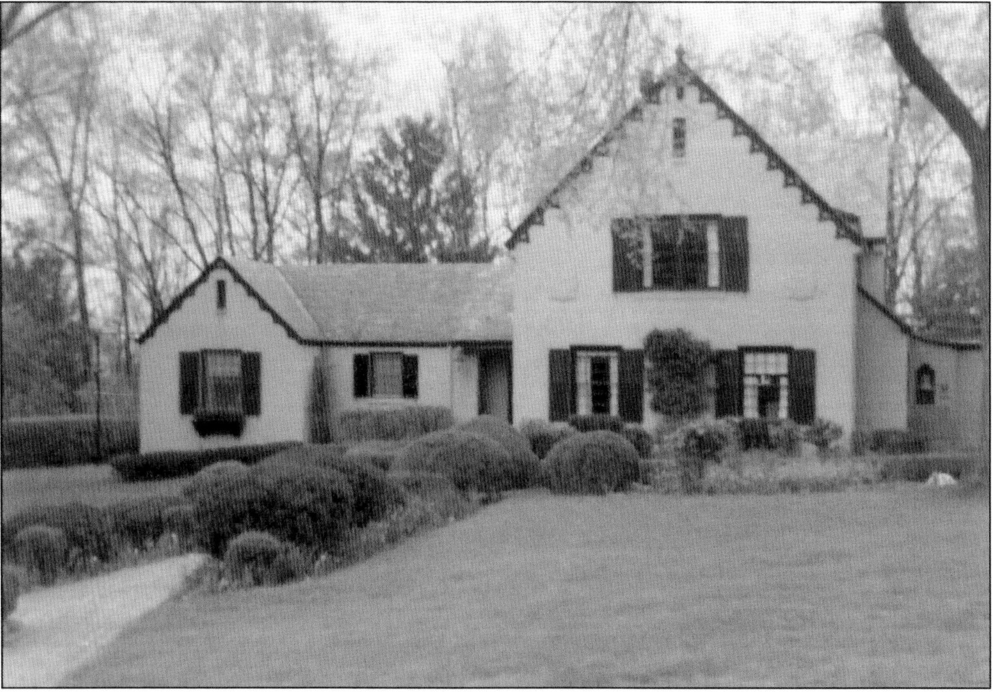

Wilcox Home. Perley Wilcox was the first general manager and chairman of the Eastman company in Kingsport. He lived in a Craftsman home built around 1930 on Linville Street. The home is surrounded by extensive landscaping and trees. According to his will, Wilcox gave the city about 14 acres of land near his house for use as a park. (Courtesy of the City of Kingsport Archives.)

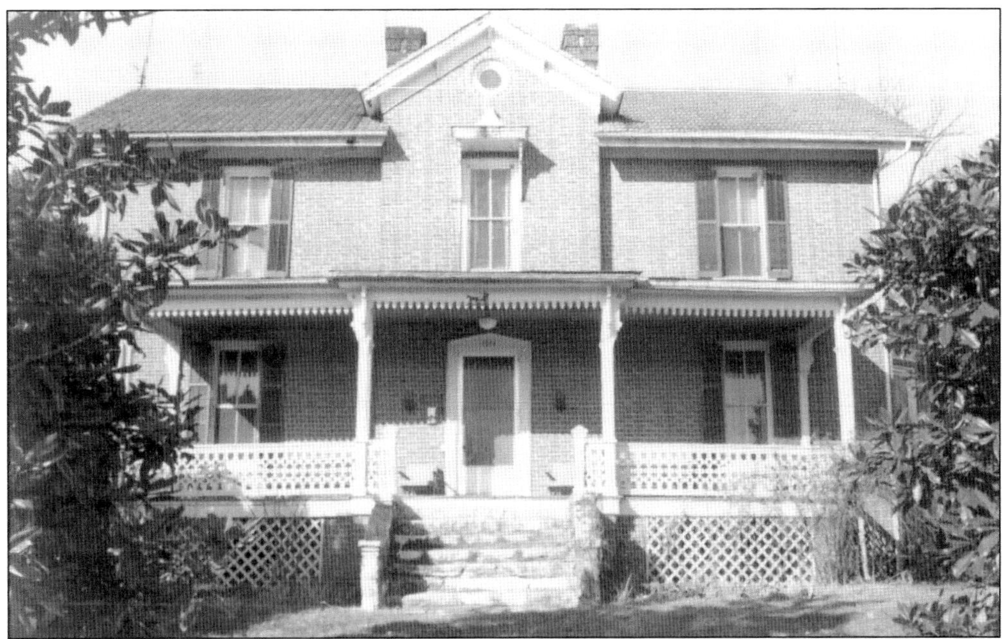

Mount Ida. The Mount Ida property, located on Sevier Terrace Drive in Kingsport, features two historic structures. The first, a log home, was built in the 1790s. Although he did not live here, the cabin was named after David Ross. In 1847, David Deaderick Sevier and his wife, Annis Netherland, bought the home. By 1884, the couple moved the cabin and constructed a two-story brick mansion. The beautiful brick residence features a large central fireplace. Sevier was the son of Valentine Sevier of Greeneville and was a distant relative of early Tennessee governor John Sevier. Annis was the granddaughter of the Netherland Inn founders. David and Annis Sevier are buried in a small grave plot at Mount Ida. (Both, courtesy of the City of Kingsport Archives.)

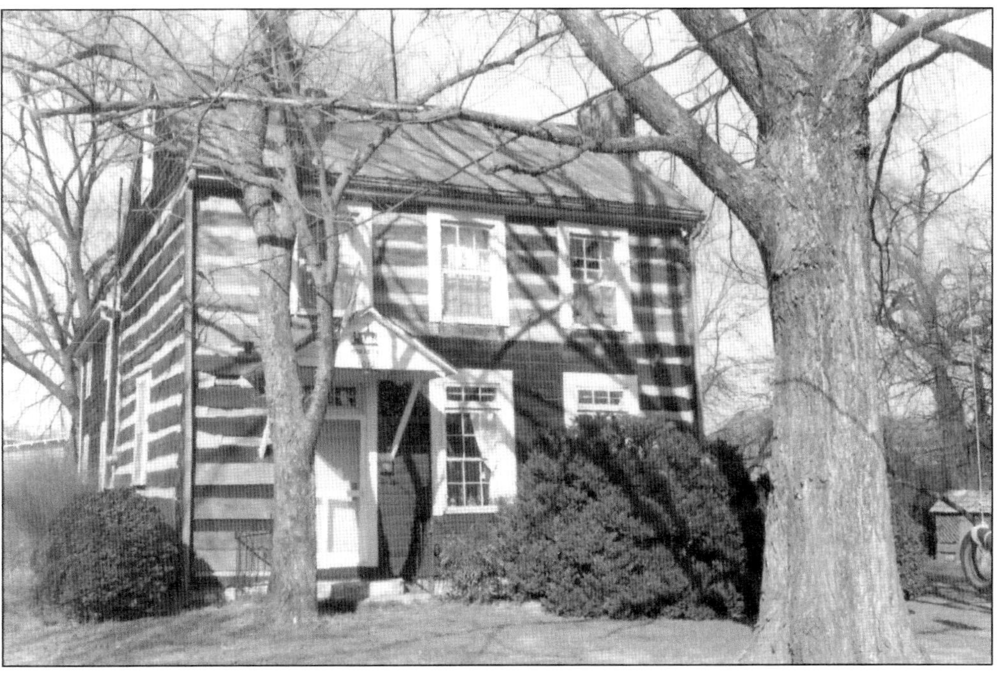

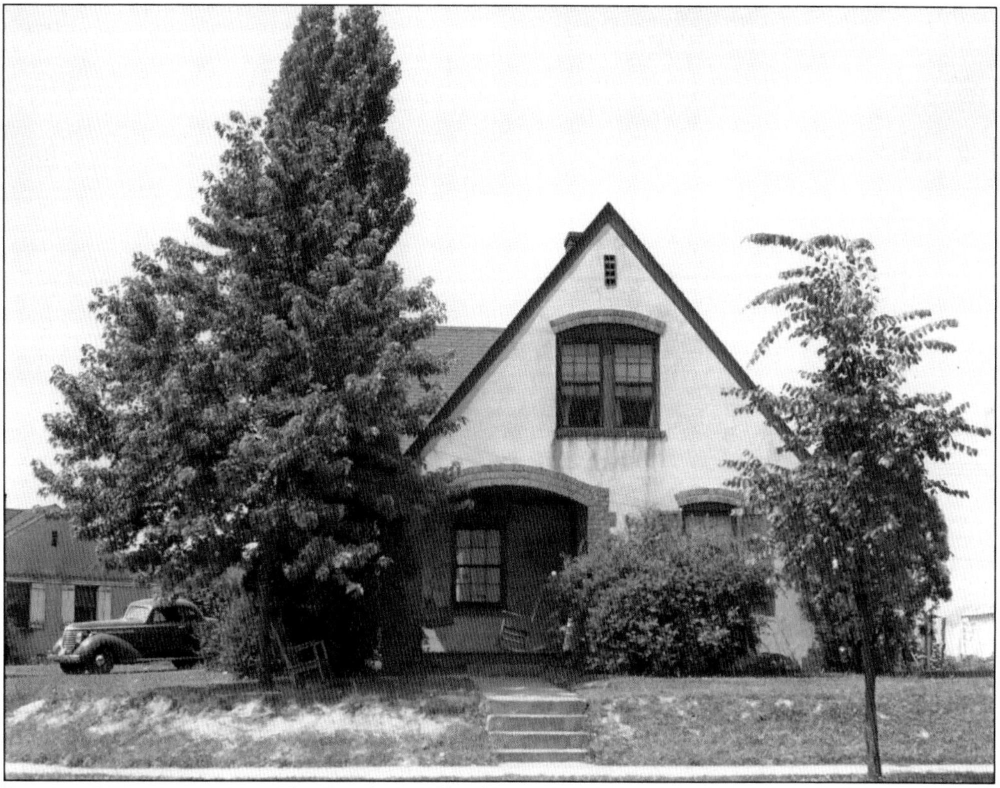

BORDEN NEIGHBORHOOD. The Borden Mills plant was established in 1924, when the owners of the American Printing Company decided to open a facility in Kingsport. A number of homes were built in the surrounding neighborhood to house the plant's employees, which reached into the thousands. The company built 277 homes. (Courtesy of the Tennessee State Library and Archives.)

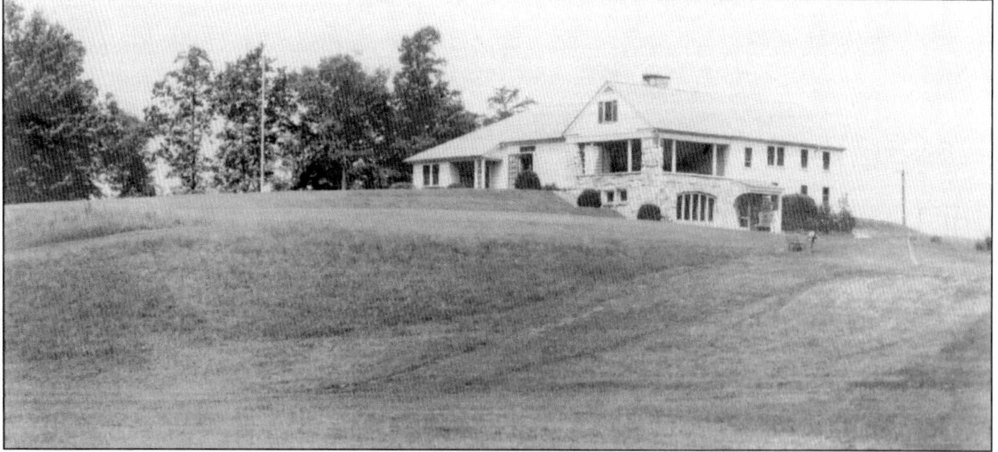

KINGSPORT COUNTRY CLUB. Well-known golf course designer A.W. Tillinghast developed the Kingsport Country Club in 1919. The course featured this clubhouse, which was located near the present intersection of Lamont Street and Pineola Avenue. The golf club closed in 1953, and the American Legion began meeting at the clubhouse. It was then torn down to build the Green Acres neighborhood. (Courtesy of the City of Kingsport Archives.)

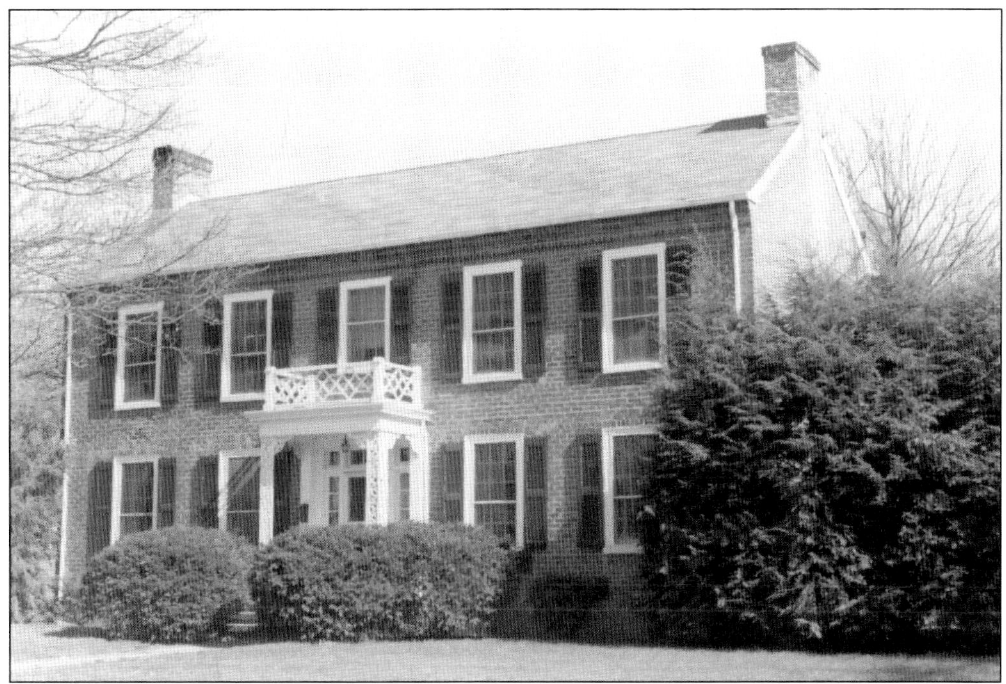

Shipley House. The Shipley House on Memorial Boulevard in Kingsport was constructed by slaves for Enoch Shipley about 1840. During the 19th century, the Shipley home became a popular stop for visitors. It was on route of the old stagecoach road. The home was designed with Federal architecture and features beautiful ornate trim and symmetrical design. (Courtesy of the City of Kingsport Archives.)

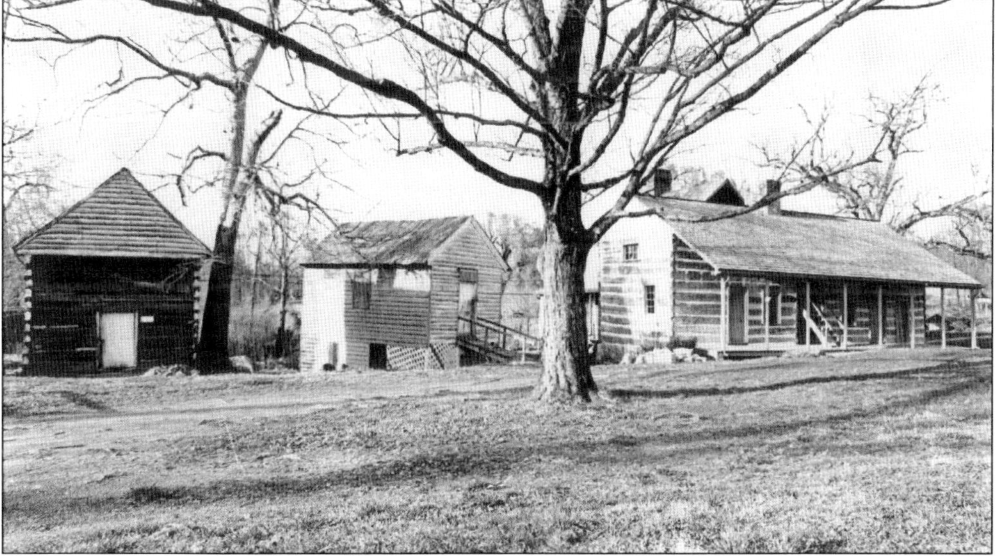

Preston Home. Exchange Place in Kingsport is the site of the historic Preston Farm. The home, built in 1820, is a saddlebag-style log house. It features two rooms with a central fireplace, gabled roof, and front porch. John S. Gaines first owned the property. There was a store, post office, blacksmith, and a woodshed. The Preston family lived here after 1847. (Courtesy of the City of Kingsport Archives.)

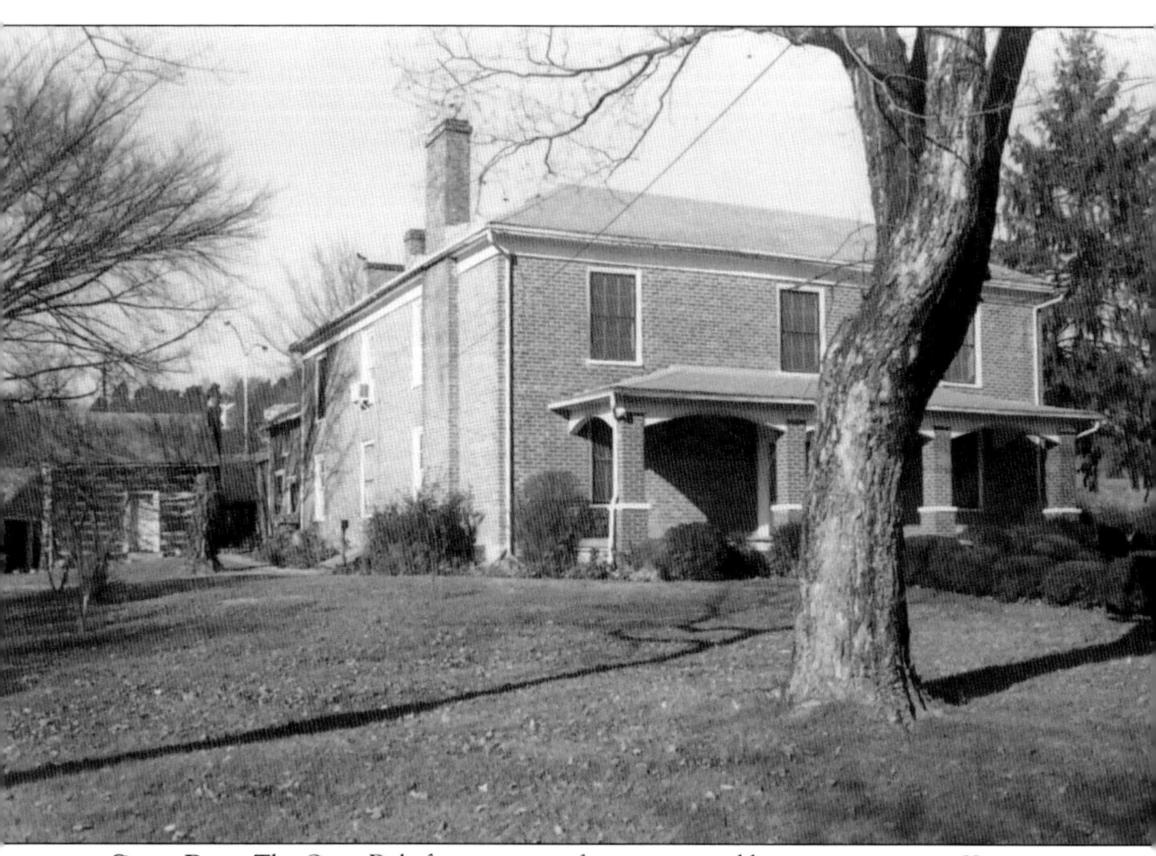

Grass Dale. The Grass Dale farm property features a grand historic mansion in Kingsport on Clinchfield Street near Stone Drive. The grounds are near the western most border of the 1750 Edmund Pendleton Land Grant, according to the City of Kingsport Archives. Pendleton sold the property to David Ross. In 1819, land was then sold to Joseph Everett. Martin Roller Jr. later purchased and sold the property again in the 1850s. Joseph Groseclose Sr. then operated a large plantation and built the Grass Dale Mansion, also known as Groseclose Mansion, in 1856. The structure, built of hand-fired brick, also features a two-story rear ell that was added in the 1880s. The current large porch was later added. Grass Dale was once a rural farm, but it is now landlocked by busy highways. (Courtesy of the City of Kingsport Archives.)

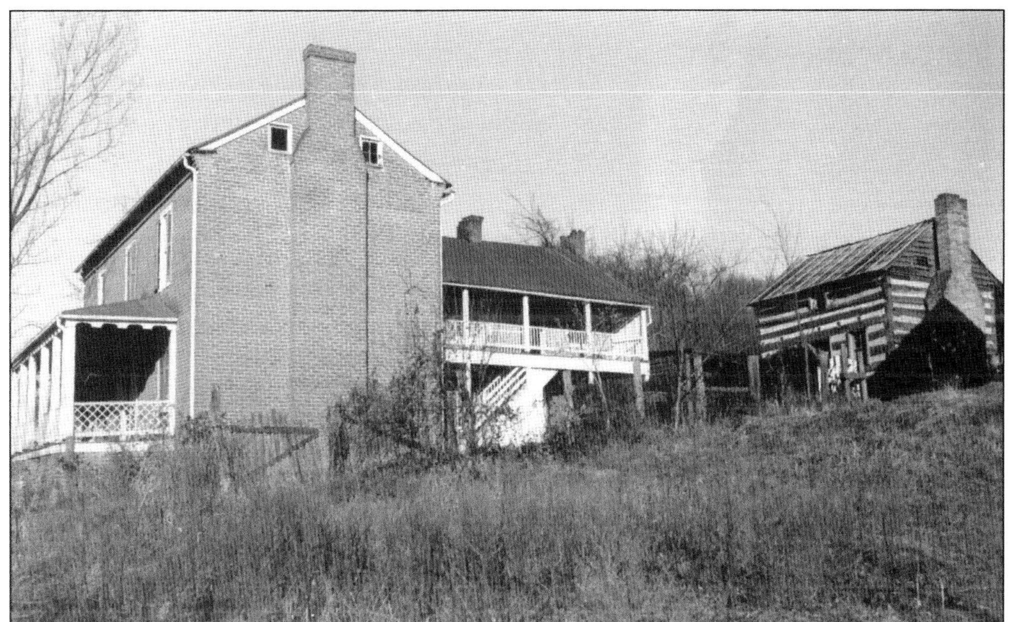

Fain Plantation/Arcadia. Thomas Fain, a Union supporter, used slaves to build his home, Arcadia, in the early 1850s. The 10-room brick home, also known as Fain Plantation, overlooks Reedy Creek. The farm also features a small utility barn, two log slave cabins, a springhouse, crib house, a log cabin study, and an old gravesite, where Fain is buried. (Courtesy of the City of Kingsport Archives.)

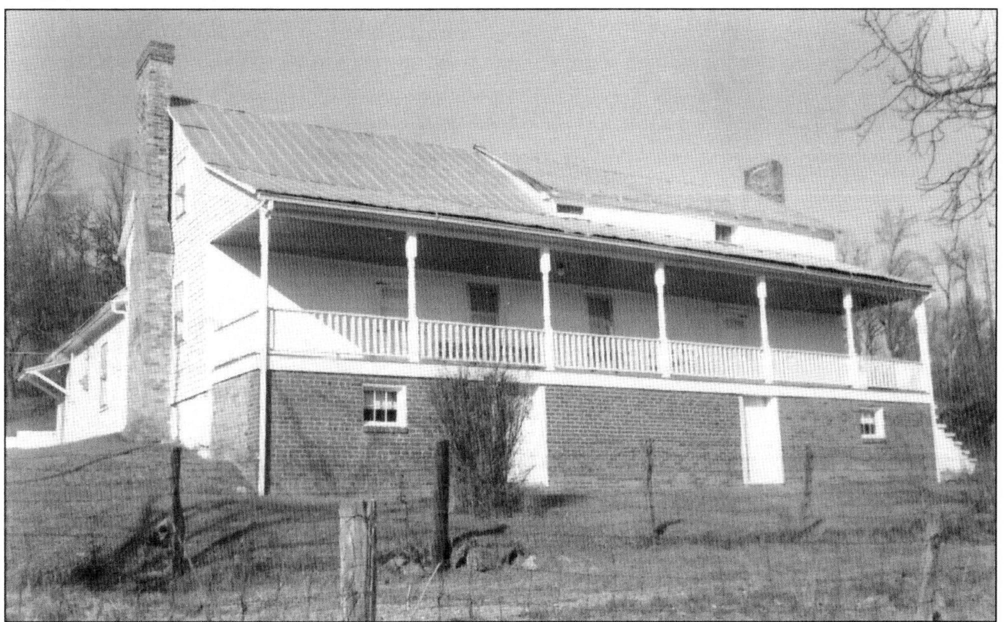

Yancey's Tavern. Yancey's Tavern was constructed of hand-hewn logs in 1779. James Hollis Sr. built the structure and the Sullivan County Commission reportedly met there. In 1784, John Yancey purchased the building and converted it into a popular tavern along the old stagecoach route. By the 1840s, John Shaver bought the tavern and it remained an inn. Shaver also clapboarded the structure. (Courtesy of the City of Kingsport Archives.)

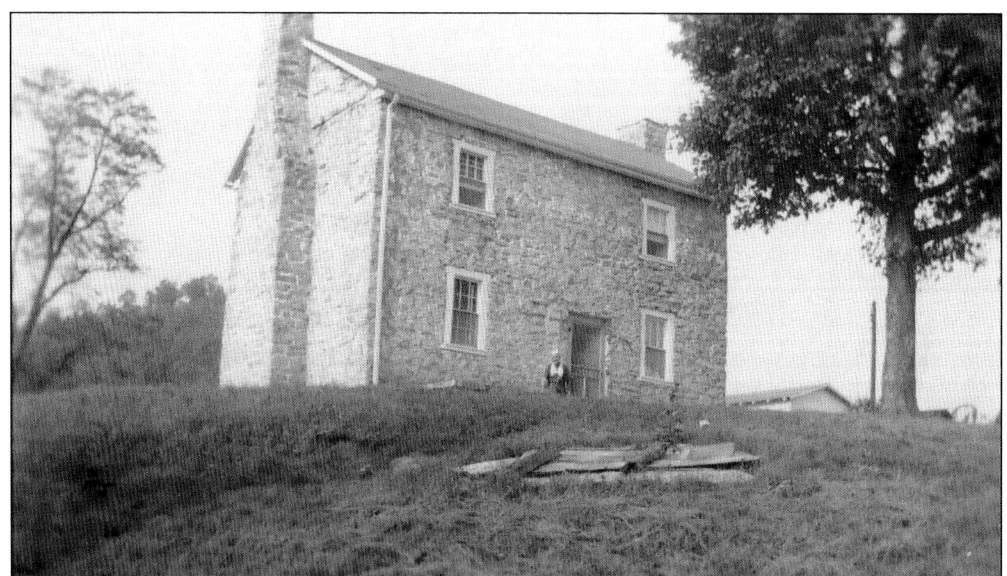

Wills-Dickey House. The Wills-Dickey House is a stone structure built around 1800 in the Carters Valley community of western Sullivan County, near the Hawkins County line. The two-story residence with two-foot-thick stone walls features a large front porch with columns. The home of Jacob and Mary Wills was added to the National Register of Historic Places in 1973. (Courtesy of the City of Kingsport Archives.)

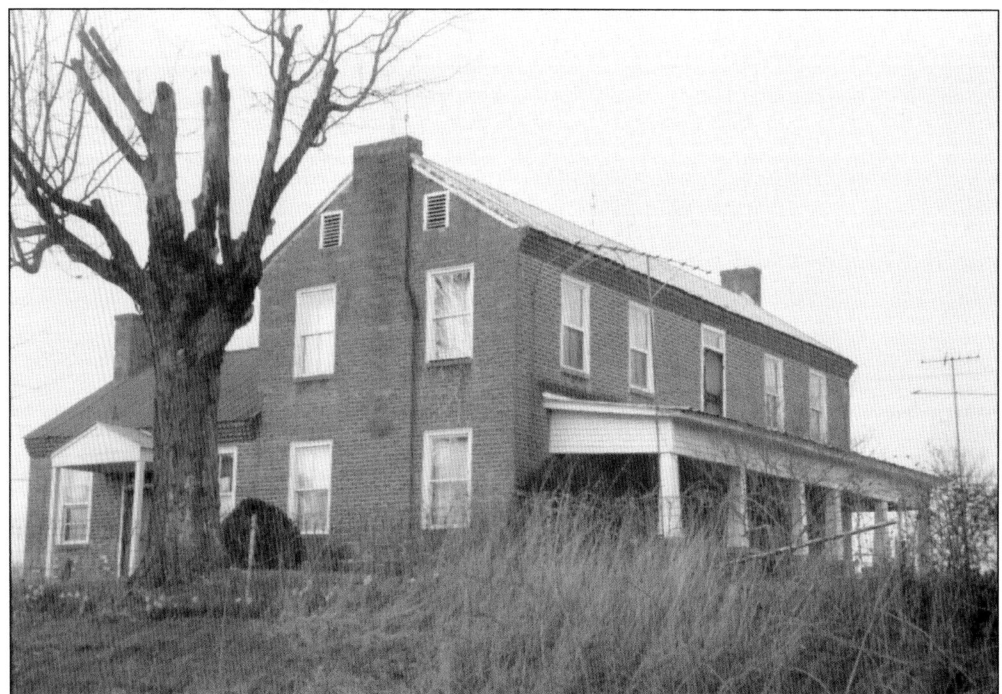

Haws House. The Haws House, a brick residence at the corner of State Route 93 and Murrell Road in the Horse Creek section of Sullivan County, was built in the mid-19th century. It is on the combined lands of Lewis Hale and his wife. The Hales eventually sold it in 1881. The home has been restored. (Courtesy of the City of Kingsport Archives.)

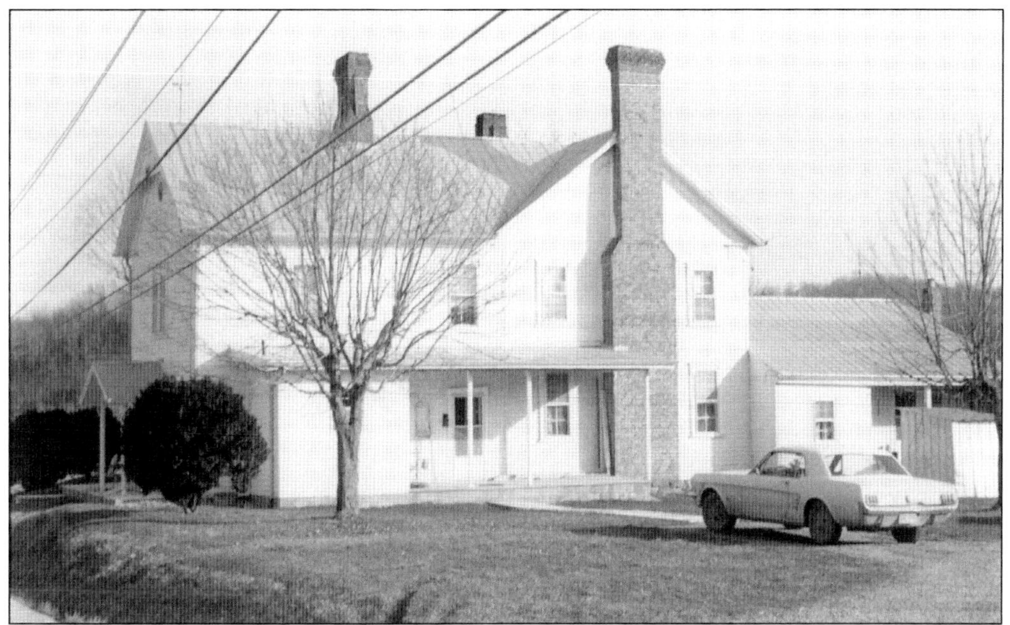

Jonathan Bachman House. Jonathan Bachman built his farmhouse in the Horse Creek section of Sullivan County in 1823. The center log section has been covered in siding and several wings have been added. Bachman family members occupied the white-sided residence on Lone Star Road for more than 150 years. Another residence, the Nathan Bachman Home, is located nearby on Sullivan Gardens Drive. (Courtesy of the City of Kingsport Archives.)

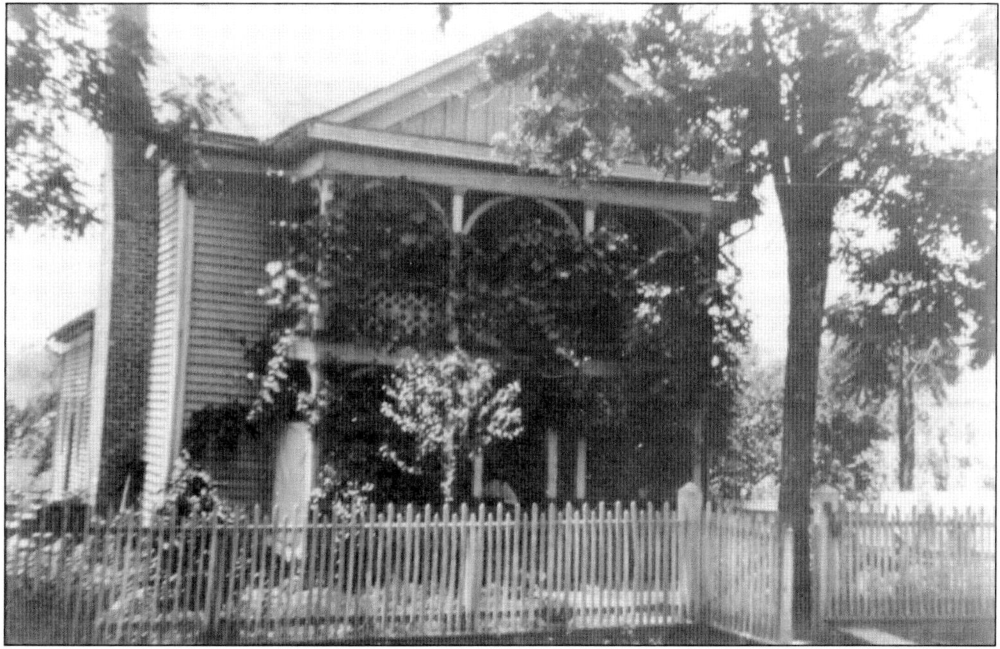

Hickman-Dolan House. The Hickman-Dolan House is located in western Sullivan County on Reservoir Road. Daniel Hickman built a log home here between 1835 and 1843, according to notes from historian Muriel Spoden. Hickman's heirs sold it to John Dolan after the Civil War. The two-story log structure now has white siding. (Courtesy of the City of Kingsport Archives.)

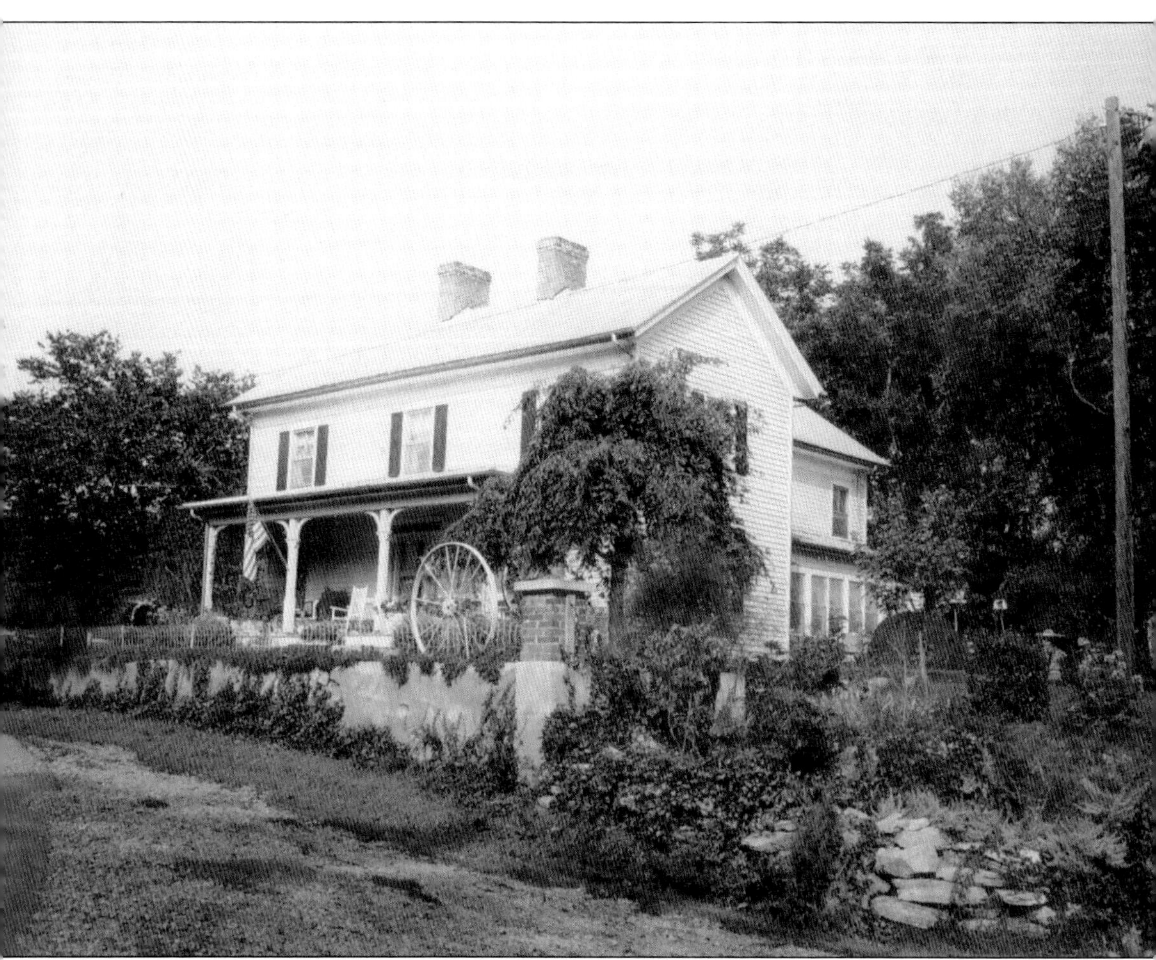

Alexander Hall Farm. The historic Hall Farm on present-day Proffitt Lane was founded in 1882 by Thomas Hall. His grandson Alexander Doak Hall built the house in the late 19th century. A stand of virgin poplar, oak, and walnut trees that grew on the land to the east of the home provided the lumber, according to the National Register of Historic Places. Built to replace an original log house, the two-story home, with an ell design, rests on a limestone outcropping and features Folk Victorian and Greek Revival elements. Inside, the Hall House retains the typical I-house plan with a center hall and a single room off each side. The farm has a number of outbuildings, including a couple unique ones. The cave house was built over a cave and used to store things such as milk, butter, and vegetables. Another unique structure is the one-story frame builders' shack. According to the owners, the structure housed the carpenter and brickmason from 1879 to 1882 when the main house was under construction. (Courtesy of the City of Kingsport Archives.)

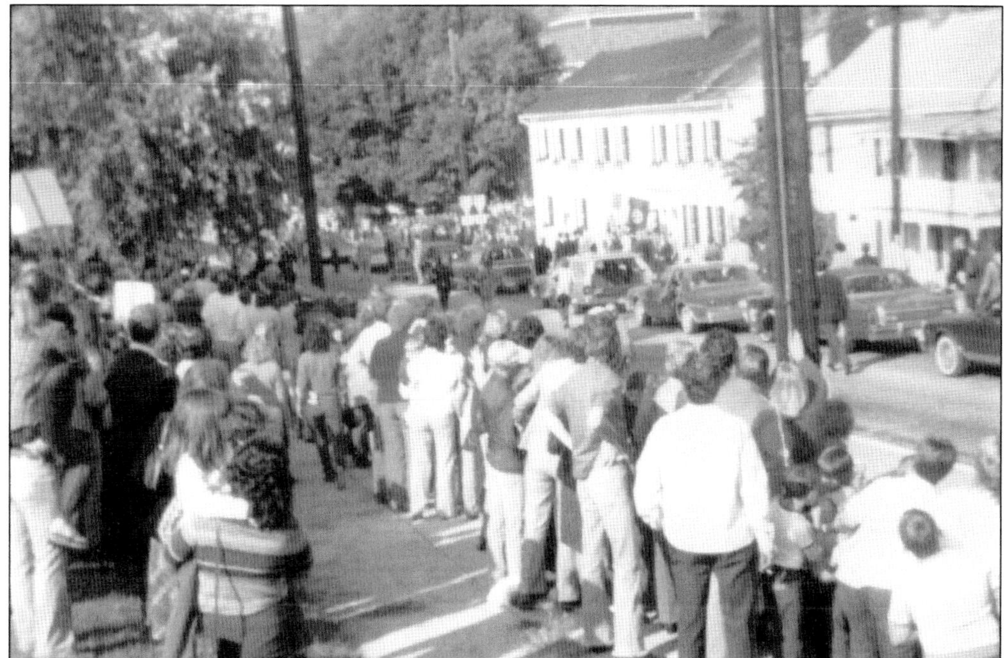

President Visits Blountville. Pres. Jimmy Carter visited historic downtown Blountville in 1981. His limousine and entourage are pictured passing the Old Deery Inn. Blountville, the county seat of Sullivan County, was laid off as a town and established as the county seat in 1795. A number of structures in the unincorporated town are listed in the National Register of Historic Places. (Courtesy of Brenda Dodson.)

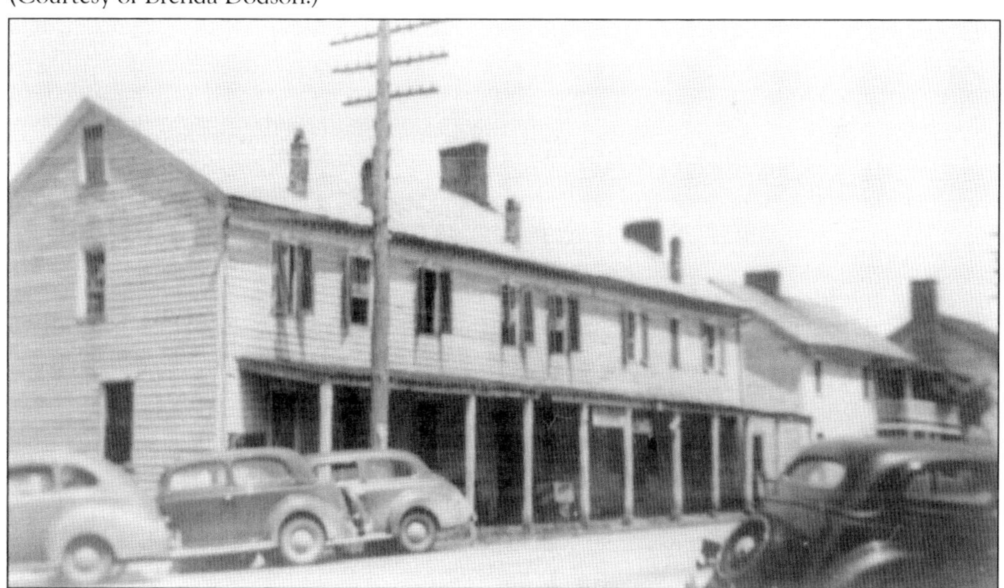

Old Deery Inn. The Old Deery Inn, built in the late 18th century, is located in downtown Blountville and served travelers on the old stage road. William Deery purchased the property in 1801. The inn features 19 rooms, three entrances, and a chimney at both ends. Presidents, generals, foreign dignitaries, and other notable guests have visited the inn. (Courtesy of the City of Kingsport Archives.)

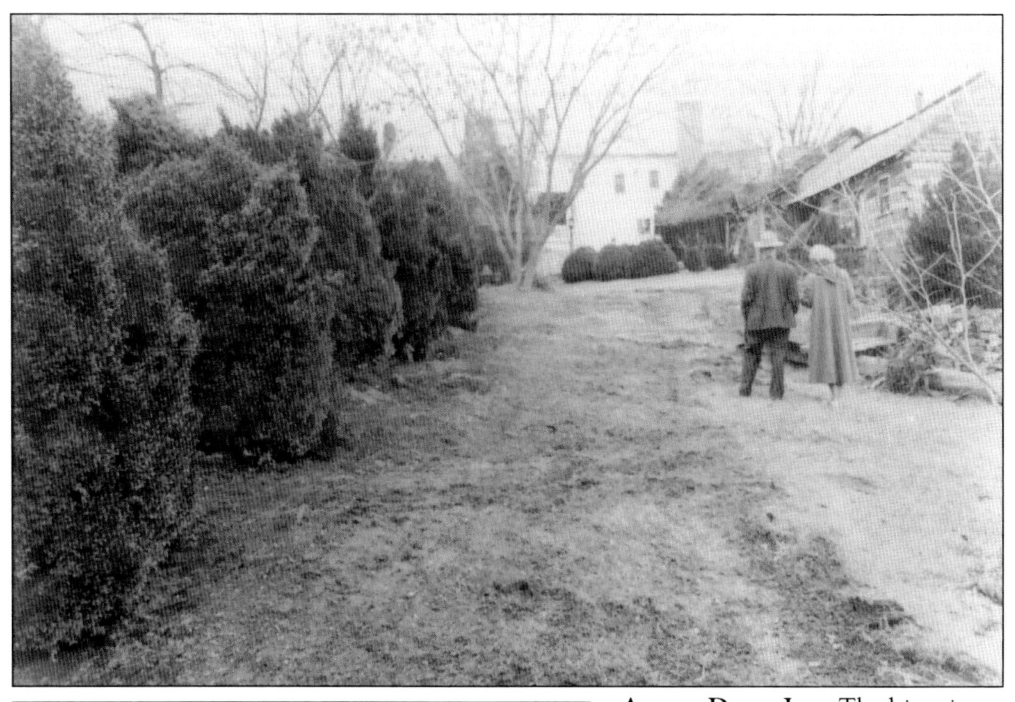

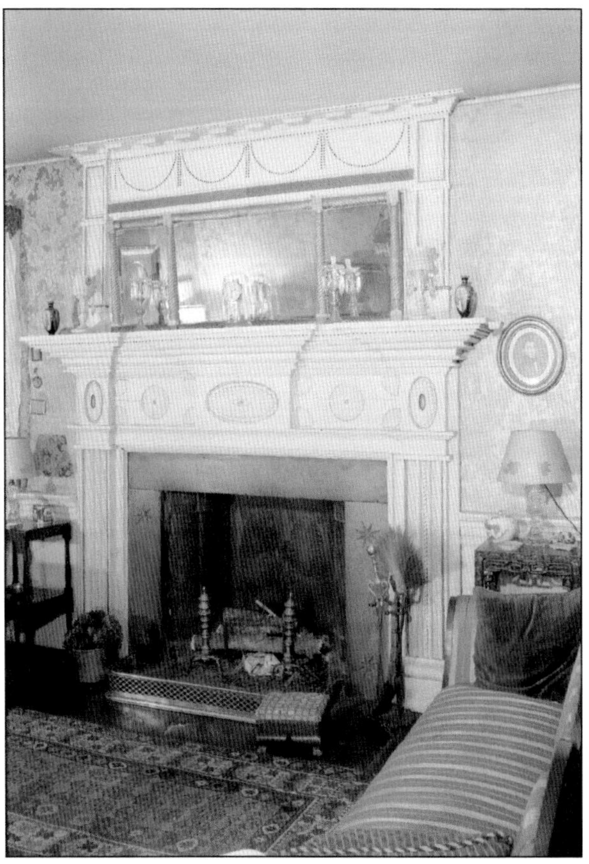

At the Deery Inn. The historic Old Deery Inn property in downtown Blountville features a number of historic structures. Virginia Byars Caldwell, who purchased the inn in 1940, added a smokehouse, the offices of the King Ironworks, a springhouse, and an early law office. The buildings, pictured above, are located behind the Federal-style inn. The photograph at left was taken inside the inn on the first floor. It shows the northeast room, with the fireplace and mantle. The local historical association has completely restored the inn, which was built in the late 18th century. (Above, courtesy of the City of Kingsport Archives; left, courtesy of the Library of Congress.)

Anderson Townhouse. Blountville's oldest home was built in 1792 of hand-hewn logs. The two-story Anderson Townhouse once housed the town's commissioners. Justices stayed here when the nearby court was in session. Besides three commissioners and judges, Presbyterian and Methodist ministers also lived here, as did Joseph Anderson, one of the founders of Bristol. (Courtesy of Brenda Dodson.)

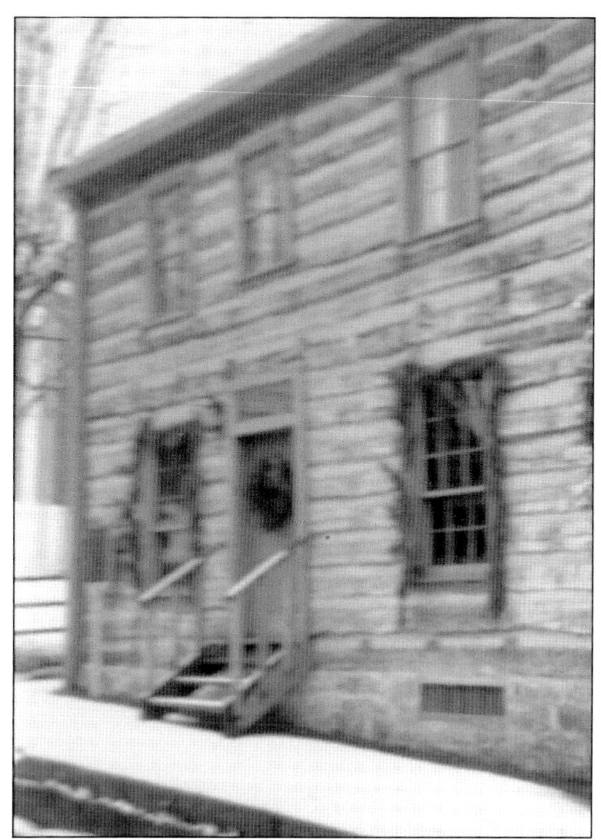

Dulaney Hall. A community parade passes by Dulaney Hall along Main Street in Blountville in this photograph. Built in 1802 by Dr. Elkanan Dulaney, the two-story home is the oldest brick structure in town. Dulaney was a physician and state legislator. William Anderson later lived here. According to historians, during the Battle of Blountville, when men fought outside, women and children stayed here for safety. (Courtesy of Brenda Dodson.)

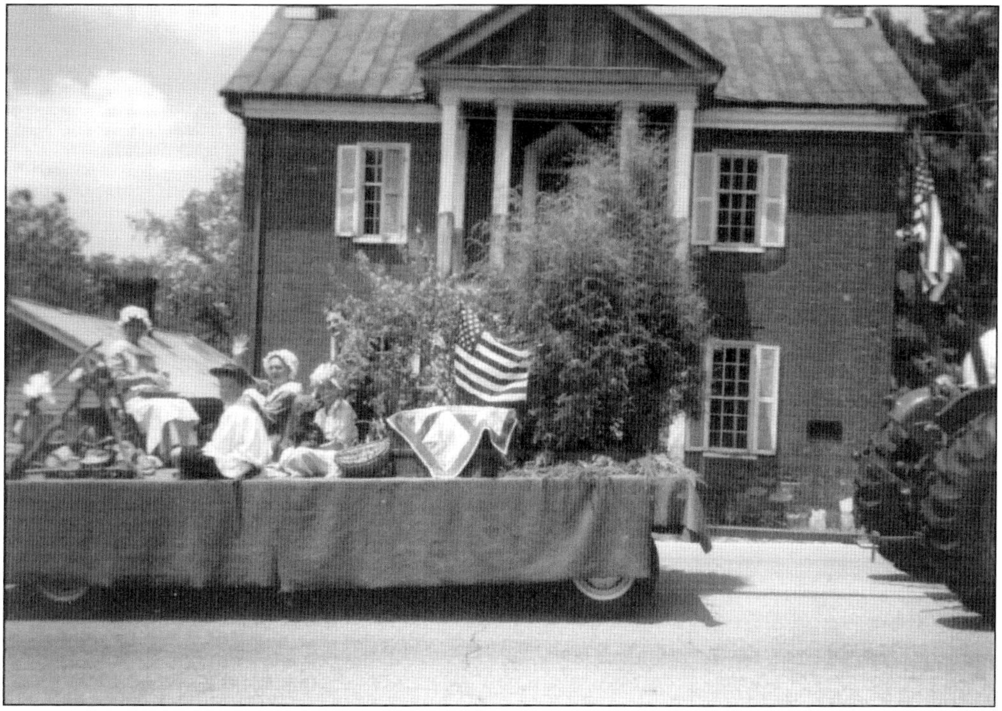

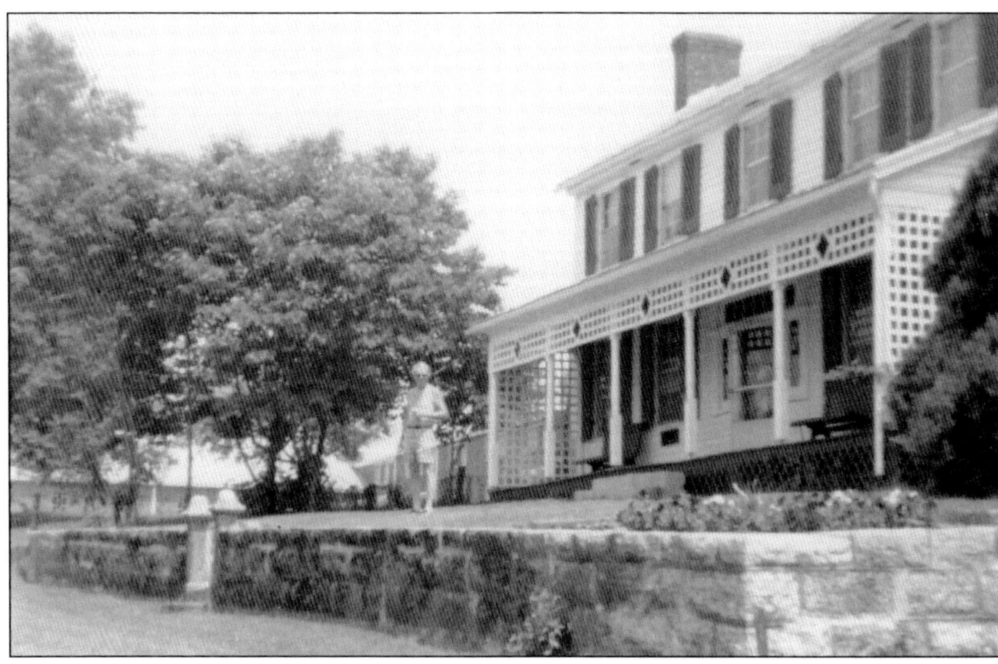

Cannonball House. Dr. Elbert Miller built his two-story, white frame house in 1848 in Blountville. It was purchased by attorney Matthew Taylor Haynes in 1855. During the Civil War, the home got its name, the Cannonball House. Haynes was a Confederate, and during the Battle of Blountville, the home was a Union target. A number of cannonballs struck the west side of the house and the chimney. The Blountville United Methodist Church purchased the Cannonball House in 1992. The front of the home can be seen in the above photograph. The rear of the Cannonball House, as well as Dulaney Hall, which is across the street, can be seen in the photograph below. (Both, courtesy of Brenda Dodson.)

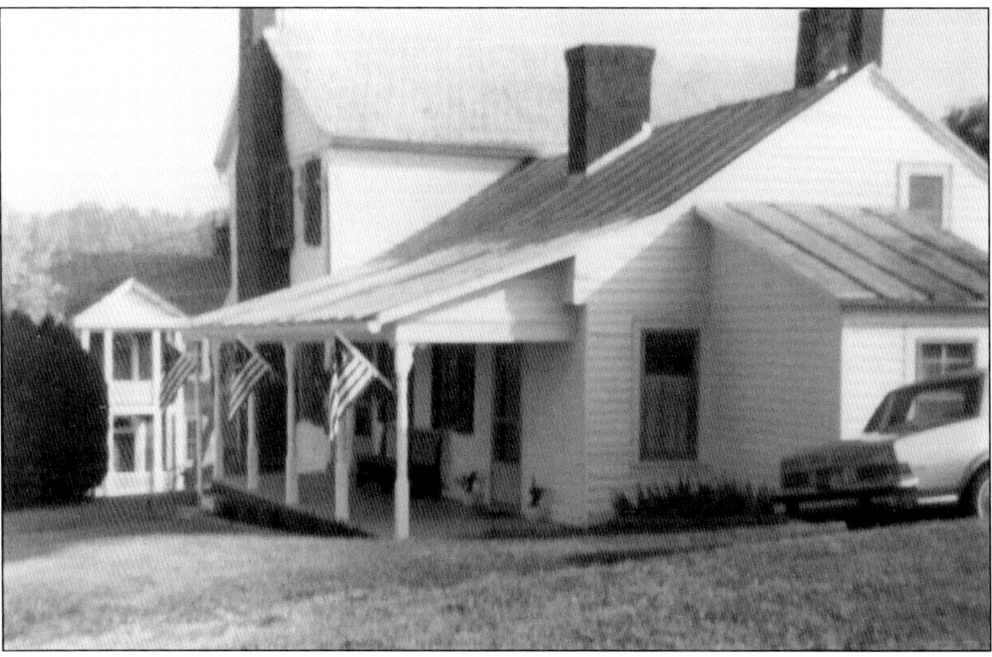

Three

Johnson City and Washington County

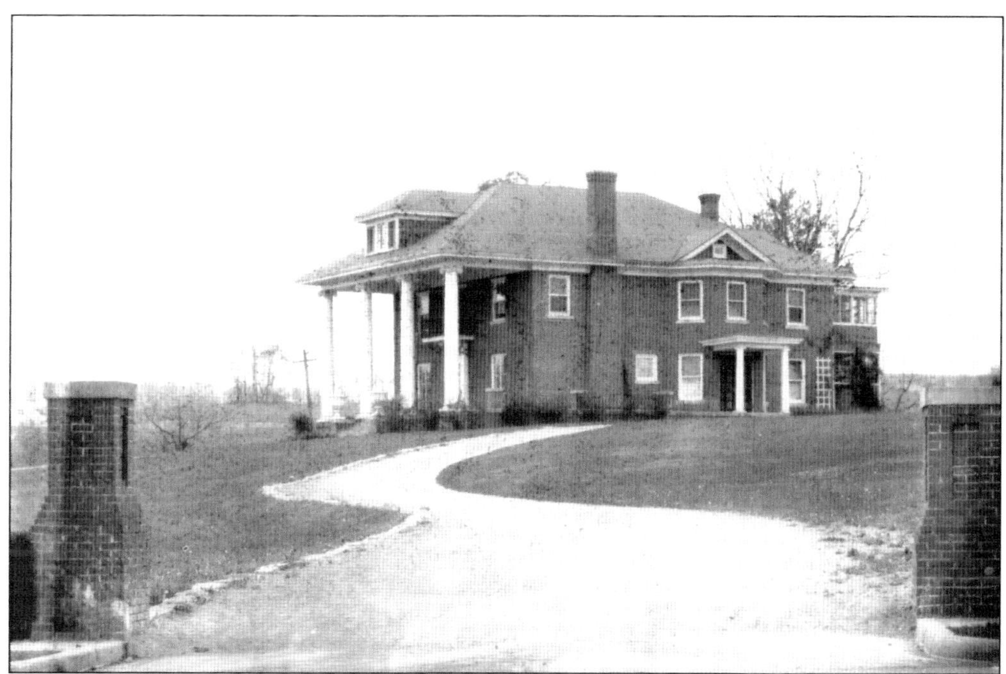

Gump House. The centerpiece of the Gump Addition in Johnson City is the home of Harry Gump. Although the surrounding residences were constructed in the early and mid-20th century, Gump's house was built in 1820. John Bowman built the home as a wedding gift for his daughter on 160 acres of land. Gump purchased the home in 1907 from the Boring family. (Courtesy of the Archives of Appalachia.)

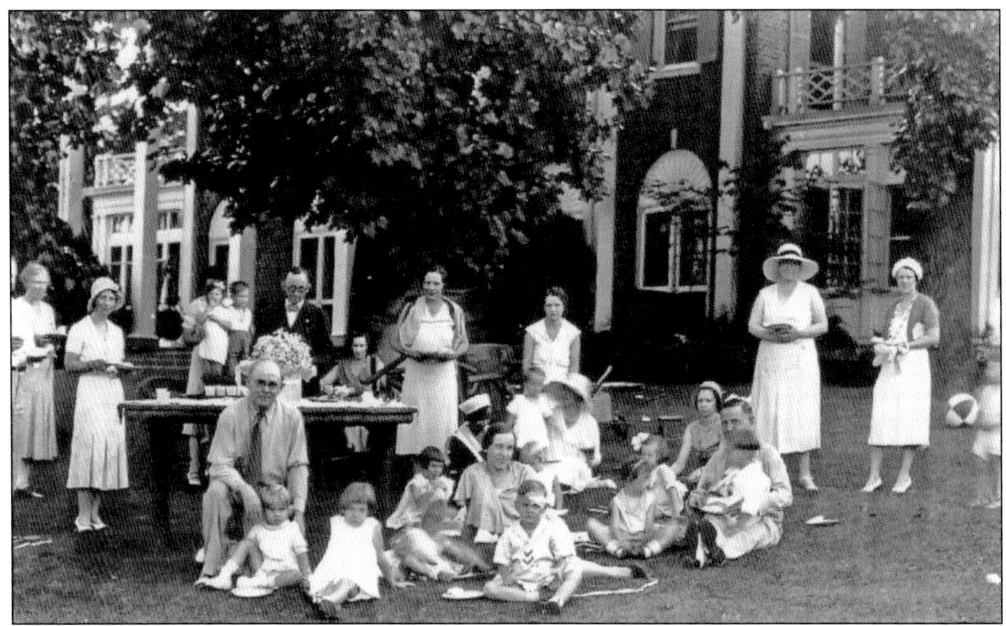

Shelbridge. Since 1973, East Tennessee State University's presidents have lived in Johnson City's historic Shelbridge on Eleventh Avenue at North Roan Street. The estate, built in 1920, was constructed for Roswell H. Spears. It was designed by notable architect D.R. Beeson. The name Shelbridge comes from the mansion's second owners. In 1928, Spears, a lumber dealer, sold the property to Henry P. Bridges and his wife, Shelby Thomas Bridges. The home is named for Shelby Bridges, and following the death of widowed Shelby, the state purchased the home in 1973. Today, the gated two-and-a-half-story home features Colonial Revival elements, extensive landscaping, and several outbuildings. (Both, courtesy of the Bridges family.)

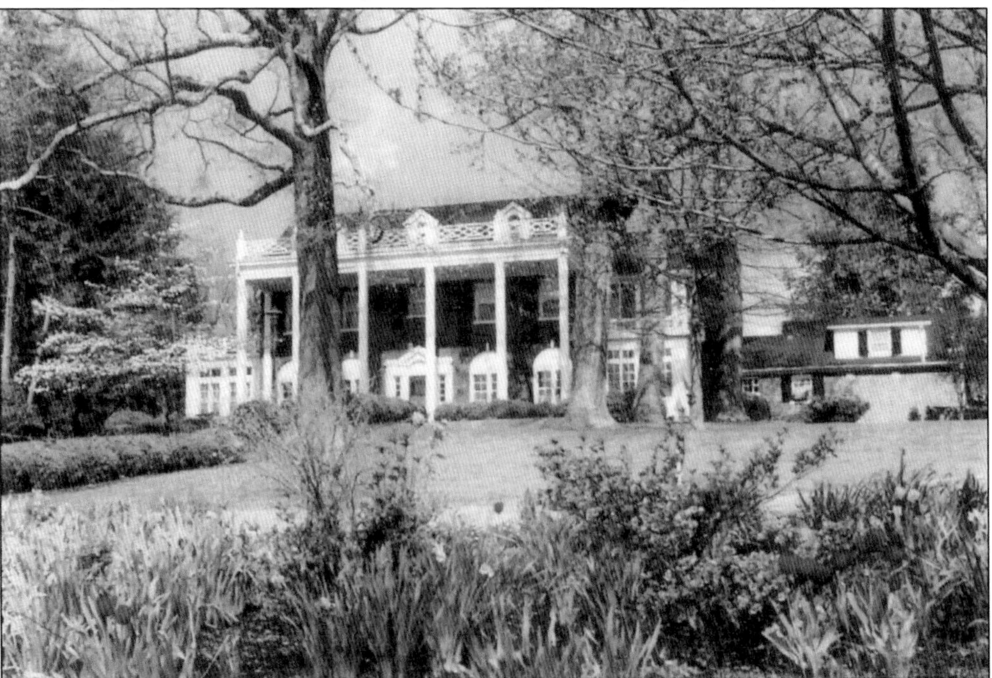

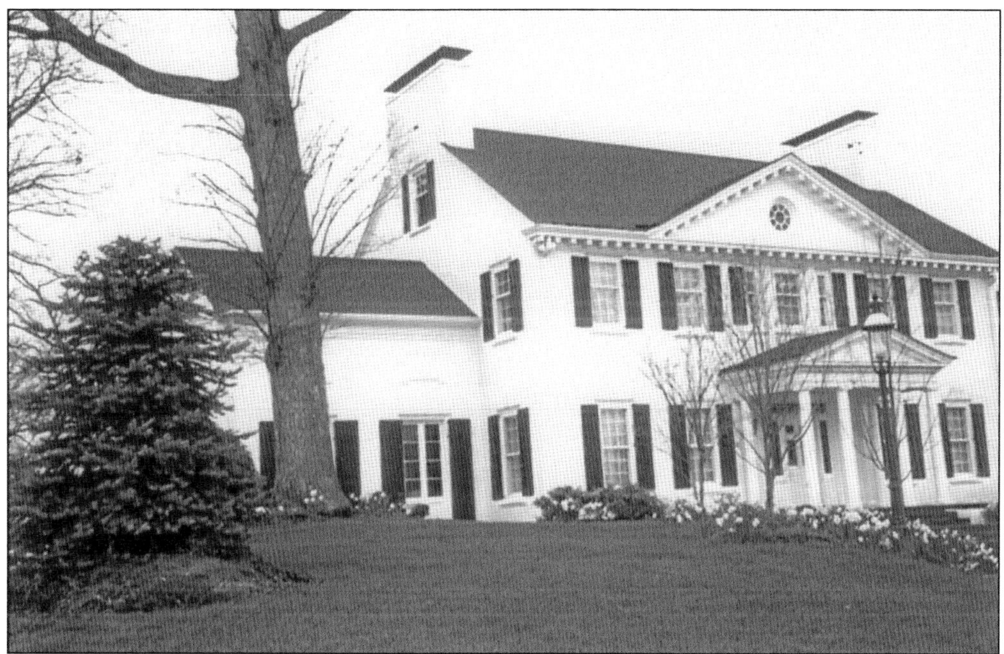

AQUONE. Aquone, an estate in north Johnson City, was built in 1925 for Samuel Cole Williams. Architect Leland Cardwell designed the home, which is based on a home in Maryland. Aquone features a two-story library, a sunroom, and a wine cellar. Williams was a judge, attorney, historian, educator, businessman, and author. (Courtesy of the Tennessee Historical Commission.)

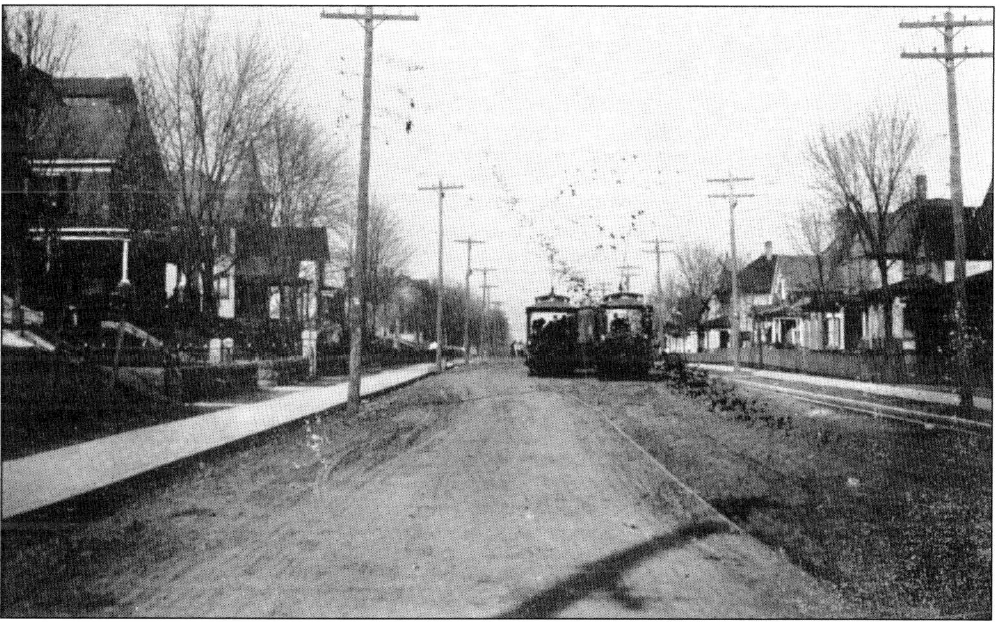

WATAUGA AVENUE IN JOHNSON CITY. This postcard features Watauga Avenue in Johnson City, which is lined with a number of historic homes. Two streetcars, which no longer operate, are pictured. The C.B. Hamilton Home, built in 1899, is located on Watauga Avenue at Baxter Street. The historic Munsey Slack Home is also on the busy thoroughfare. (Courtesy of Betty Jane Hylton.)

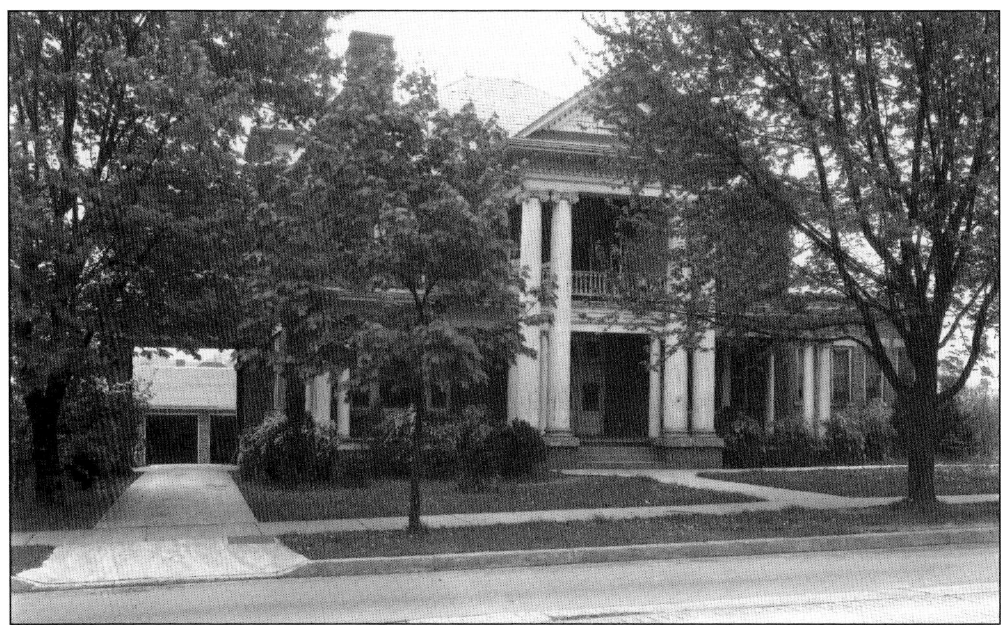

Munsey Slack Home. The Munsey Slack Home is located on Watauga Avenue in Johnson City. The large Neoclassical-designed house was built in 1904. Slack owned an early 20th-century newspaper called the *Johnson City Staff-News*. His father owned the *Bristol Courier*. By the 1940s, the residence housed student nurses from Appalachian Hospital and Memorial Hospital. It has also been a funeral home. (Courtesy of the Archives of Appalachia.)

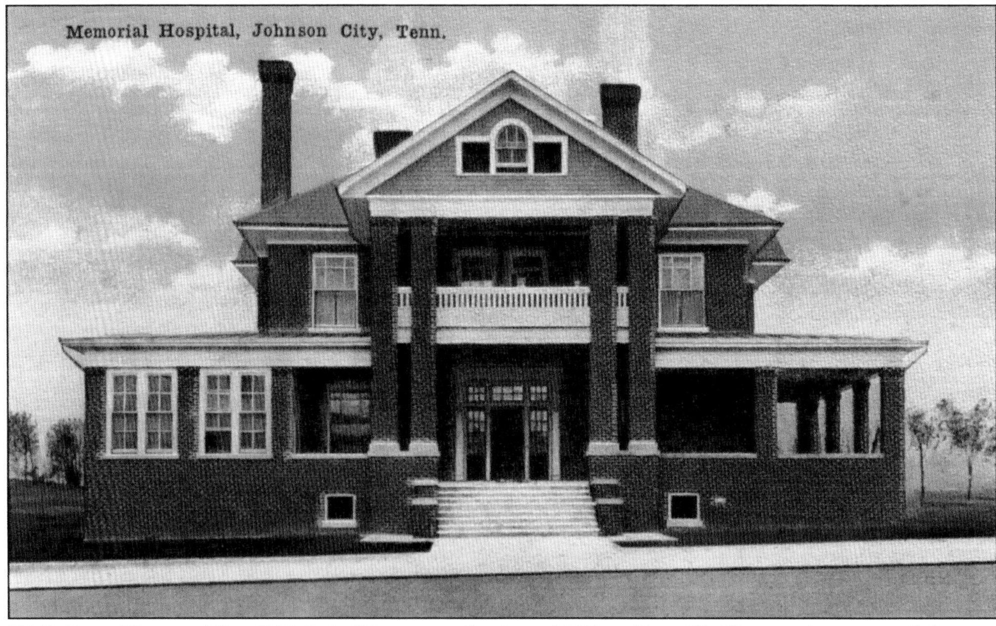

C.H. Lyle House. The C.H. Lyle House was built in 1915 on East Chilhowie Avenue in Johnson City. Lyle, editor of the *Comet* newspaper, needed a large home to accommodate his family. After the home's completion, he accepted a job at the National Soldiers' Home and resided there. The home then became Memorial Hospital. Lyle moved into the house in the 1930s, after the hospital relocated. (Courtesy of Betty Jane Hylton.)

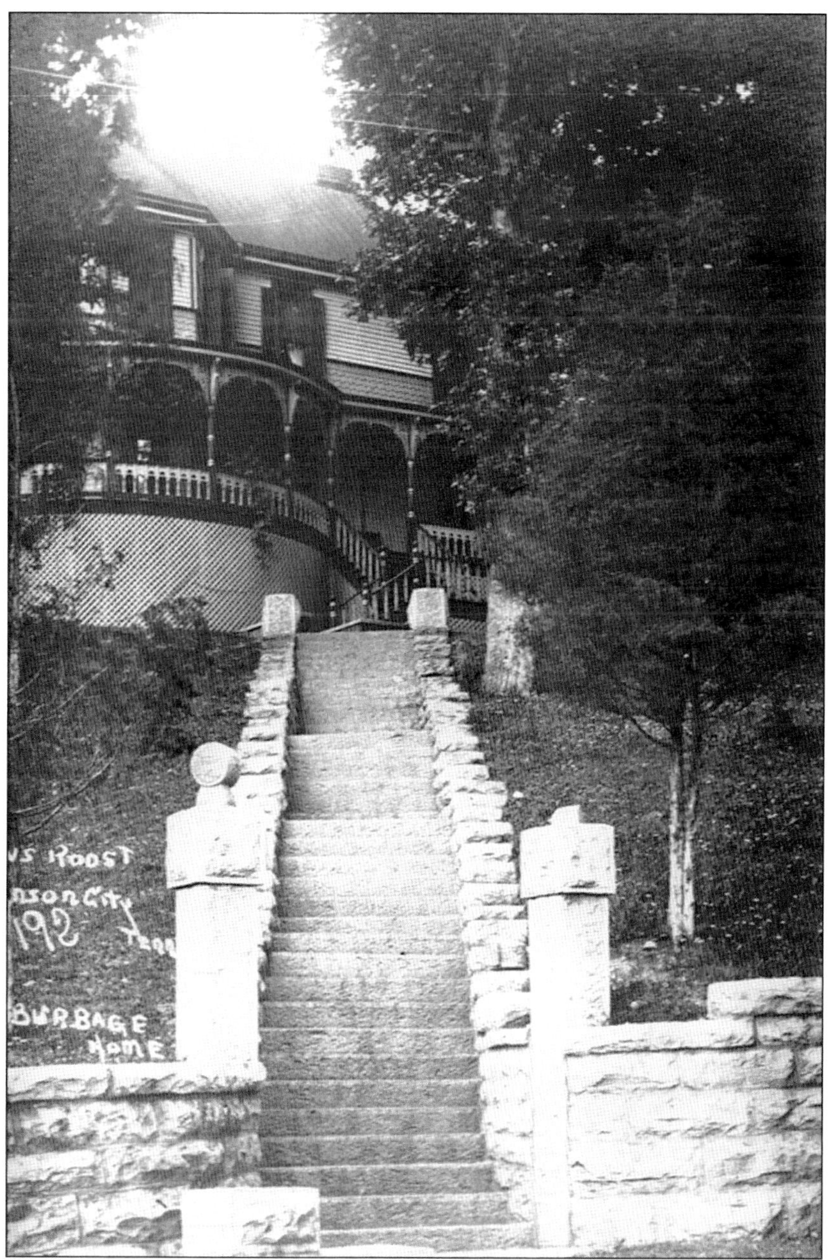

Robin's Roost. Constructed by professional builder William T. Graham in 1890, Robin's Roost, a Queen Anne residence on South Roan Street in Johnson City, was purchased in 1892 by Robert Love Taylor, a Tennessee governor, according to a listing in the National Register of Historic Places. Hordes of robins gathered there, and Taylor frequently invited his friends to the house, saying, "Let's go where the robins roost." Taylor lived here until 1897. His brother Alfred A. Taylor, who later served as governor in the 1920s, lived here from 1900 until 1903. The two brothers are known to have run against each other for governor in 1886 in the so-called War of the Roses. Robert was a Democrat, and his brother was a Republican. The two-story residence features a wraparound porch, a band of textured trim between floors, and an asymmetrical facade. (Courtesy of the Tennessee State Library and Archives.)

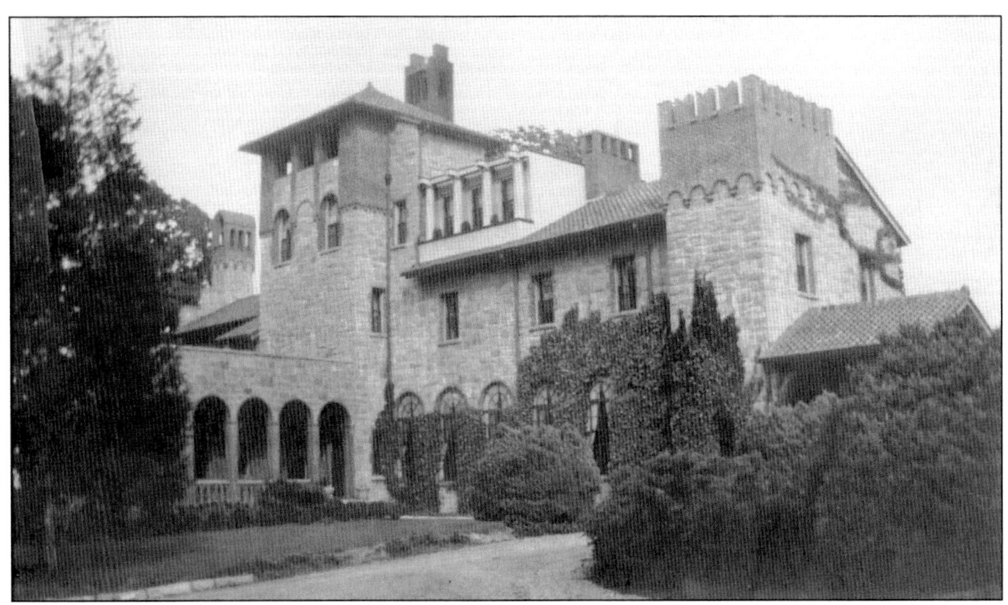

Oaks Castle. The Oaks Estate in Johnson City was built in the 1920s by Tennessee Supreme Court judge Thaddeus Abraham Cox. The castle is located near the intersection of South Roan Street and University Parkway. Architect James Green designed the house and landscape with the help of Pearle Painter Cox. The unique Italianate structure constructed of handcrafted stone and brick has served as a private residence and various offices. A number of structures have been built on the Coxes' property, including condominiums, apartments, and a couple small houses, which he gave to his tenants and chauffeur. (Both, courtesy of the Archives of Appalachia.)

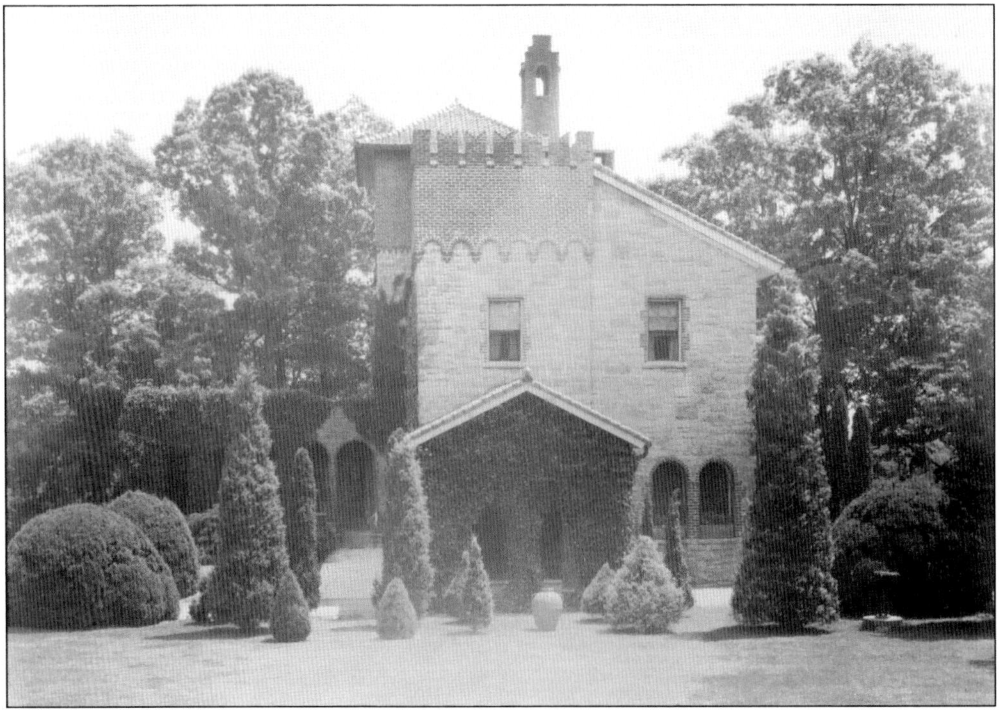

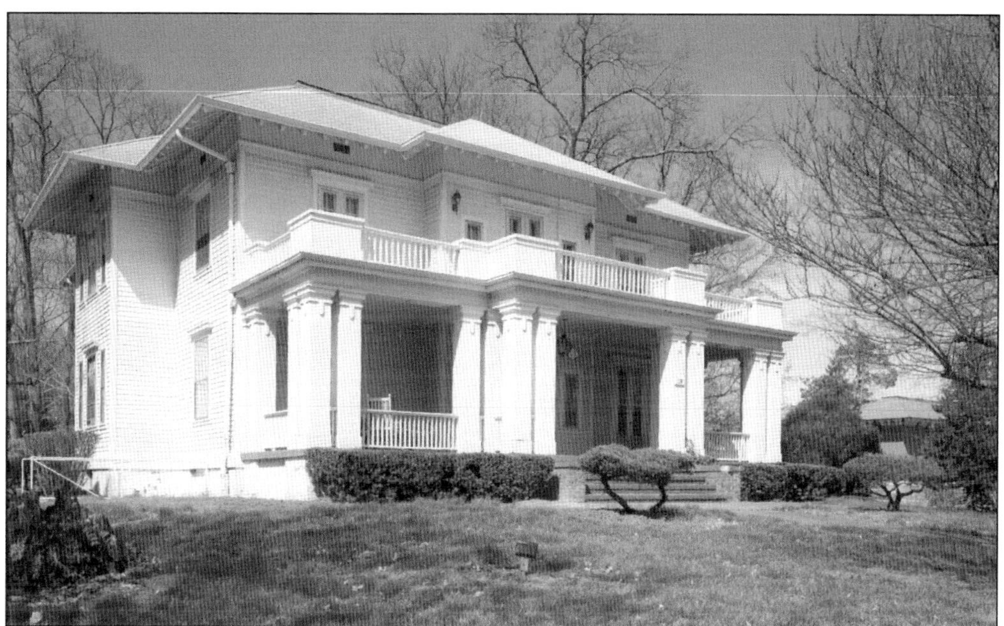

Superintendent's Residence at Mountain Home. The superintendent of the Veterans Affairs campus in Johnson City lived in this home. In 1901, the Mountain Branch of the National Home for Disabled Soldiers was created by an act of Congress introduced by Walter P. Brownlow. A number of buildings on campus are more than 100 years old, including the superintendent's residence. (Courtesy of the Library of Congress.)

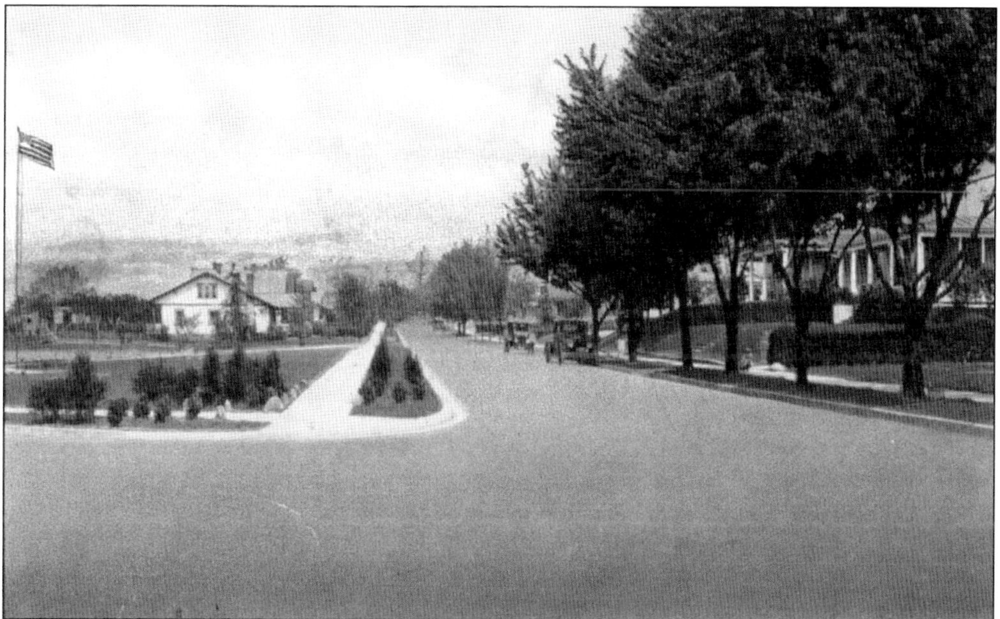

Tree Streets. The Tree Streets Historic District, featured on this postcard, is one of the largest historic residential neighborhoods in Tennessee. In 1909, George Carter developed the neighborhood, also known as the Southwest Addition. Notable residents have included Civil War general John T. Wilder, businessman J. Fred Johnson, illustrator and artist John Alan Maxwell, and author Catherine Woods Marshall. (Courtesy of Betty Jane Hylton.)

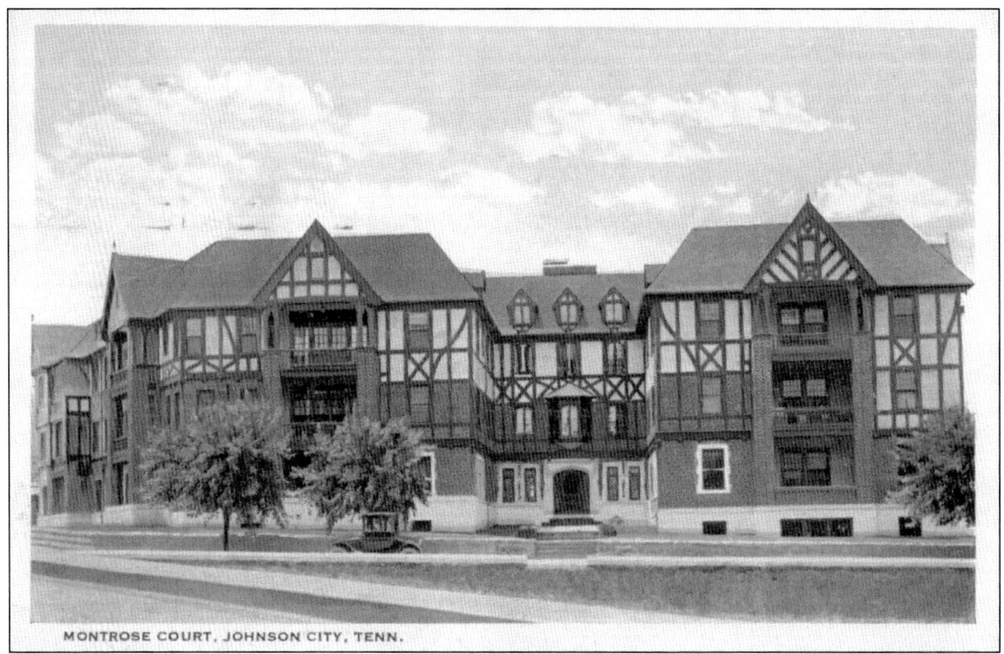

MONTROSE COURT. Montrose Court Apartments, featured on this postcard, is located in the Tree Streets neighborhood of Johnson City. Designed by architect D.R. Beeson Sr., the 28-unit complex was originally planned in 1922. It was rebuilt following a 1928 fire and was renovated in 1983. Johnson City was known as the Chicago of the South during Prohibition. Legend has it that Al Capone frequented the complex. (Author's collection.)

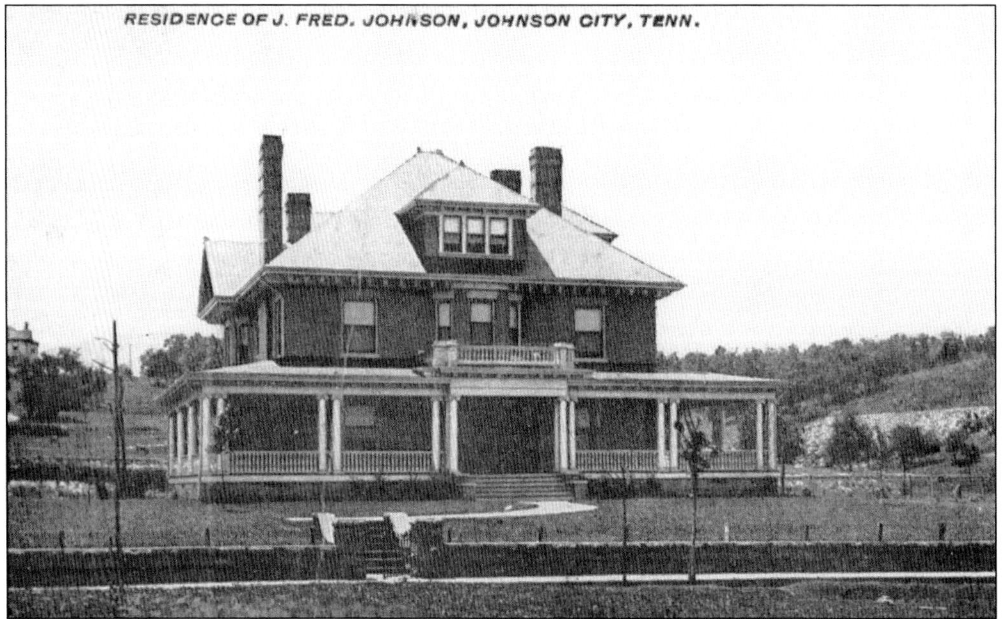

J. FRED JOHNSON HOUSE IN JOHNSON CITY. Businessman J. Fred Johnson resided in a large home on West Locust Street in Johnson City's Tree Streets neighborhood. His Queen Anne residence is two-and-a-half stories and has a slate roof, dentil trim, transoms, and a Colonial Revival porch. Johnson eventually moved to Kingsport. (Courtesy of Kathy Serago.)

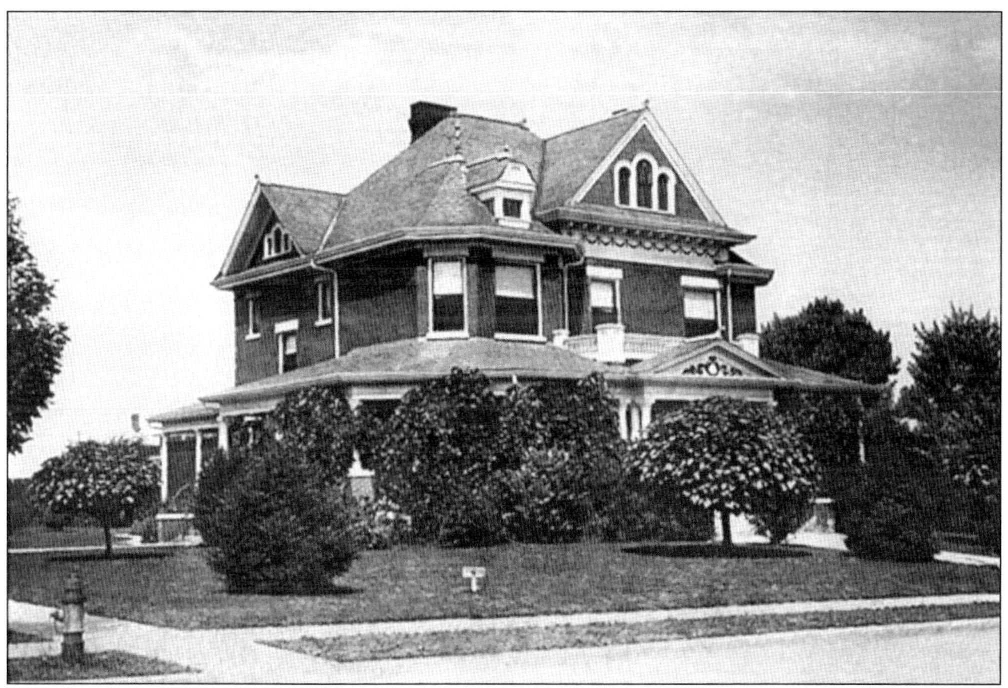

Ring-Myron House. The first president of Model Mill, Joshua Ring, built his Queen Anne Victorian home in 1919 on Locust Street. The house, with its original slate roof, copper gutters, and wavy glass, has also been owned by the Jones and Myron families. (Courtesy of Kathy Serago.)

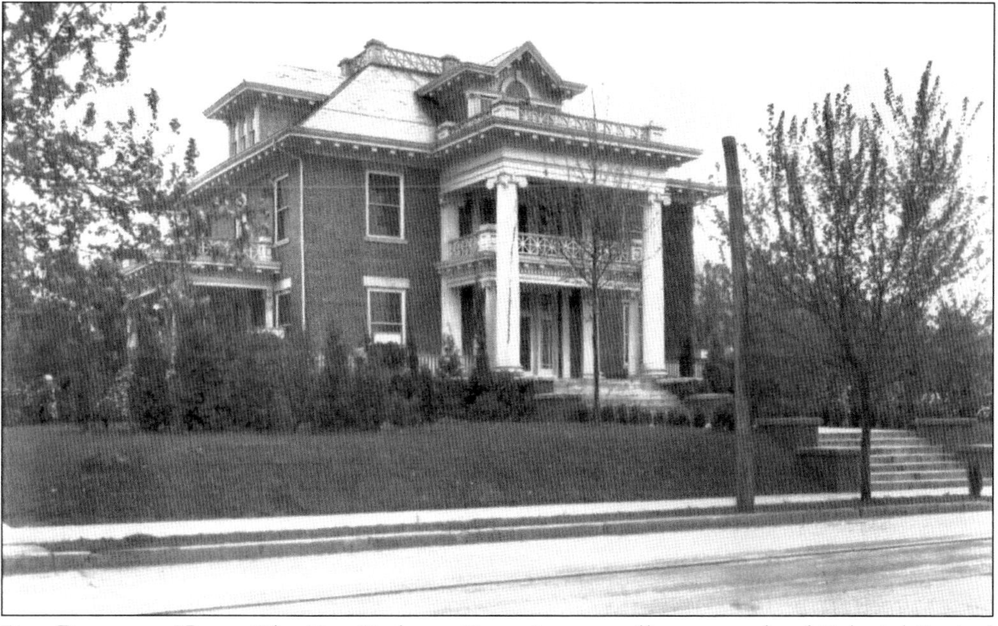

Dew-Burleson Home. The Dew-Burleson Home is an excellent example of Colonial Revival style. It is a large brick residence with imposing columns at the corner of Pine Street and Cherokee Street in the Tree Streets of Johnson City. It was built for Mary Henly Dew Burleson and her husband, David Sinclair Burleson, a charter faculty member at the Normal School (now East Tennessee State University). (Courtesy of Kathy Serago.)

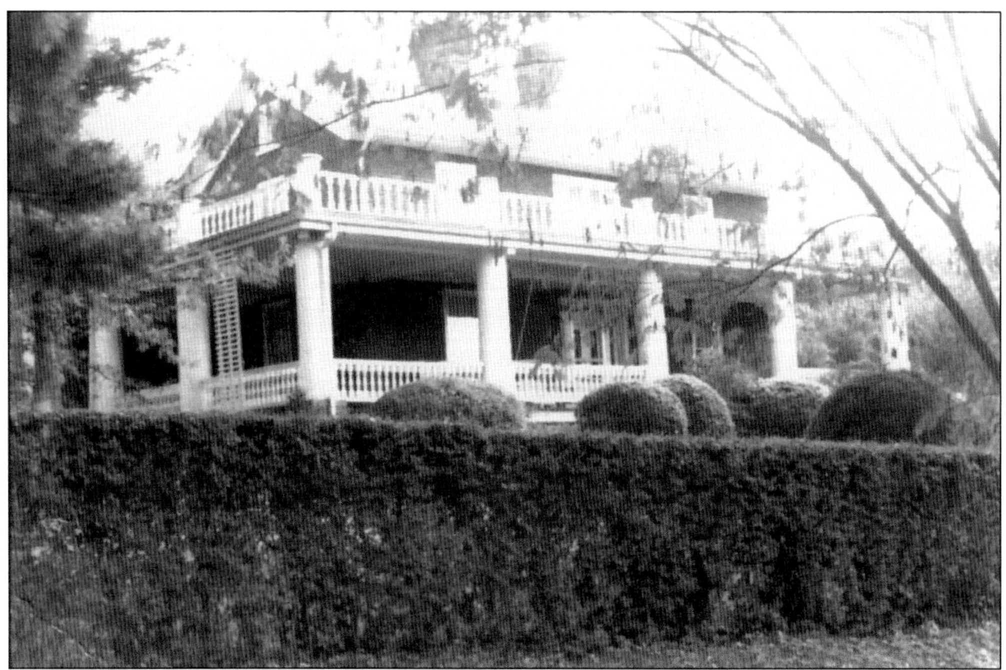

Cedar Place. Cedar Place, one of Johnson City's oldest homes, was constructed sometime before the Civil War. James T. Young, the son of Robert Young Jr., built the house. The original home, a log structure, was erected adjacent to the cemetery in 1780. By 1812, James Young built Cedar Place, a Colonial home featuring four-brick-thick walls and a large front porch. (Courtesy of Marion Davis.)

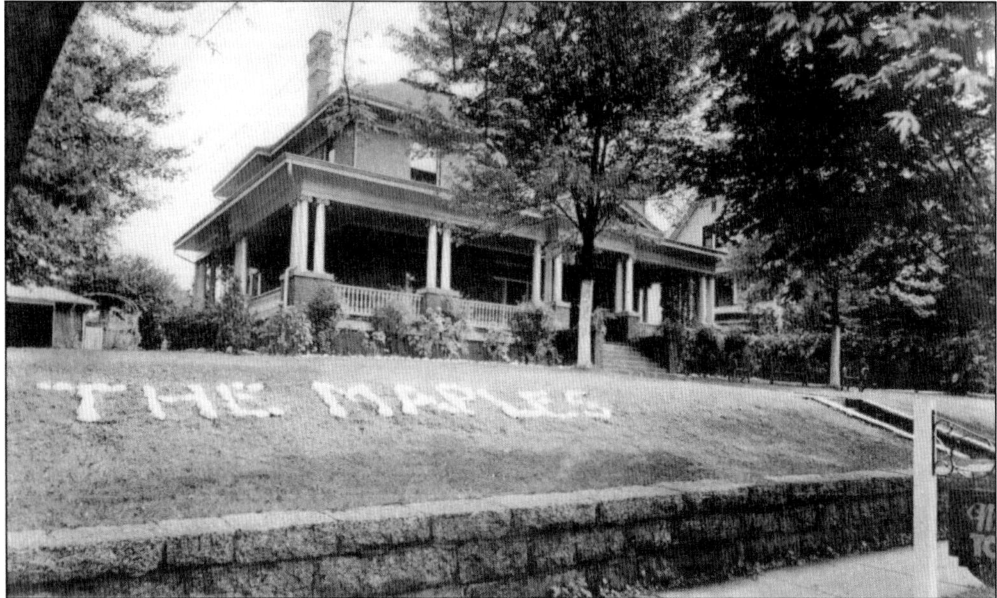

The Maples. The Maples Tourist Home, a large brick residence on Maple Street in the Tree Streets neighborhood of Johnson City, is featured on this postcard. The residence, built in 1920, was used as a home for guests. It is currently a private residence and the letters on the lawn have been removed. (Courtesy of Betty Jane Hylton.)

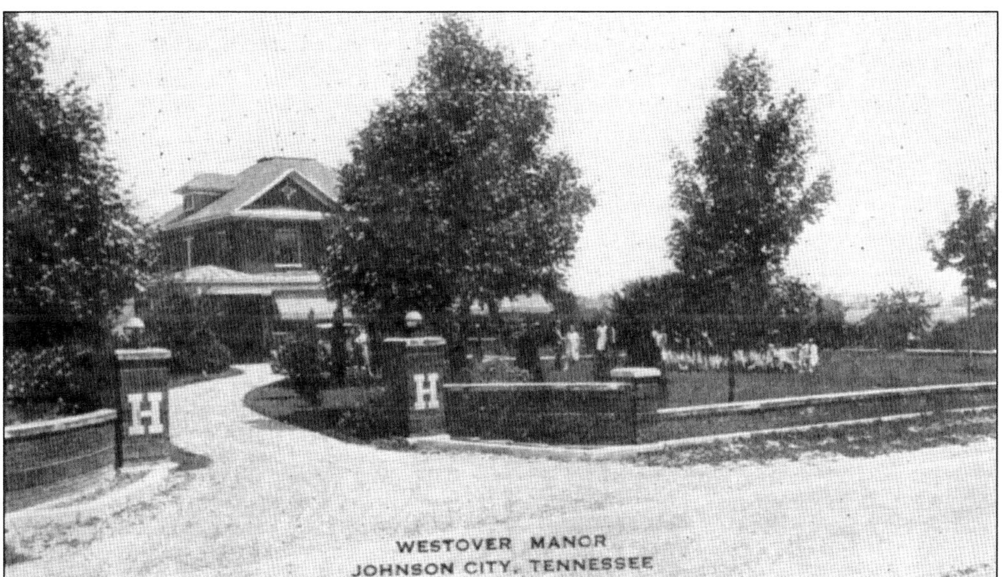

WESTOVER MANOR. This postcard advertises the former Westover Manor in Johnson City. It reveals that Mrs. George S. Hannah was the proprietor of the establishment. According to Johnson City historian and author Bob Cox, the two-story brick inn was located on West Walnut Street off State of Franklin Road. (Courtesy of Betty Jane Hylton.)

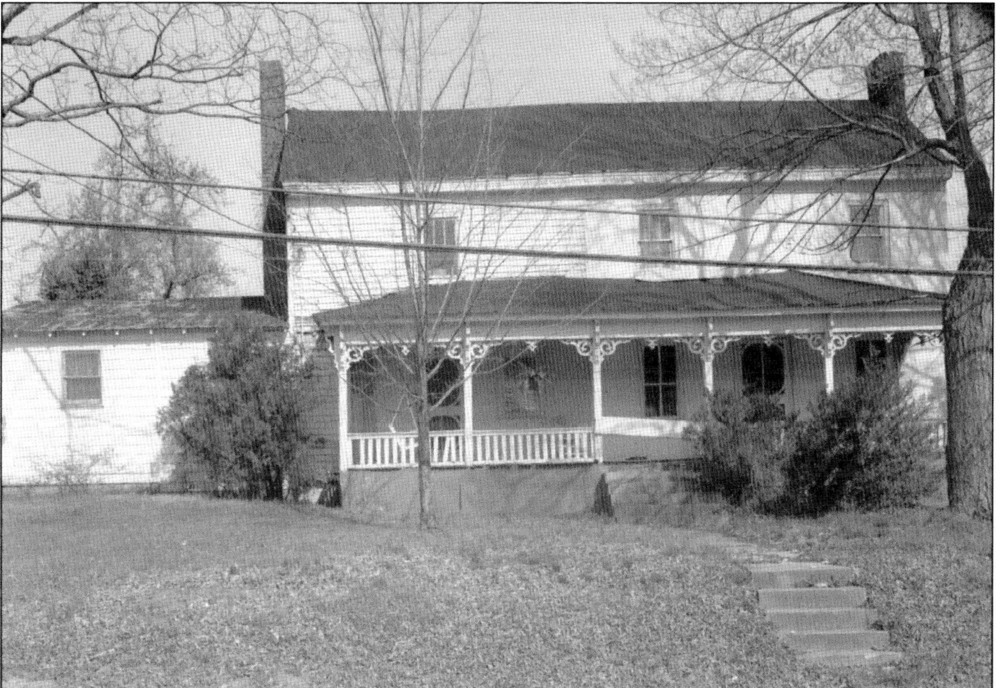

HAMMER-TAYLOR HOUSE. The Hammer-Taylor House is a double-house with end chimneys in north Johnson City. It is significant as an unusual example of hybrid construction that incorporates a log section built about 1806 with a later brick addition in 1844. The home was studied by the Historic American Buildings Survey, a federal project that featured historic properties around the country. (Courtesy of the Library of Congress.)

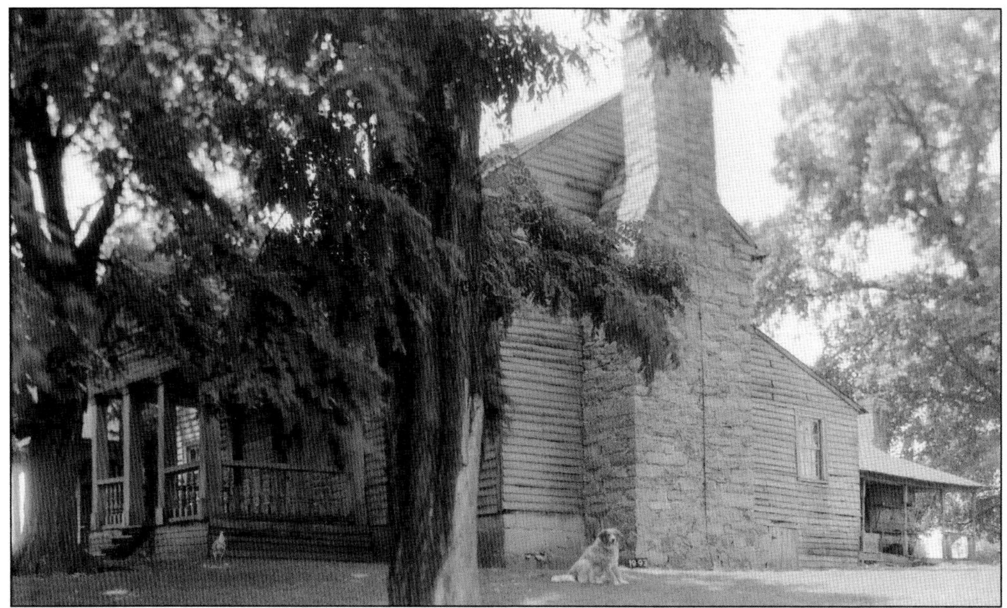

TIPTON-HAYNES. The property on which the Tipton-Haynes home is located was first documented in 1673 by English traders James Needham and Gabriel Arthur. In 1784, Col. John Tipton purchased the property and built a large log cabin. The home was later expanded and clapboarded. David Haynes purchased the farm in 1837 and became a political leader in the area. It is currently open to the public as a historic site. The site includes 45 acres, 11 historic buildings, a historic cemetery, a limestone cave, a natural spring, a buffalo trace, a nature trail, and a visitor center. Landon Carter Haynes's law office was said to be the first law office in the area that was stand-alone and on the solicitor's home property. It is located next to the house. (Both, courtesy of the Tipton-Haynes State Historic Site.)

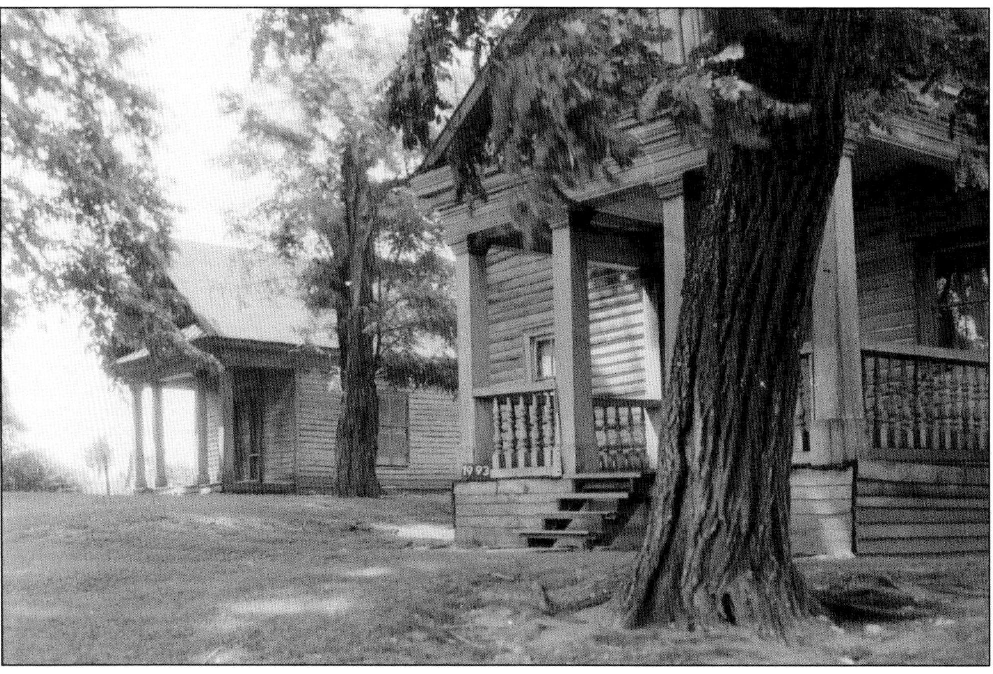

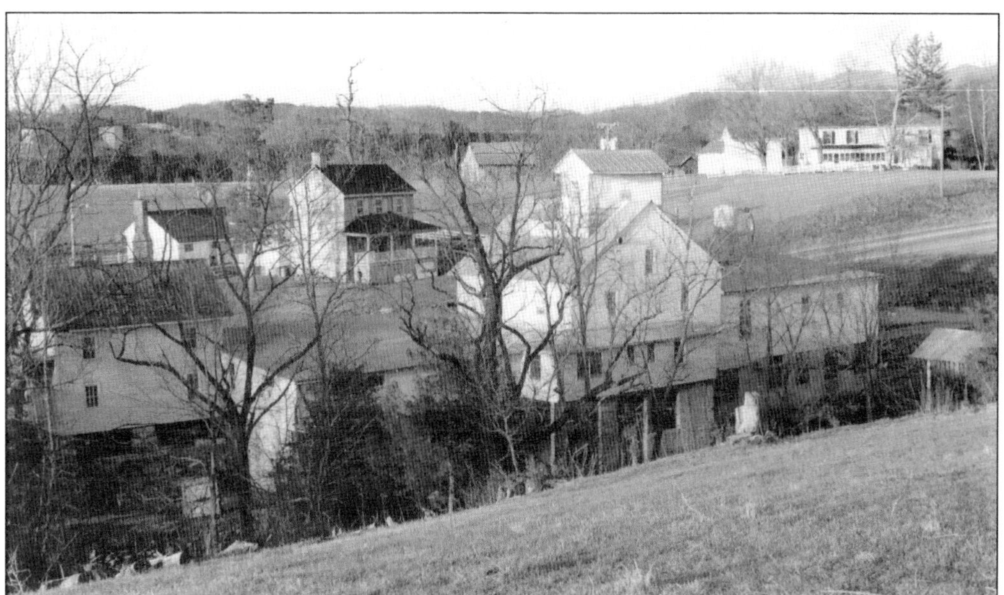

Homes at St. John's Mill. Jeremiah Dungan, from Pennsylvania, purchased property along the Watauga River in 1784. He built his three-story stone house and adjacent mill within a couple years. Henry Bashor bought the mill and house in 1847. His nephew George W. St. John bought them in 1866. Today, St. John descendants still own the property. The mill is the oldest continuously operating business in Tennessee. St. John also built a large white residence nearby for his wife around 1880. While living in the Dungan stone house, his wife became ill, and St. John wanted to make her feel at home, so he built the large St. John's mansion. The home is of Federal design but features touches of Italianate and Greek Revival architecture. (Both, courtesy of Ron Dawson.)

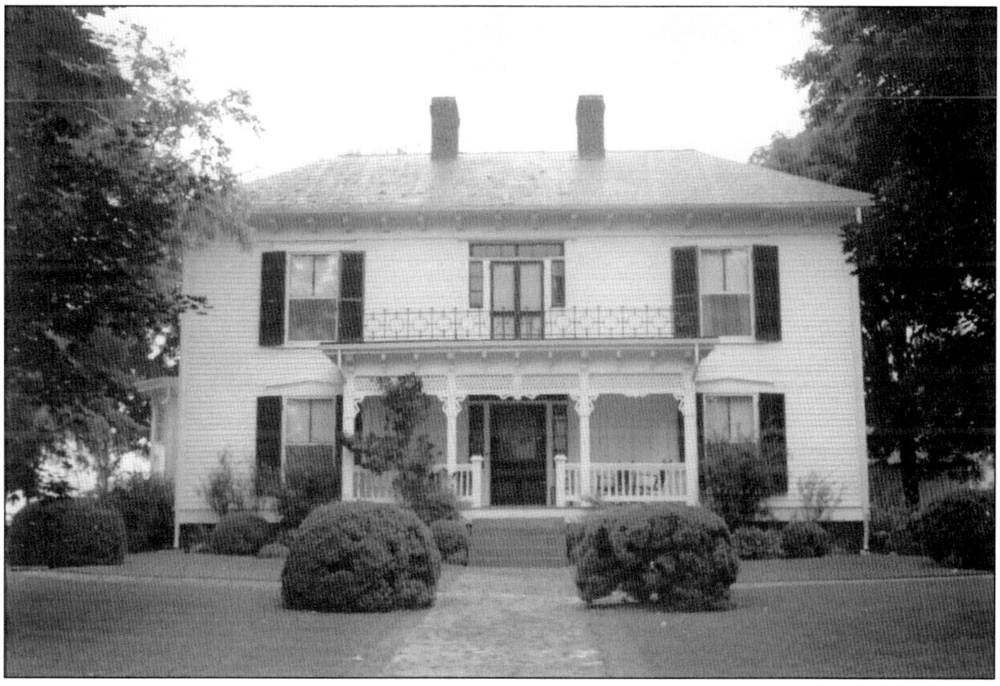

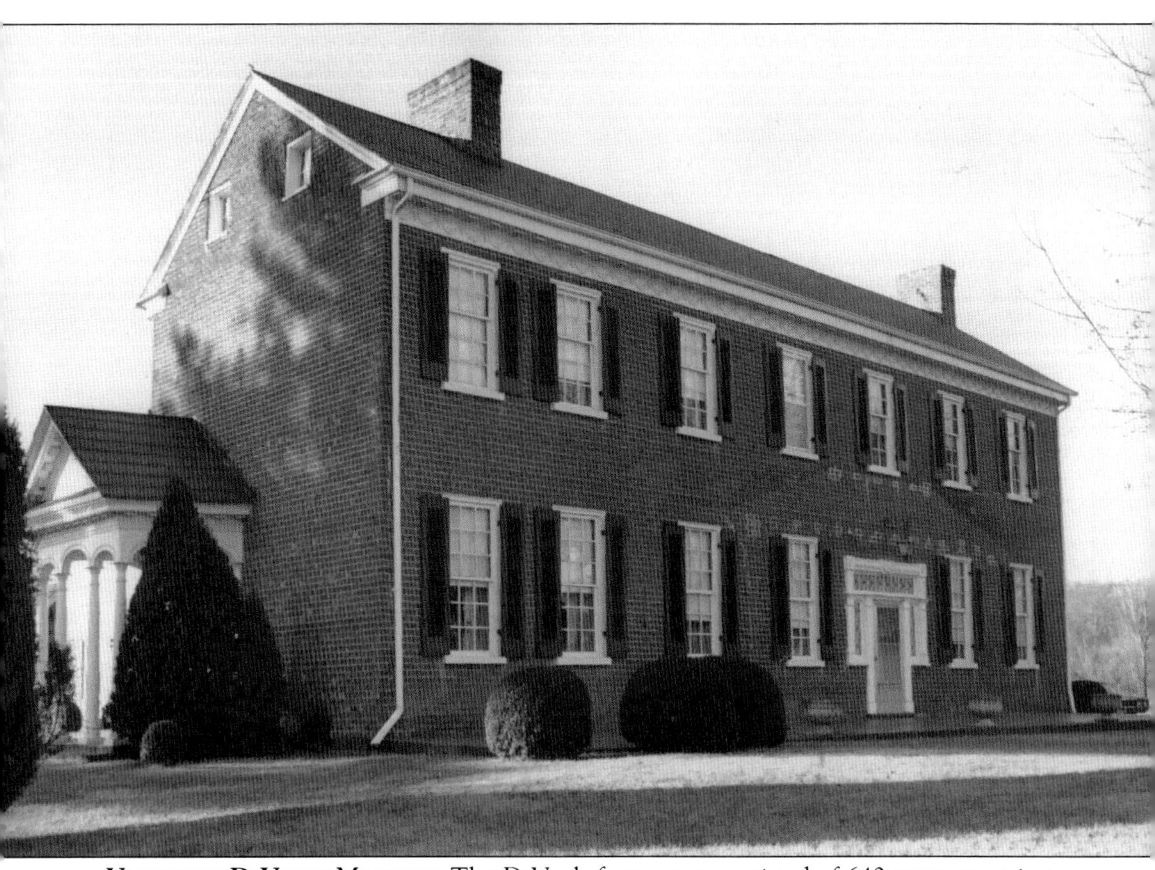

Valentine DeVault Mansion. The DeVault farm once consisted of 640 acres, covering one square mile north of Johnson City. The 14-room DeVault Mansion was constructed in 1820 by Valentine DeVault. According to a listing in the National Register of Historic Places, the original plan consisted of a two-story rectangular shape, seven-bay structure, one room deep with an attached wing extending out from the center of the rear wall. Built of brick and frame, the wing replaces an earlier addition and the former original kitchen. Henry DeVault had purchased the land prior to passing it to his son Valentine. DeVault's property also included the nearby DeVault-Massengill House. Valentine's brother Frederick built a large tavern house in Leesburg in 1821. The homes feature similar architectural details, according to the National Register. Today, the DeVault Mansion sits at the end of Degrasse Drive, overlooking Boone Lake, and is surrounded by newer, modern luxury homes. (Courtesy of the Tennessee Historical Commission.)

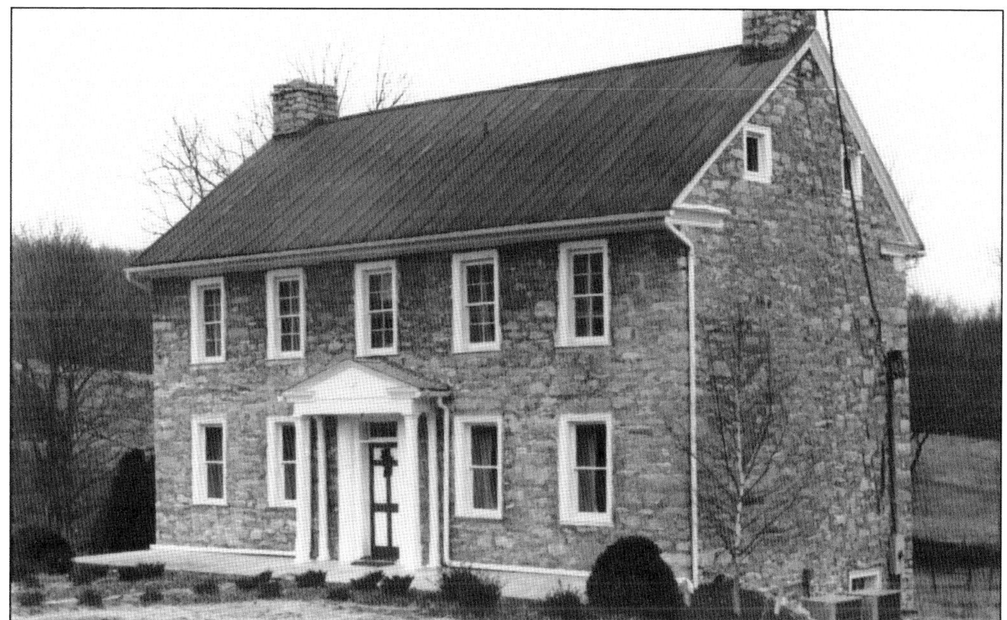

Martin Kitzmiller Home. Martin Kitzmiller was a religious leader in early Tennessee. He built his home in the early 19th century in Boone's Creek along present-day State Route 36. This rare home is one of the country's only five-bay stone houses. According to historians, it was a popular stagecoach stop. After the Kitzmillers, the Pearce family lived here. (Courtesy of the Tennessee Historical Commission.)

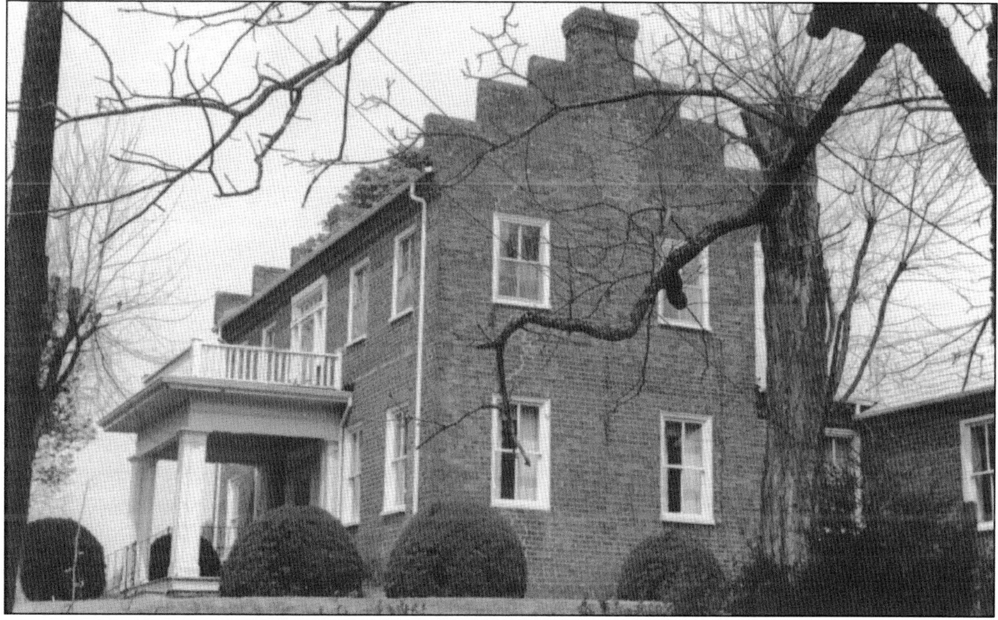

Henry Hoss House. The Henry Hoss House on Old Boone's Creek Road near Jonesborough was built in 1875 by physician Thomas Rhea. It is a large Federal-style home, which has been meticulously preserved by each of the successive owners. After the Rhea family, another prominent doctor, Henry Hoss, lived here. Hoss served as the president of Milligan College. (Courtesy of the Tennessee Historical Commission.)

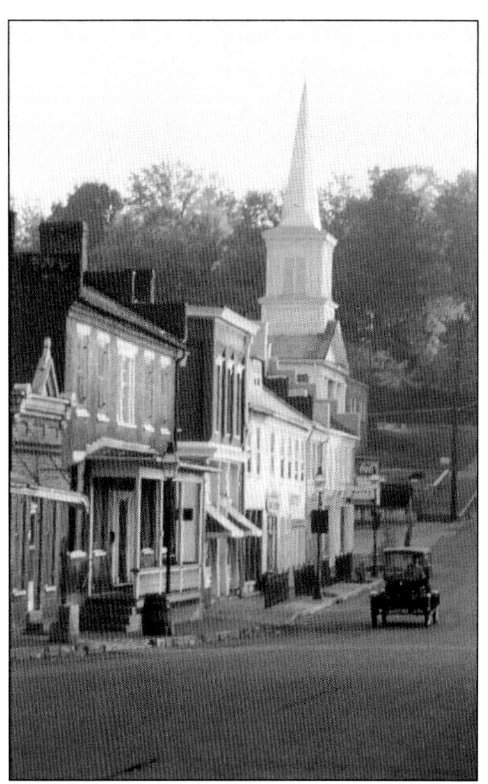

NAFF-HENLEY HOUSE. The Naff-Henley House, seen in this street scene of downtown Jonesborough, was built in 1840 by local tailor Jacob Naff. The tailor lived in the structure's top floors, while his tailor business occupied the basement. This home includes a stepped gable roof, delicate, symmetrical trim, and Federal-style windows. Following the Naffs, the Baxter, Crouch, Fain, and Henley families lived here. (Courtesy of Betty Jane Hylton.)

MANSION HOUSE. J.W. Simpson, a farmer, built the Mansion House along Main Street in Jonesborough in 1851. The large Georgian style home was built without the present porch. It was designed to attract guests who traveled on the stagecoach road. Since the Civil War, the home has been used as a private residence. (Courtesy of the Tennessee State Library and Archives.)

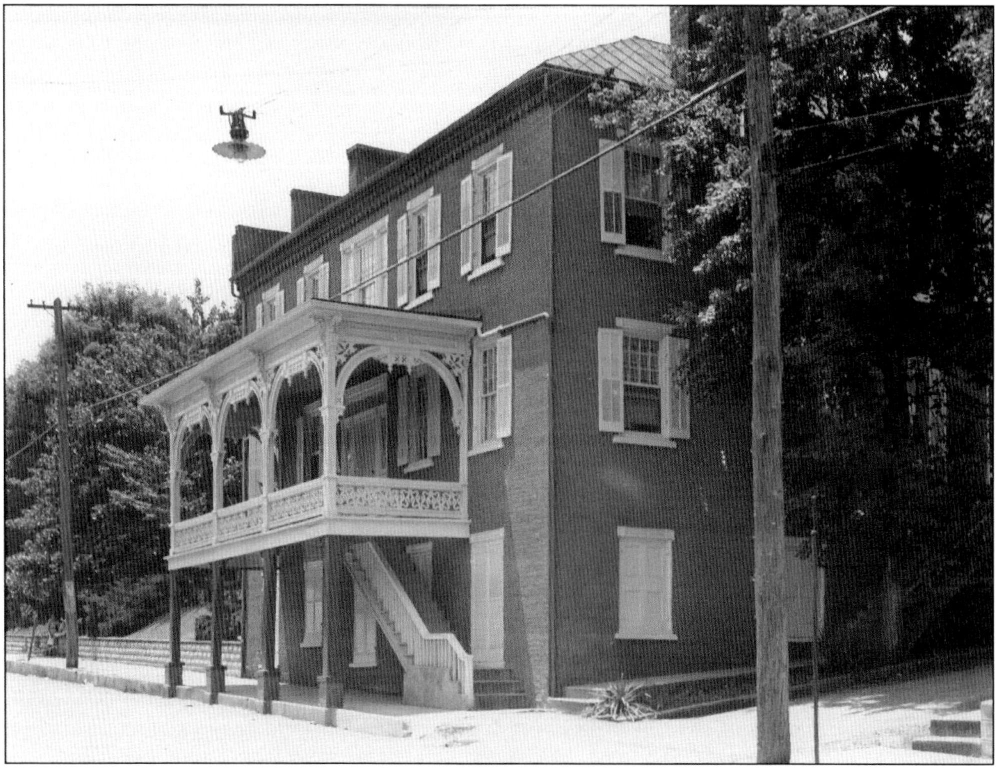

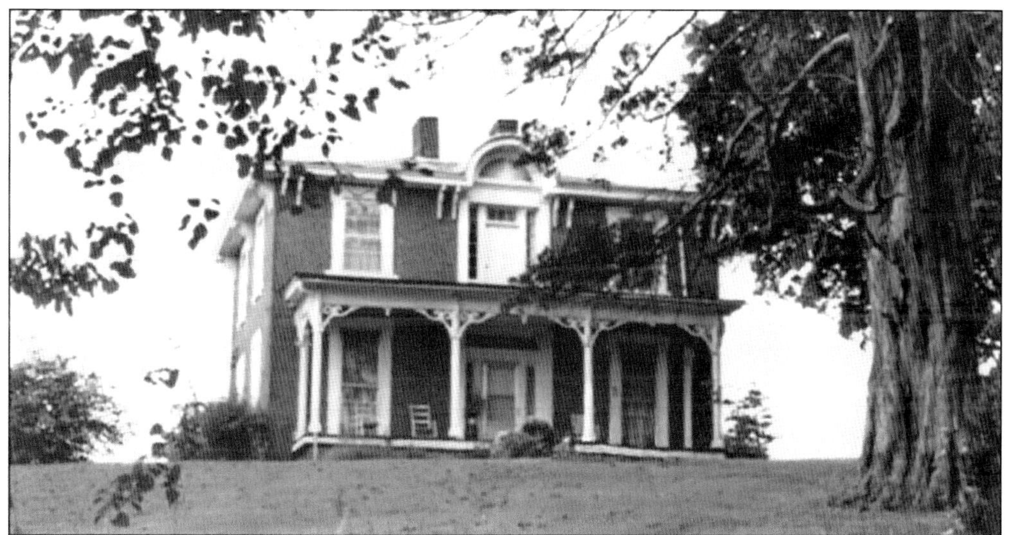

Old Sabin House. Before the Civil War, the Reverend Rufus Wells built a large brick residence at the site of the present-day AmericInn on US Highway 11E in Jonesborough. The hotel's development forced the old Wells home to be torn down piece by piece. It was moved to a new location at the corner of Washington Drive and College Street on Academy Hill. (Courtesy of Pat Sabin.)

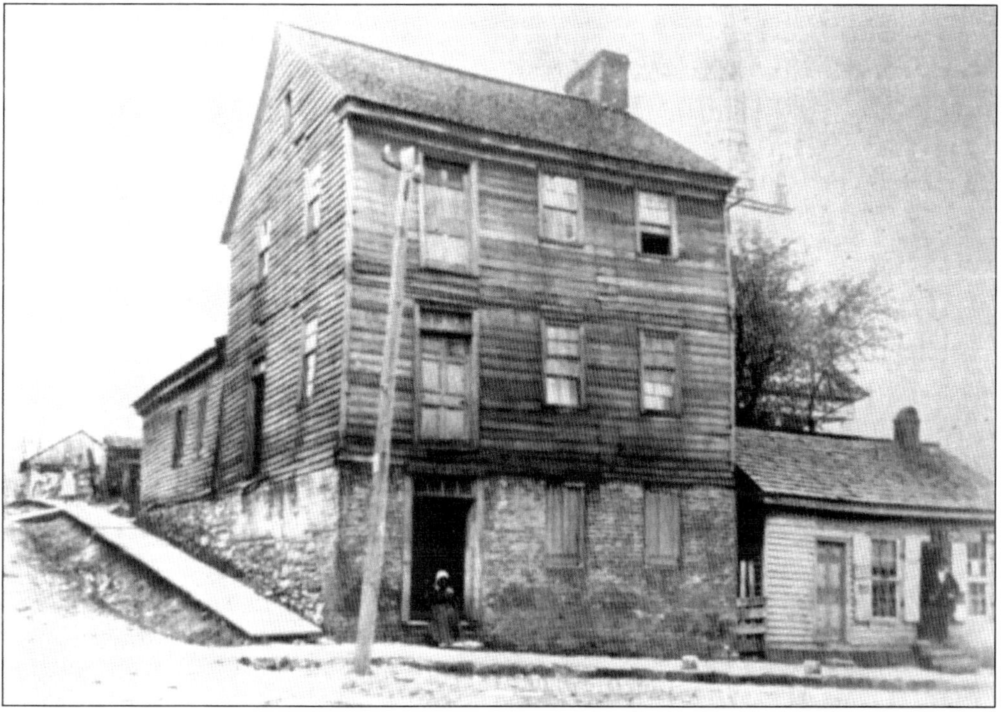

Abolition Newspaper Building Site. The site of Jacob Howard's print shop, where the country's first abolitionist papers were created, is now home to the May-Rice House. The Victorian home was constructed in 1905, long after the original wood structure was built. Elihu Embree printed copies of the *Manumission Intelligencer* and the *Emancipator* at this site. (Courtesy of Betty Jane Hylton.)

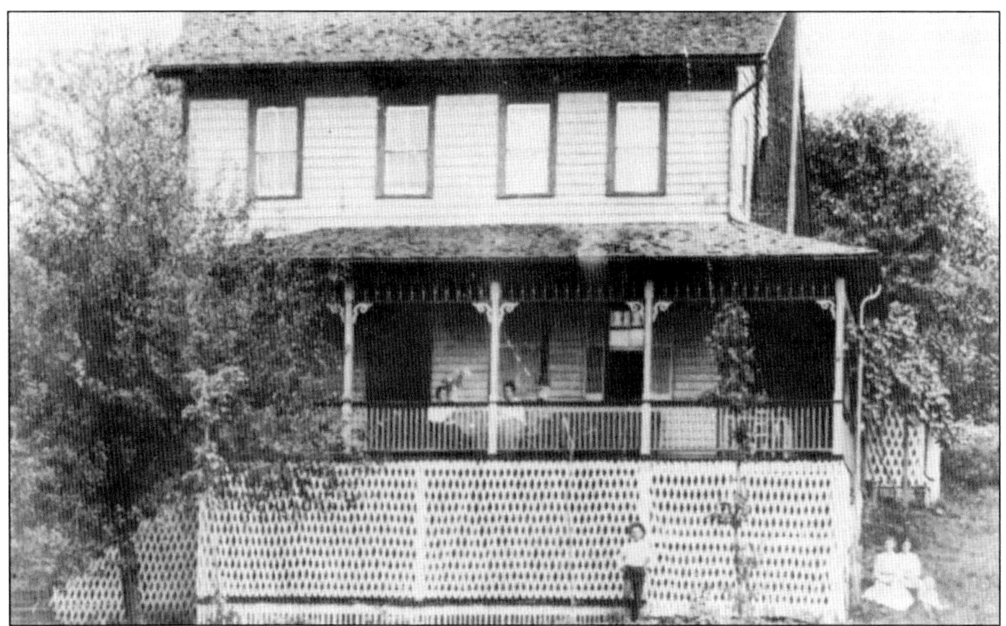

Emmerson House. John Joseph Jacobs built his unique three-story home around 1830 in Jonesborough. The home's first floor is made of stone, and the two upper floors are made of wood. The main entrance is on the second floor. Shortly after Jacobs built the home, Thomas Emmerson purchased the property. Emmerson was the first mayor of Knoxville and a member of the Tennessee Supreme Court. (Courtesy of Betty Jane Hylton.)

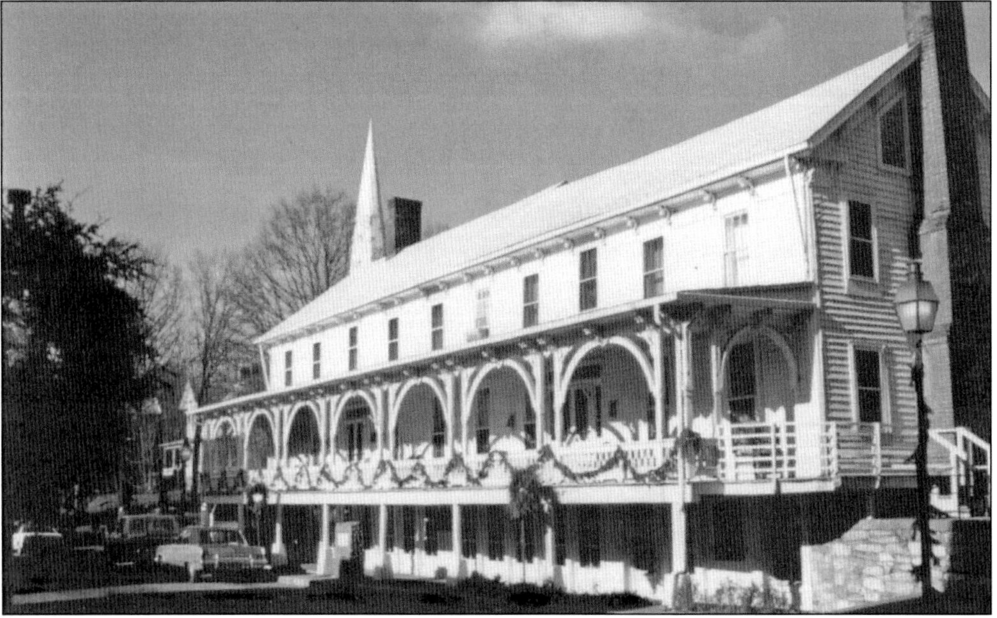

Chester Inn. The Chester Inn, Jonesborough's oldest structure, was built in the late 18th century by Dr. William P. Chester. The physician wanted to open an inn on the Great Stage Road that traversed the town. Local historians say that over the years, guests have included Andrew Johnson, James Polk, and Andrew Jackson. The building has also acted as a private residence. (Courtesy of Betty Jane Hylton.)

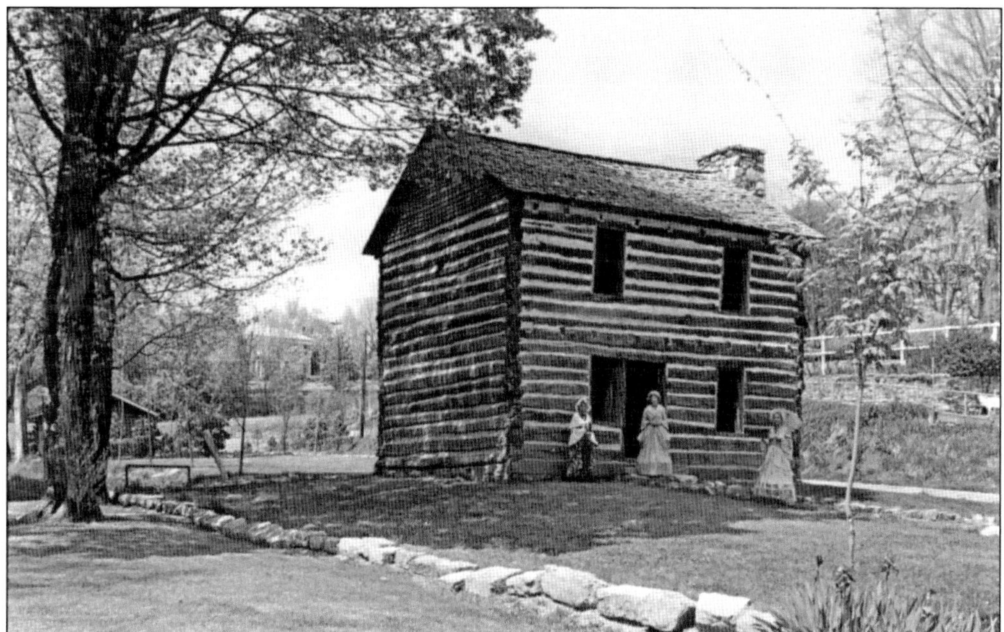

Taylor House and Dossett Home. Two homes can be seen in this photograph of Jonesborough's historic district. The Christopher Taylor House, an 18th-century cabin, is in the foreground. The Dossett Home can be seen in the background. It was built in 1832 by Congressman John Blair. The Febuary family and Burgin Dossett, a former East Tennessee State University president, also lived here. (Courtesy of Betty Jane Hylton.)

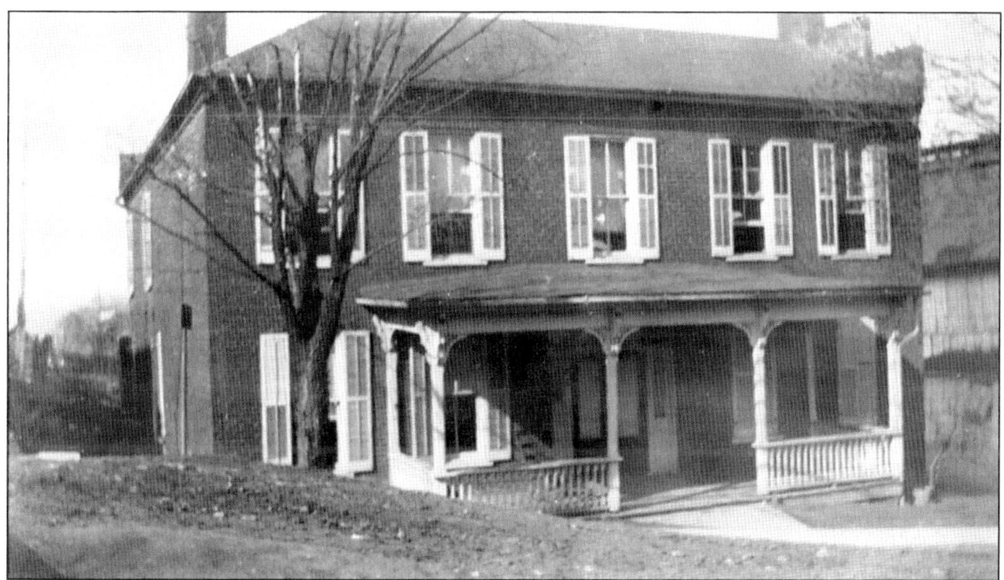

Willet-Stephenson House. The Willet-Stephenson House is located on Cherokee Street in Jonesborough near the Washington County Courthouse. It was built by the Willet family about 1830. The Stephenson family later lived here. This photograph, taken in 1920, shows the unique stepped roof. (Courtesy of the Tennessee State Library and Archives.)

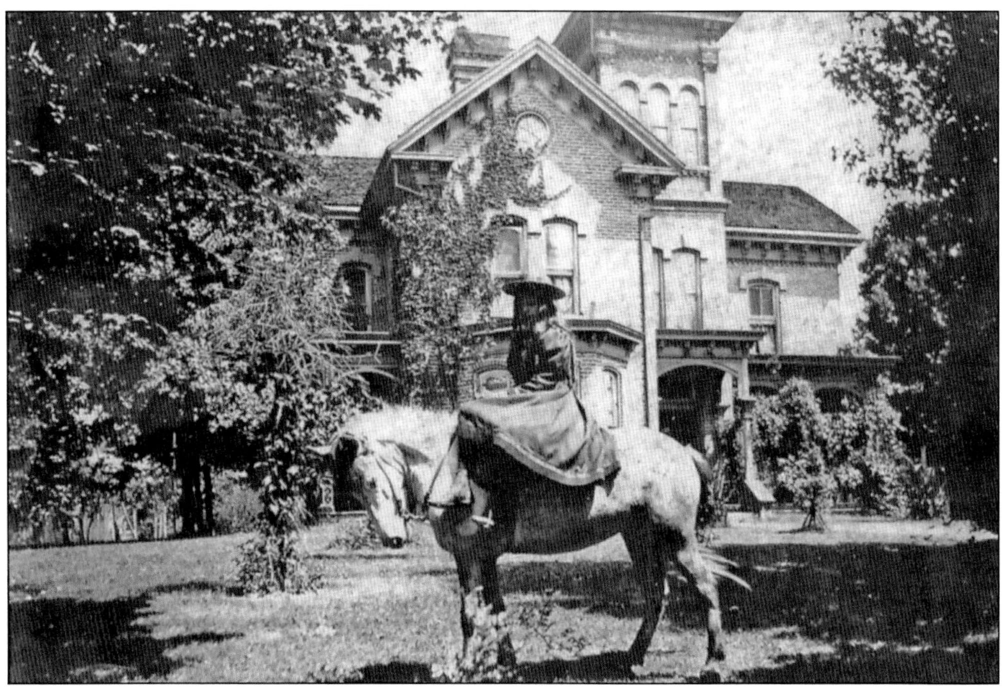

Dosser Homes of Jonesborough. James Dosser built a number of elaborate and colorful homes in Jonesborough. The above photograph features the Reeves-Hankins House on College Street. This impressive Italianate house was built for Dosser's daughter Mary and her husband Isaac E. Reeves. Dosser also built a similar Italianate home on Depot Street for his son Charles Edwin Dosser. Both houses are characterized by towers, large porches, narrow windows, ornate arches, and other Italianate influences. The homes were built before 1900. Dosser was a prominent merchant, builder, and community leader. (Above, courtesy of the Heritage Alliance; below, author's collection.)

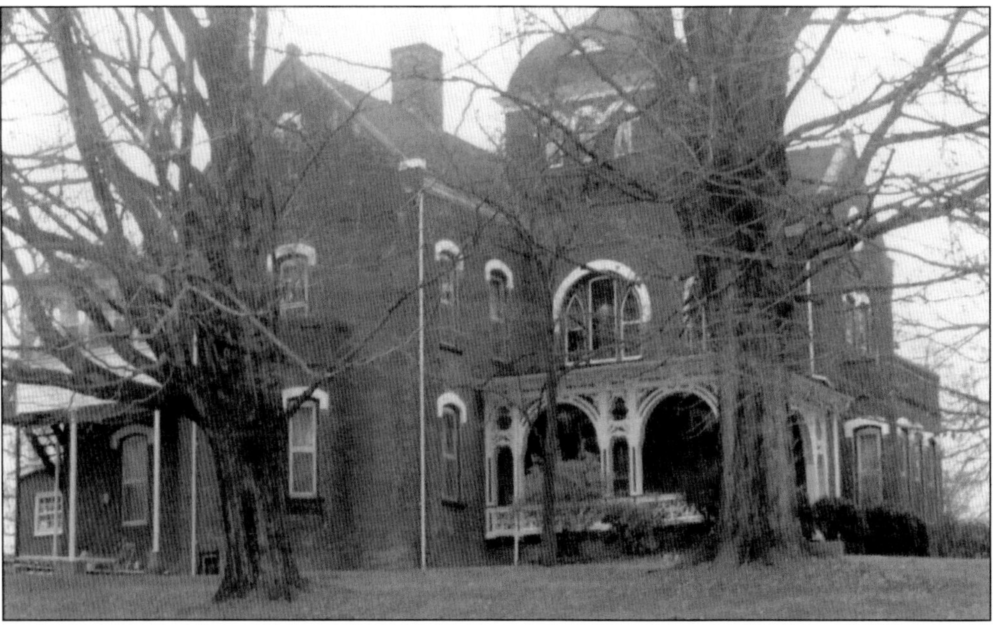

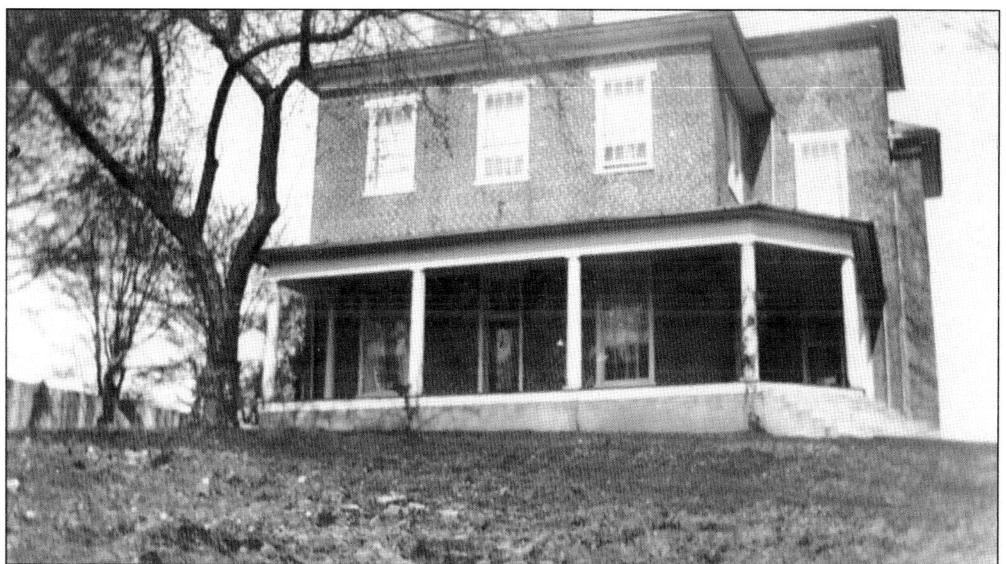

WARNER INSTITUTE. According to a historical marker, the Warner Institute in Johnson City, built in 1854, was originally constructed as the Holston Baptist Female Institute and later became Tadlock's School for Boys. In 1876, Yardley Warner bought the building and formed Warner Institute, to "educate colored persons and train colored teachers." It has also been a private residence and boardinghouse. (Courtesy of the Tennessee State Library and Archives.)

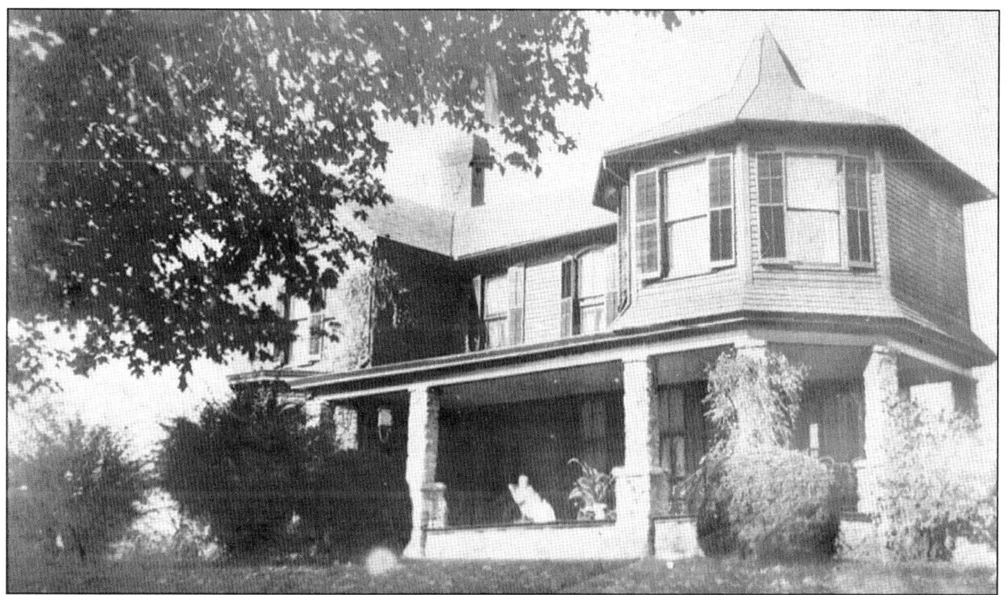

POPLAR GROVE. Jonesborough's Deaderick family built Poplar Grove, a large brick residence on College Street, in 1850. The two-story structure was built by James F. Deaderick, the son of David Deaderick. David, who owned a store and office nearby, previously built a home on this site. James was a merchant, attorney, politician, and a state chief justice. (Courtesy of the Tennessee State Library and Archives.)

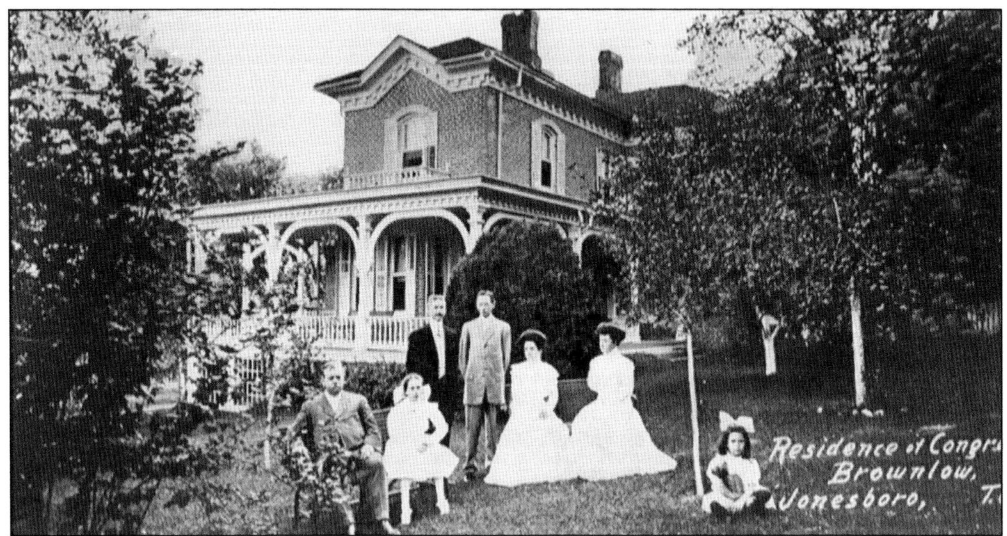

Brownlow House. Walter Preston Brownlow purchased the *Jonesboro Herald & Tribune* in 1876. He also served as the town's postmaster and was elected to the US House of Representatives. The man, who was also instrumental in establishing a soldiers' home nearby, lived in a home in Jonesborough. He was a nephew of William Gannaway Browlow, another prominent Jonesborough newspaperman and politician. (Courtesy Tennessee State Library and Archives)

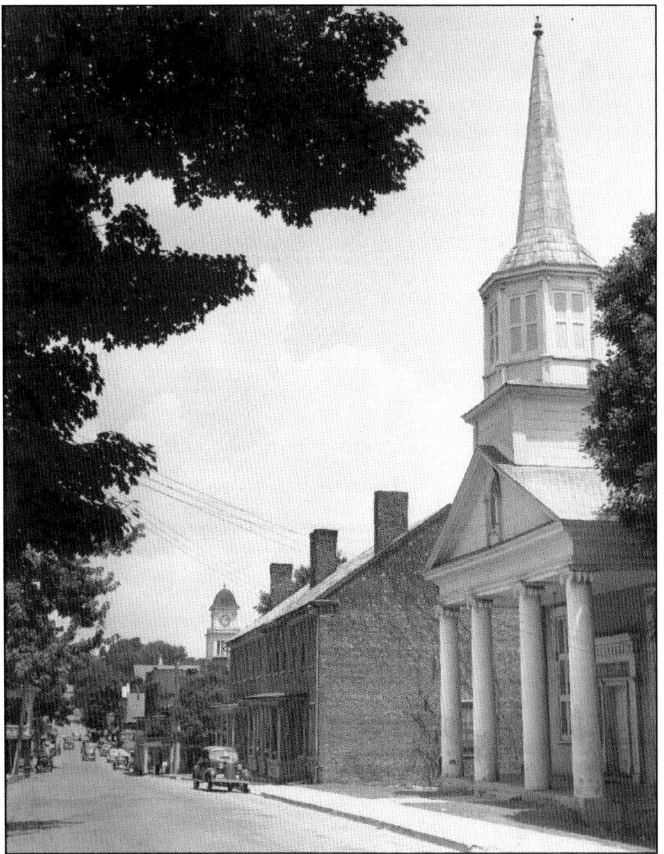

Sisters' Row. Located on Main Street in Jonesborough, Sisters' Row is a three-unit Federal-style row house. Samuel Jackson and contractors John Smith and Elijah Embree built the structure in 1820. It features original wide-plank floors, a rock wall basement, and two fireplaces. (Courtesy of the Tennessee State Library and Archives.)

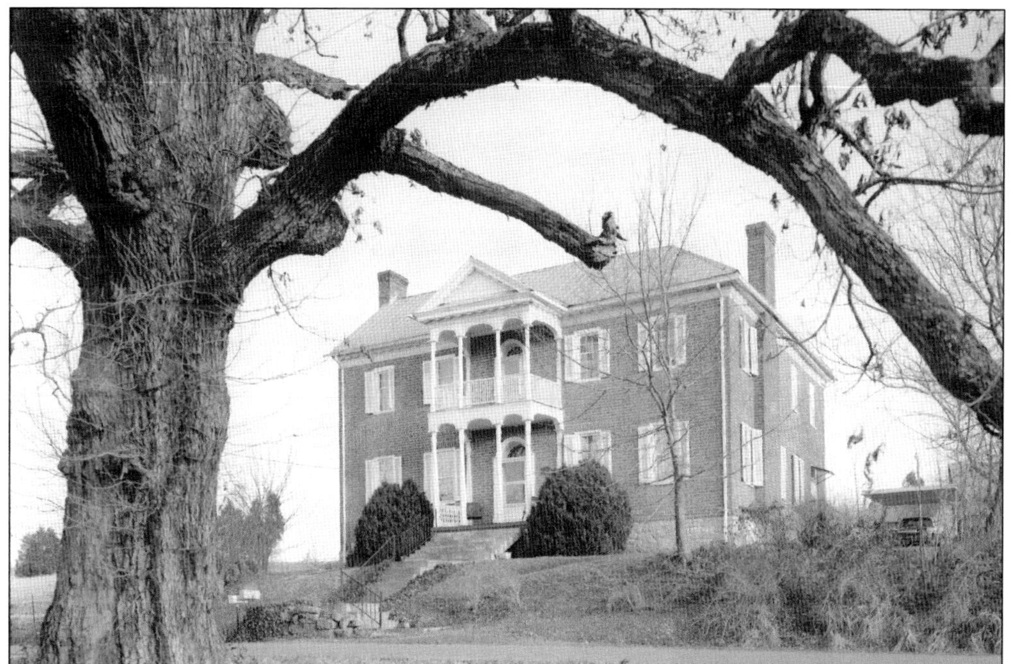

DeVault Tavern. The DeVault Tavern, a historic structure in the Leesburg community of Washington County, was built in 1821 by Frederick DeVault as an inn. It stands on what was the Great Stage Road between Abingdon, Virginia, and Knoxville, Tennessee. It is a two-story brick building in the Federal style. The home featured several large rooms on the second floor, all unconnected without doors. They could only be reached from two stairwells leading downstairs. DeVault's brother, Valentine, built a similar home on present-day Boone Lake in Johnson City. The exterior of the imposing home can be seen in the above photograph, and an interior bedroom is pictured in the photograph below. (Both, courtesy of the Tennessee State Library and Archives.)

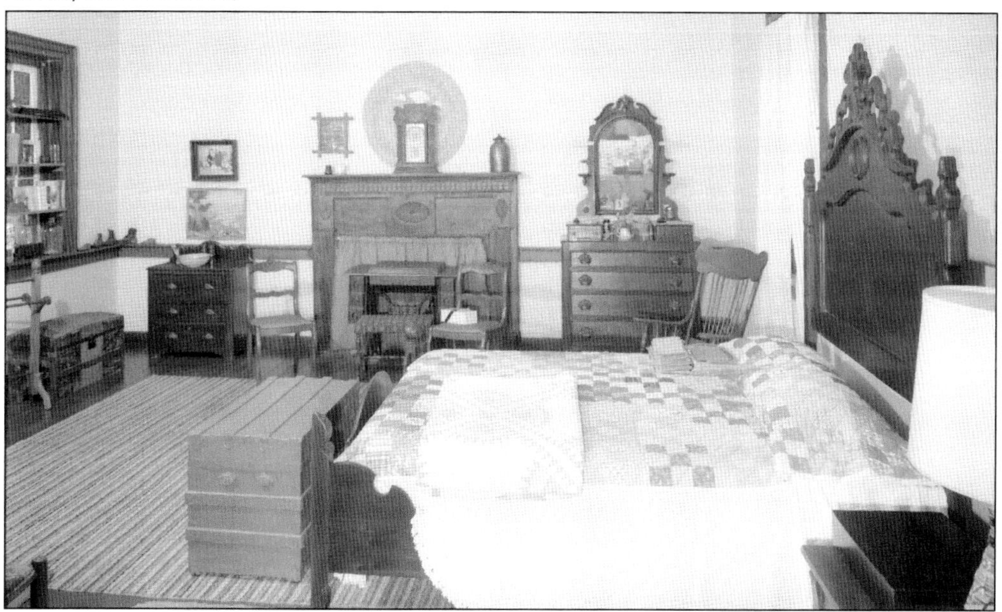

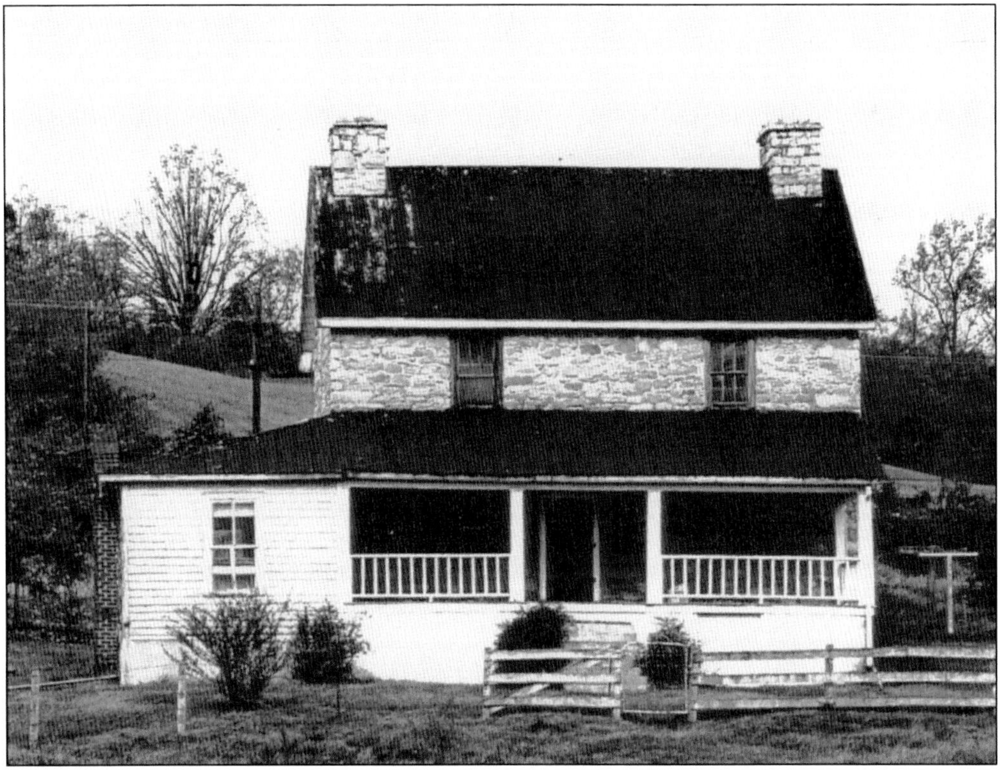

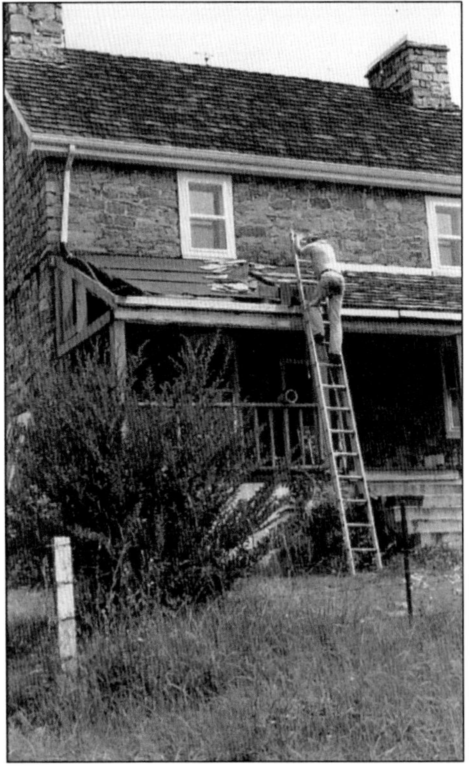

Embree Stone House. The Thomas Embree home in Telford was built by stonemason Seth Smith in 1791. Embree, the first owner, had two very influential sons in the region. Elijah Embree was a wealthy ironmaster in the Bumpass Cove area. Elihu Embree was the first person to publish a newspaper for the abolitionist movement. The Embree House, located at the site of a Civil War battle, features two identical fireplaces in the living room and cellar, which also was the original location of the kitchen. Over the years, additions have been built. The most recent owners, the Sterns, have also purchased the nearby Wassem Home, a brick antebellum house, and a mid-20th-century farmhouse. (Both, courtesy of Patrick Stern.)

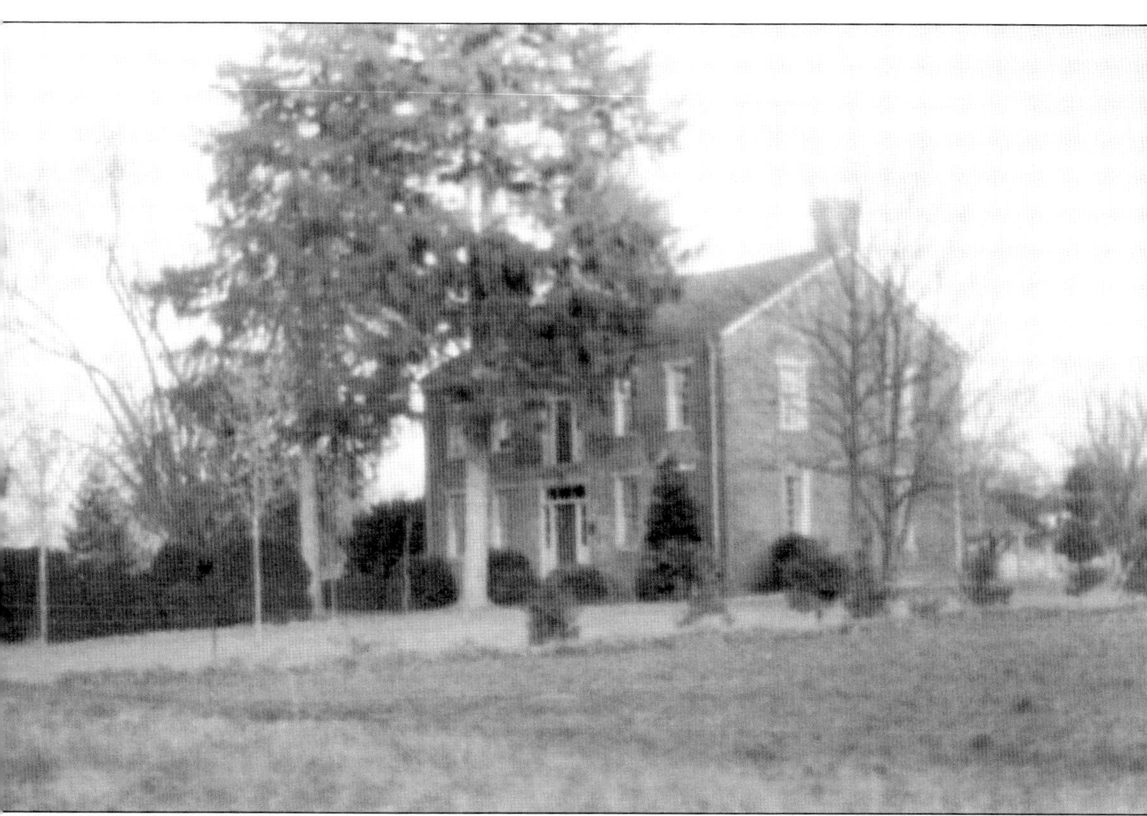

THOMAS TELFORD HOUSE. Listed in the National Register of Historic Places, the Thomas Telford House, situated near the old Broylesville community in Washington County, Tennessee, was constructed in 1815. Thomas Telford, an early settler to the area, came from Charleston, South Carolina, and purchased land from Samuel Broyles. (Courtesy of Patsy Green.)

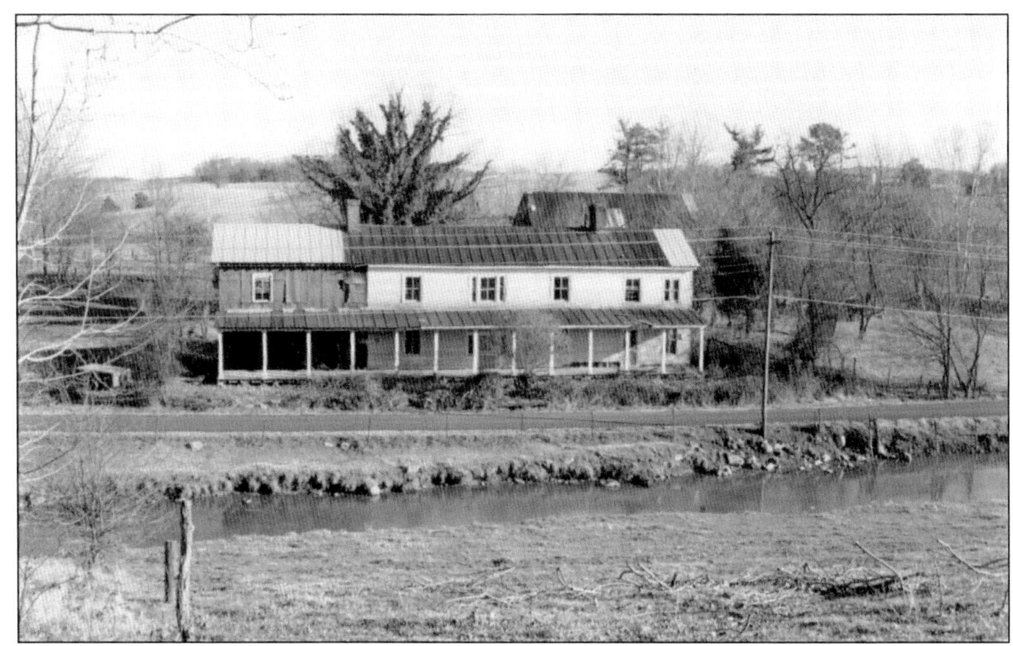

Broylesville Inn. The Broylesville Historic District features a number of structures, including homes, a mercantile building, and a mill. It was once the site of the Broylesville Inn, built by Adam Broyles in 1797. The large inn burned down during a suspicious fire in 2004. Broyles lived nearby in a large brick Federal-style home, which still stands. (Courtesy of Patsy Green.)

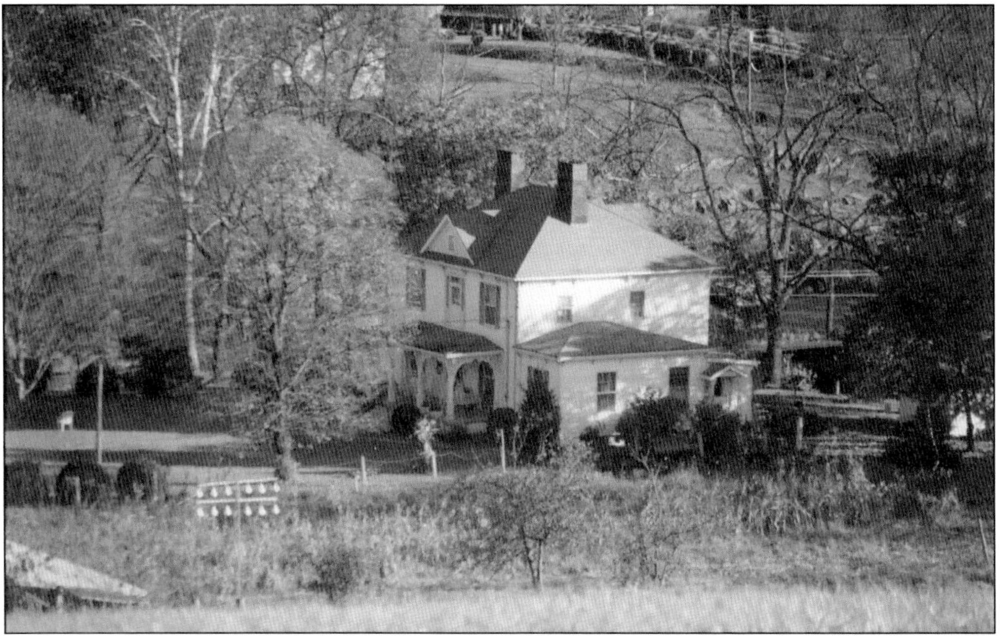

Green House. Broylesville settler Ira Green built a large two-story frame home in 1812. The vernacular home with Italianate details features a large front porch and a one-story wing at both ends. The home is one of a few remaining structures built in the 19th century in the historic town of Broylesville. In 1829, Green petitioned the legislature to clear the nearby Nolichucky River for commodities. (Courtesy of Patsy Green.)

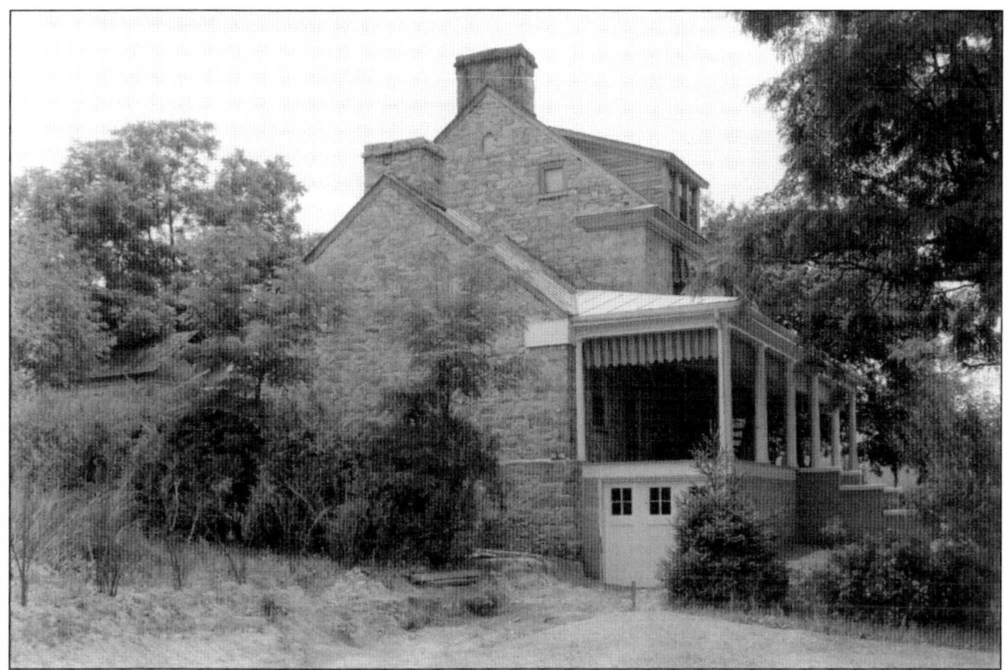

Gillespie Stone House. Col. George Gillespie had his stone home built in 1792 in the town of Limestone. Stonemason Seth Smith designed and constructed the home, which also acted as a safe fort for residents. The home served as a hospital temporarily during the Civil War when the Battle of Limestone was fought nearby. Its owners, the Kleppers, helped bring the nearby railroad through Northeast Tennessee. During the second half of the 20th century, the home was abandoned, except for a few days when it was used to shoot the Walt Disney movie *Goodbye, Miss 4th of July*. In the 21st century, the abandoned house was purchased by Doug and Donna Ledbetter, who have completely restored the unique structure. (Both, courtesy of the Library of Congress.)

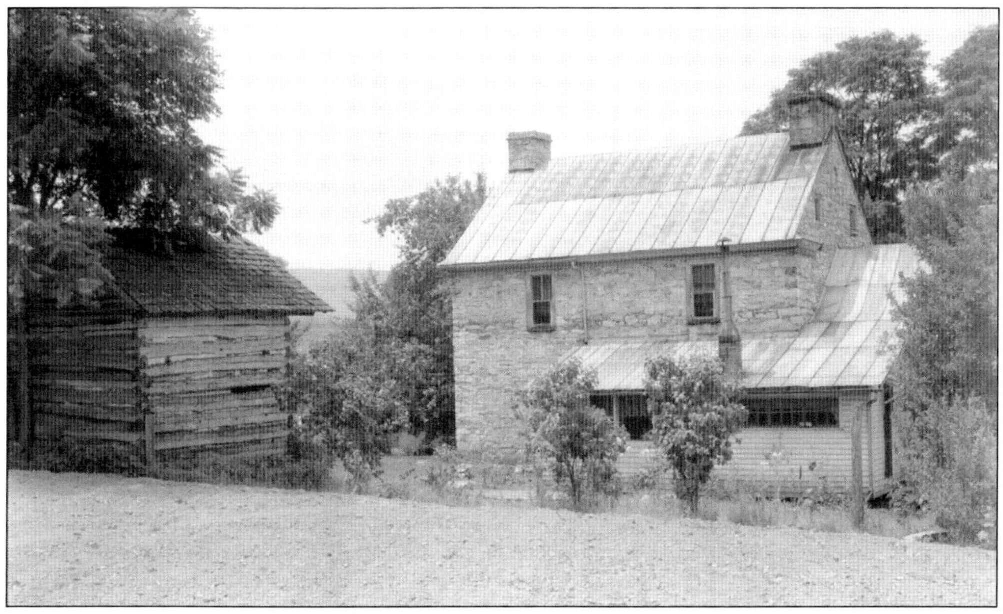

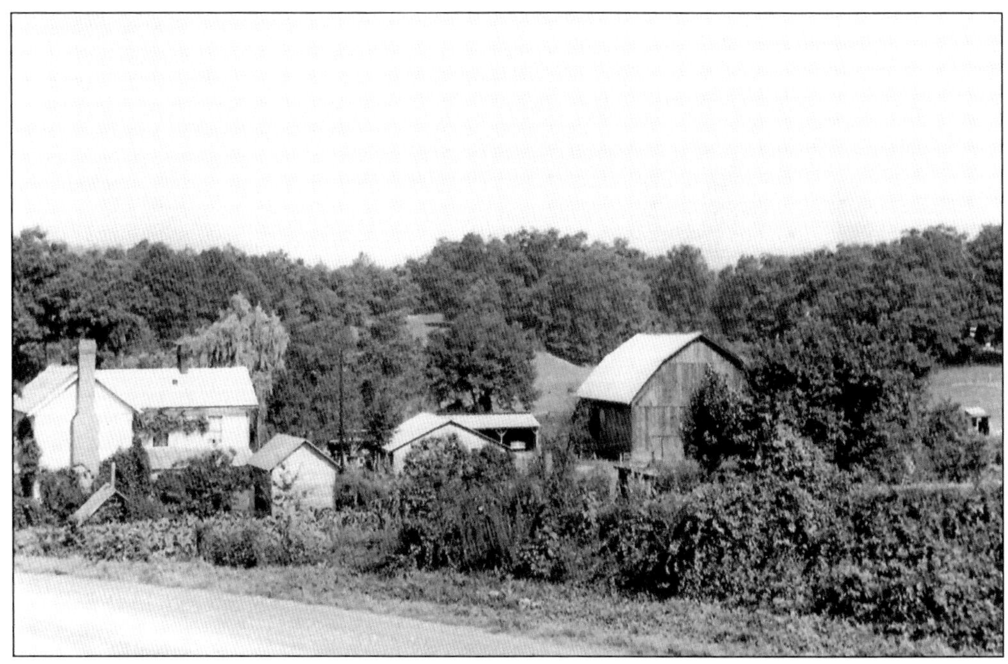

Squibb Farm. In the Sulphur Springs community, the Squibb Farm, which has remained in the family for more than a century, features a home built around 1890. According to the family, the house is of the original size with the porches on the east and west being turned into living spaces. It is the second house known to have been on the farm. The first house was torn down in 1943. The original home's foundation still remains. A crib and tobacco barn were built from the wood of the first house. (Both, courtesy of the Squibb family.)

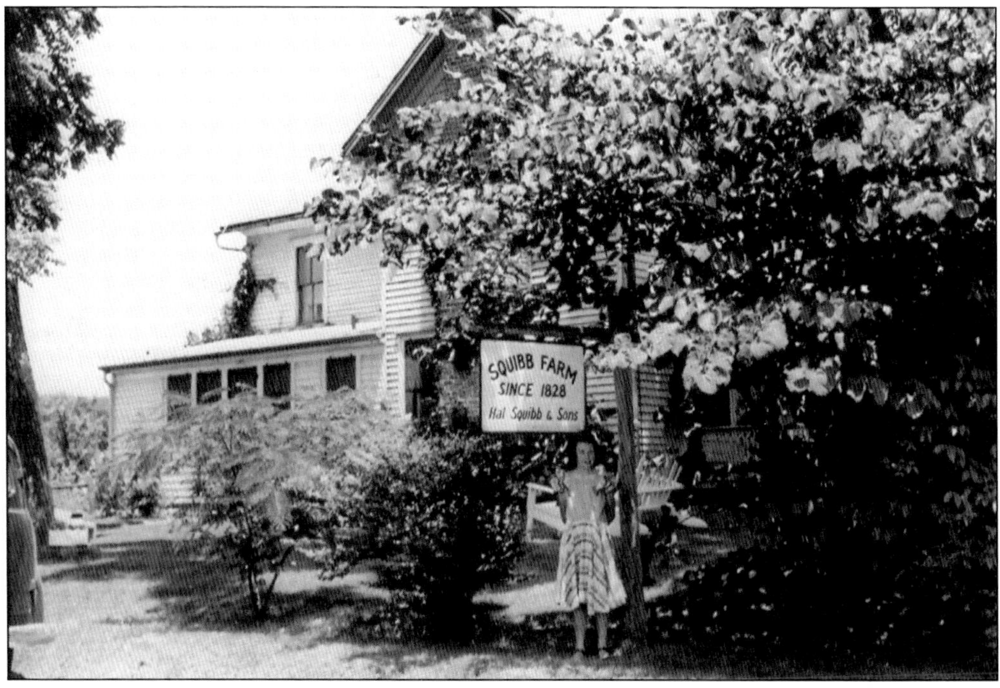

Four

Elizabethton and Carter County

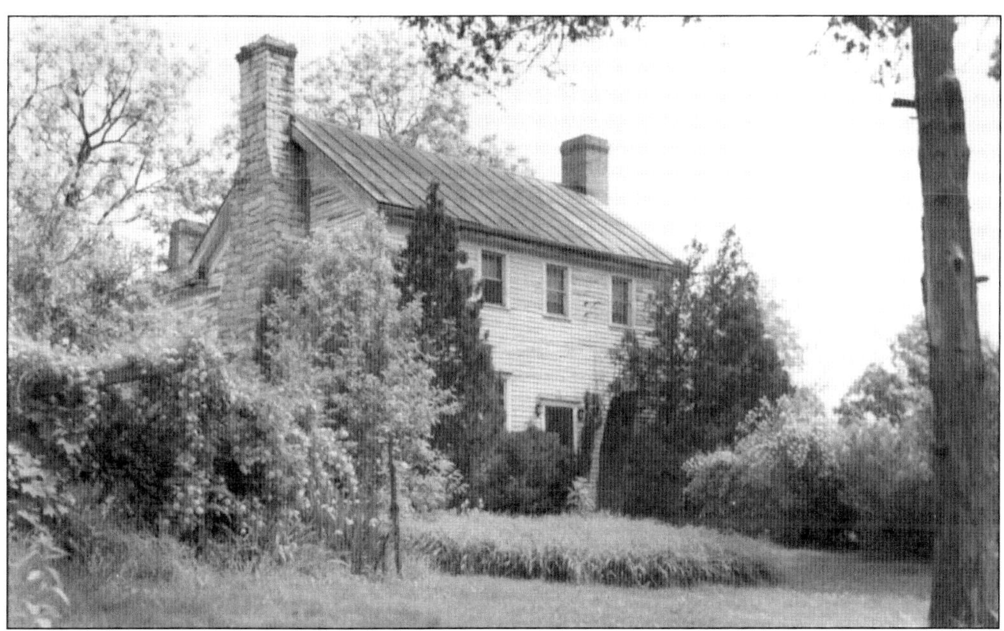

Carter Mansion. The Carter Mansion of Elizabethton is considered as the oldest frame house in the state of Tennessee. It was built by pioneers John and Landon Carter between 1775 and 1780. The remarkable home with intricate woodworking is a bit out of place, as its architecture resembles homes built in the Virginia Tidewater and Europe, rather than on the frontier. (Courtesy of the Tennessee State Library and Archives.)

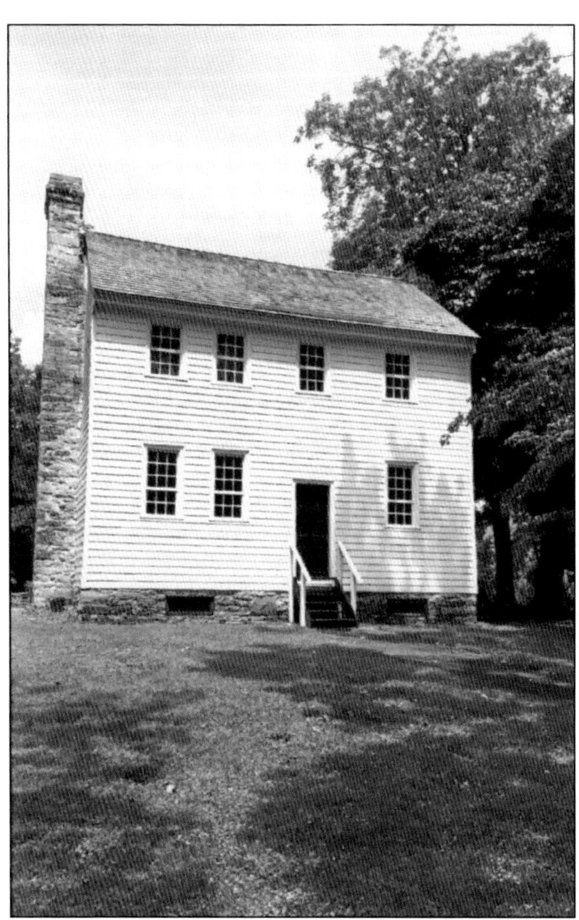

Carter Mansion. Sycamore Shoals State Historic Area operates the historic Carter Mansion in Elizabethton as a house museum. The state purchased the property and restored the once dilapidated home in the 1970s. A number of archaeologists and historians studied the property during restoration efforts. The property also features a family cemetery and gardens. (Courtesy of Jennifer Bauer.)

Historic Elizabethton. The town of Elizabethton was established near the confluence of the Doe and Watauga Rivers. The town's historic district can be seen in this photograph taken from Lynn Mountain. One important residence, the Alfred Moore Carter Mansion, can be seen in the foreground, next to the courthouse. Carter was the son of the town's namesakes, Landon and Elizabeth Carter. (Courtesy of Betty Jane Hylton.)

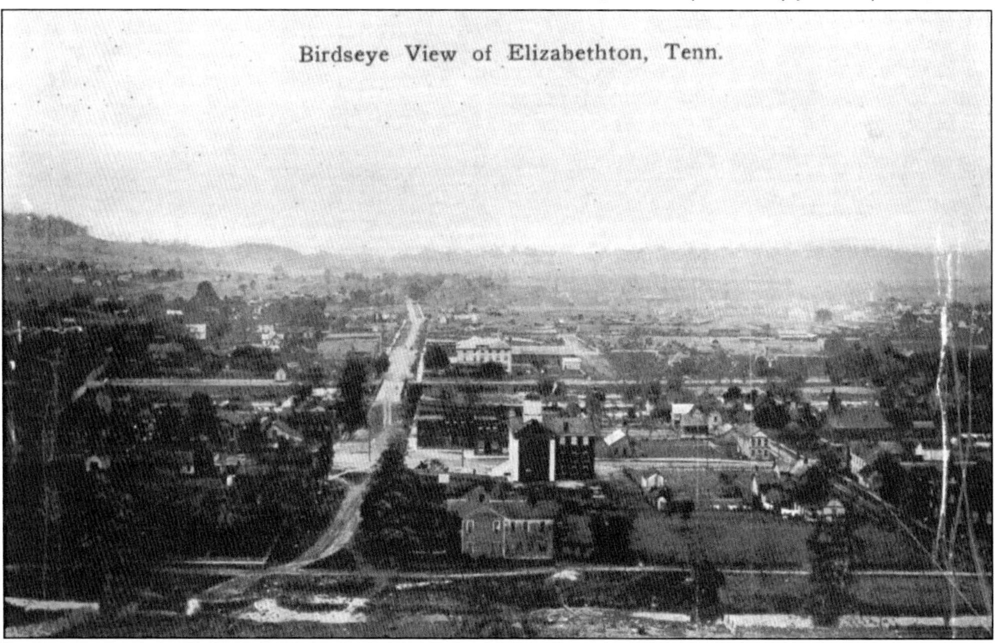

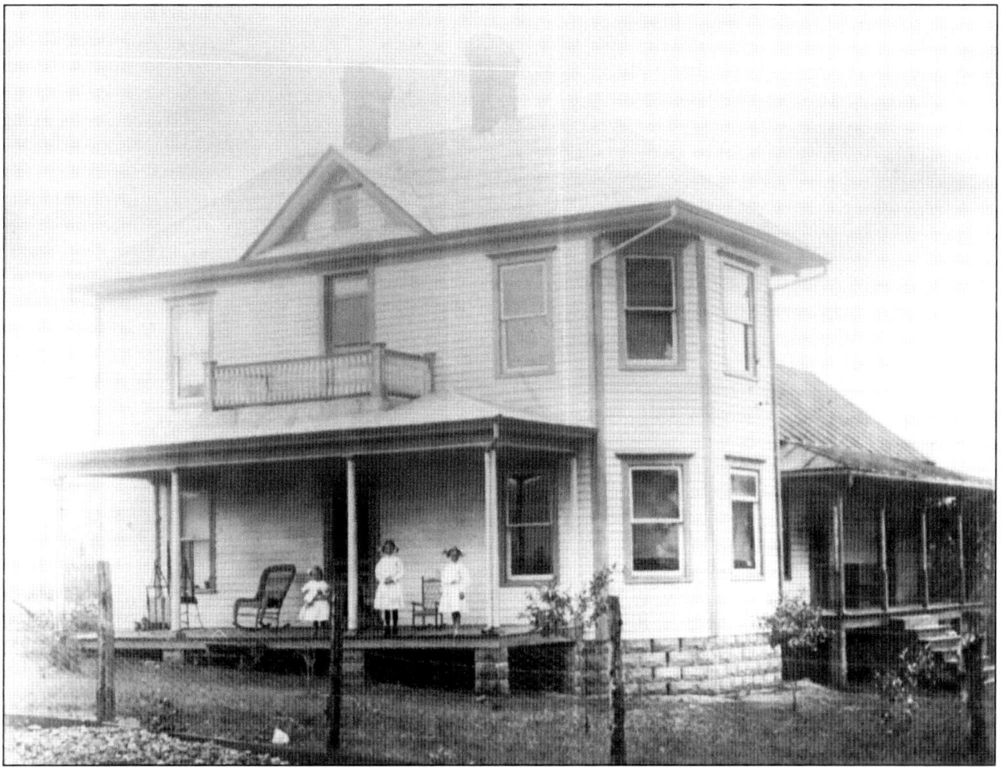

DUGGER HOUSE. The Dugger House, which still stands in Elizabethton, was constructed about 1905 at the intersection of Maple and Cedar Streets. This photograph, taken about 1910, shows the Dugger girls on the front porch of the home. The Moreland family later lived in the home. (Courtesy of the Tennessee State Library and Archives.)

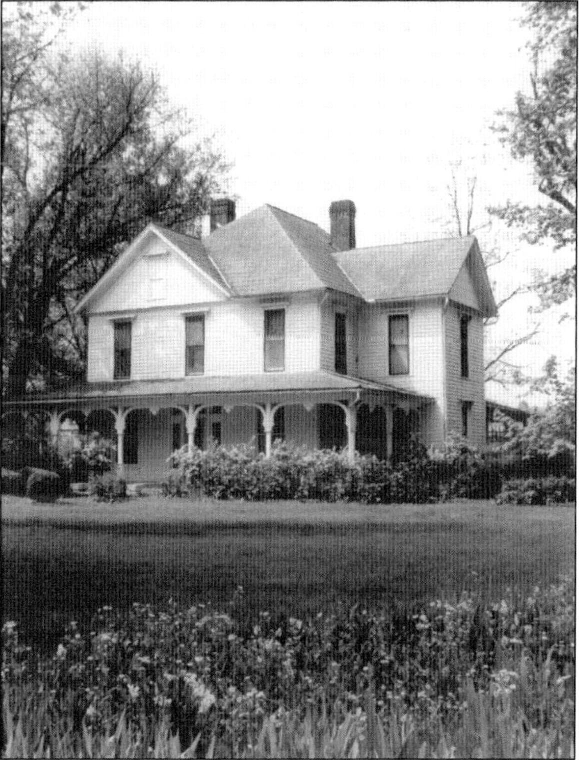

RANGE HOUSE. The Range House was built in the mid-19th century along the Doe River in Elizabethton. Its most famous owner was Tennessee governor Robert Taylor in the 1880s. The Victorian home was constructed by Dr. Abraham Jobe, who once owned the land on which the covered bridge is now located, across the street from the Range House. (Courtesy of the Tennessee State Library and Archives.)

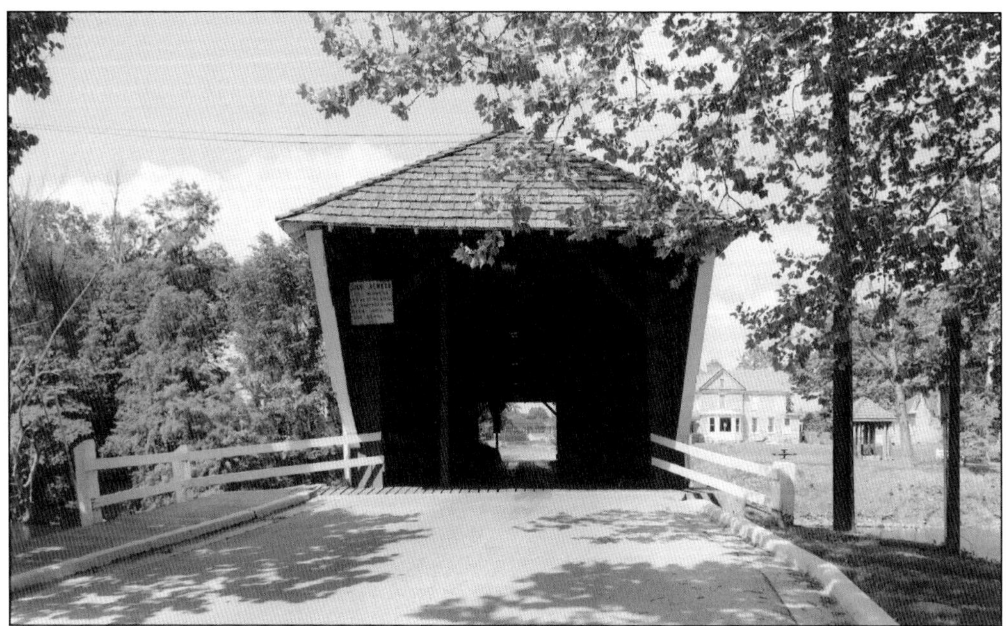

DUNGAN HOUSE AND COVERED BRIDGE. The Dungan House, built in 1892 by Judge W.P. Dungan, and the covered bridge, built in 1882, can be seen in this photograph. The elaborate 14-room mansion was one the town's first to feature electric lights, a residential telephone, and its own water system. The bridge, which connects Third Street and Hattie Avenue, is now only open to pedestrians. (Courtesy of the Library of Congress.)

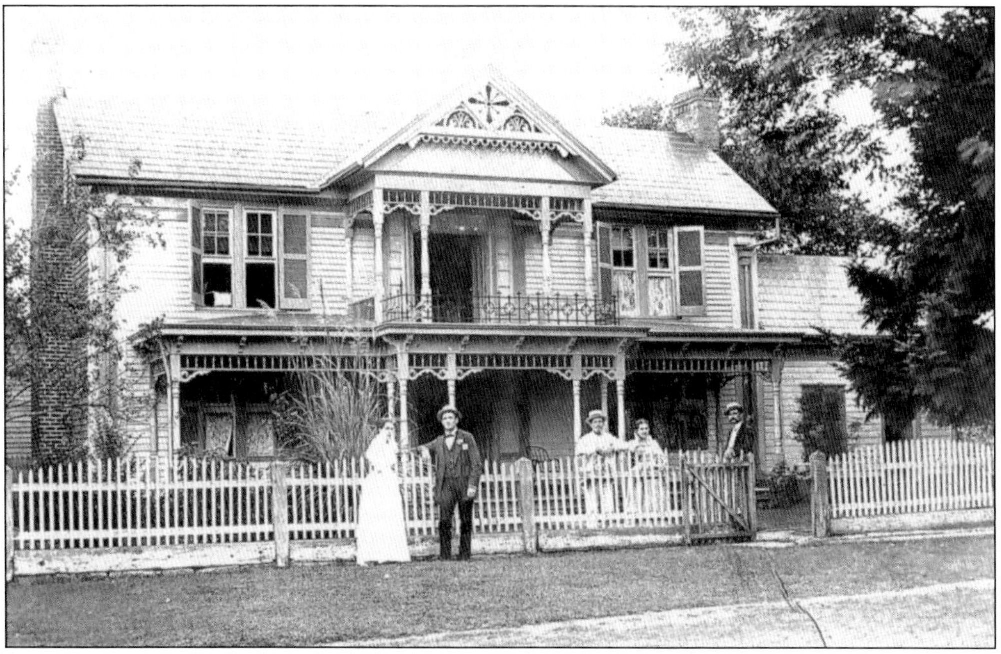

FOLSOM HOUSE. The clapboard-sided Folsom House was built in 1861 by Confederate army major Henderson Folsom. It is of the Greek Revival style and features an ornate two-story portico with columns. While residing here, Folsom planted a significant fir tree on his property. Today, the fir is the tallest in Tennessee and the second-tallest in the United States. (Courtesy of Keith Hart.)

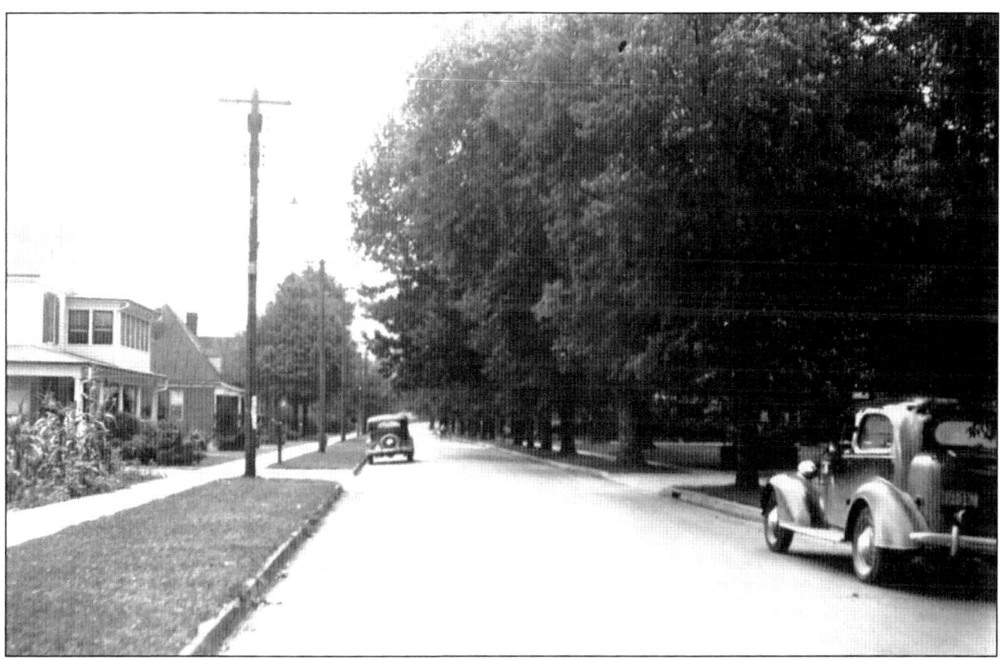

Main Street. Tree-lined Main Street in Elizabethton is home to several historic houses, including the Alexander House, pictured below. Edwin C. Alexander, who lived in the home, was a well-known businessman and served as city manager during the 1930s and 1940s. The Alexander House was built in 1900. Another notable residence on North Main Street is known as the Old Main Manor, which was built in the early 1900s. It is a unique brick structure with asymmetrical design. A number of cottages and bungalows can also be found along Main Street. (Both, courtesy of the Alexander family.)

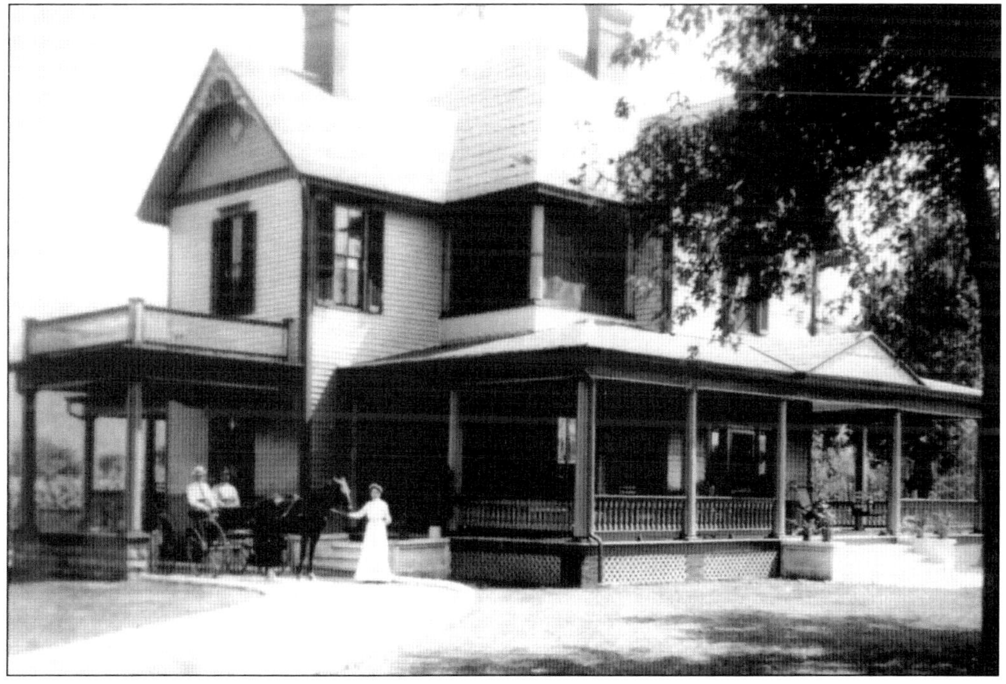

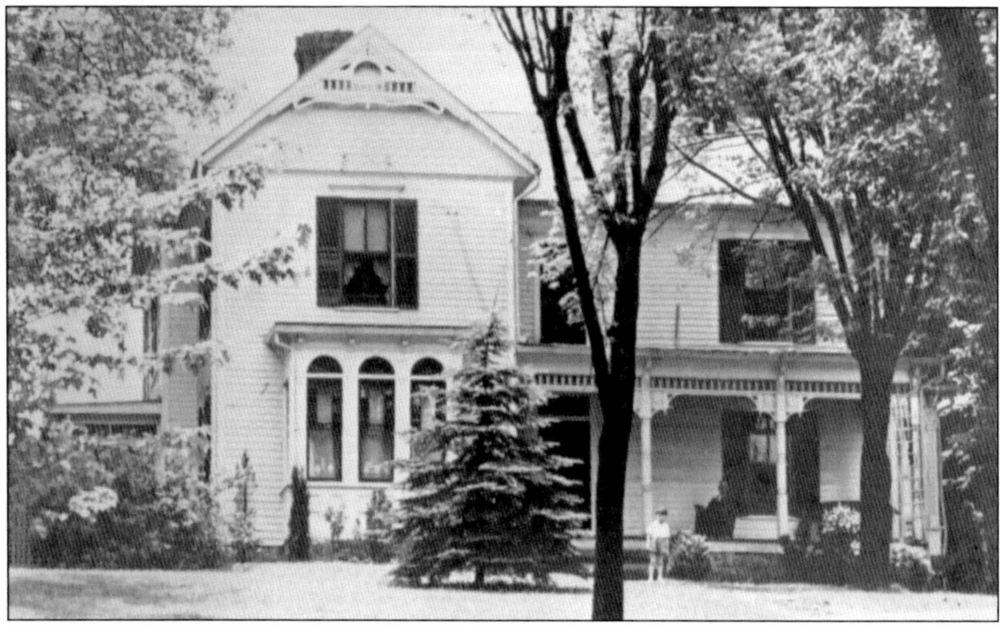

HENDRICKSON HOUSE. The Lon Hendrickson House was located on Doe Avenue in Elizabethton before it was demolished in the 1970s. This photograph, taken in the 1930s, shows Hendrickson on the front porch and a boy, Richard Lovett, in the front yard. Hendrickson was president of the Watauga Bottling Works, which was located a few blocks away on East Elk Avenue. (Courtesy of the Tennessee State Library and Archives.)

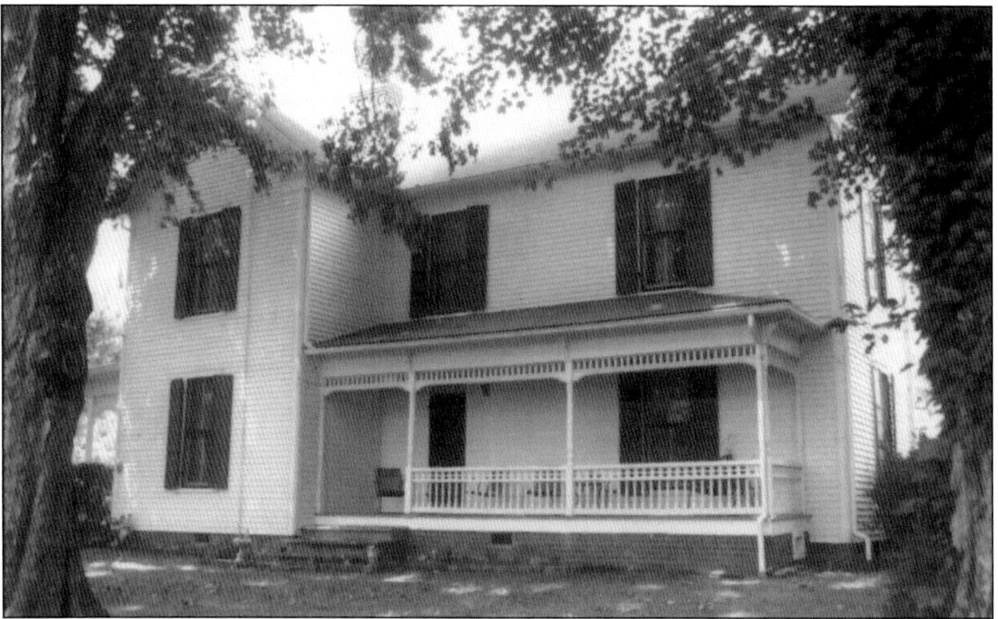

RENFRO-ALLEN HOUSE. The historic Renfro-Allen Farm in Stoney Creek was founded in 1840 by Issac H. Brown of Virginia. The landmark house was built in 1897 by James Renfro. Judge Ben Allen, a prominent criminal court judge, later lived here. Allen retreated to his home, a white Folk Victorian structure, which has received few alterations over the years. (Courtesy of the Tennessee Historical Commission.)

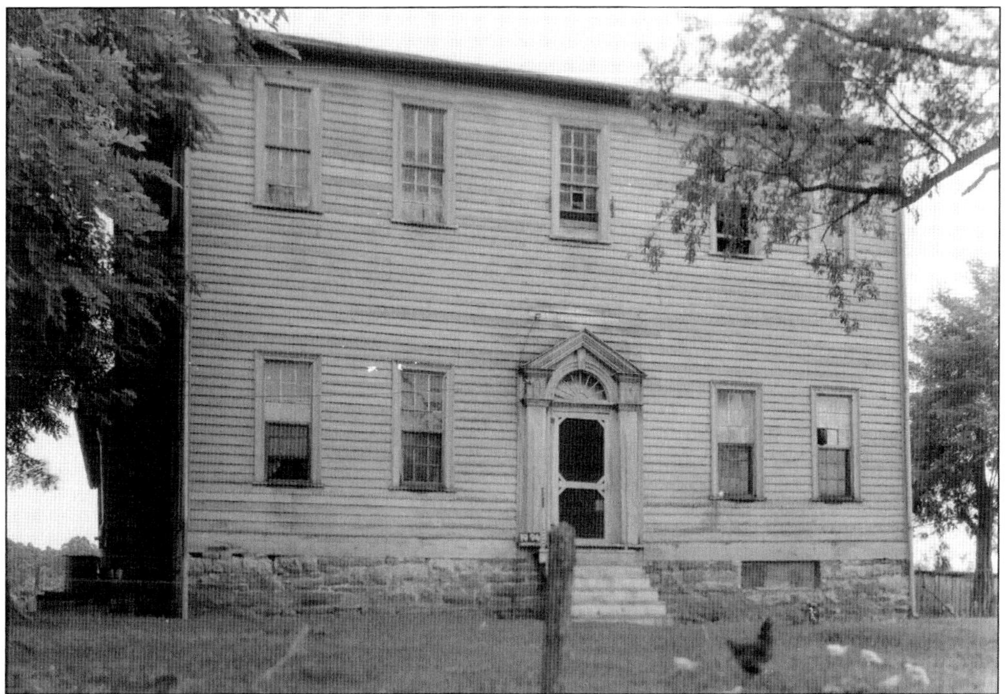

Sabine Hill. Brig. Gen. Nathaniel Taylor and his wife built a Federal, two-story home on Sabine Hill in present-day Elizabethton. Taylor died in 1816, before the home was finished. His wife, Mary Patton Taylor, lived here for 37 years after his death and raised numerous children—her own and others. The wood-frame home has been restored and is currently owned by the State of Tennessee. Historians and architects have said the home is one of the country's finest examples of Federal-style architecture. The Historic American Buildings Survey visited the home in the 1930s and noted that the structure had delicate and almost elaborately carved wood elements. The Taylor family is one of Carter County's most famous; it includes governors, generals, sheriffs, and wealthy landowners. (Both, courtesy of the Library of Congress.)

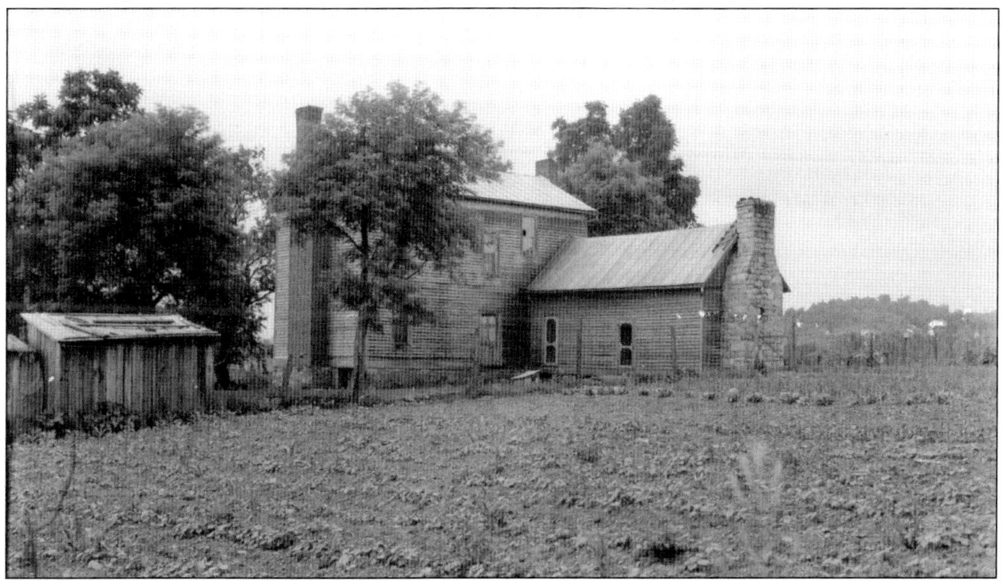

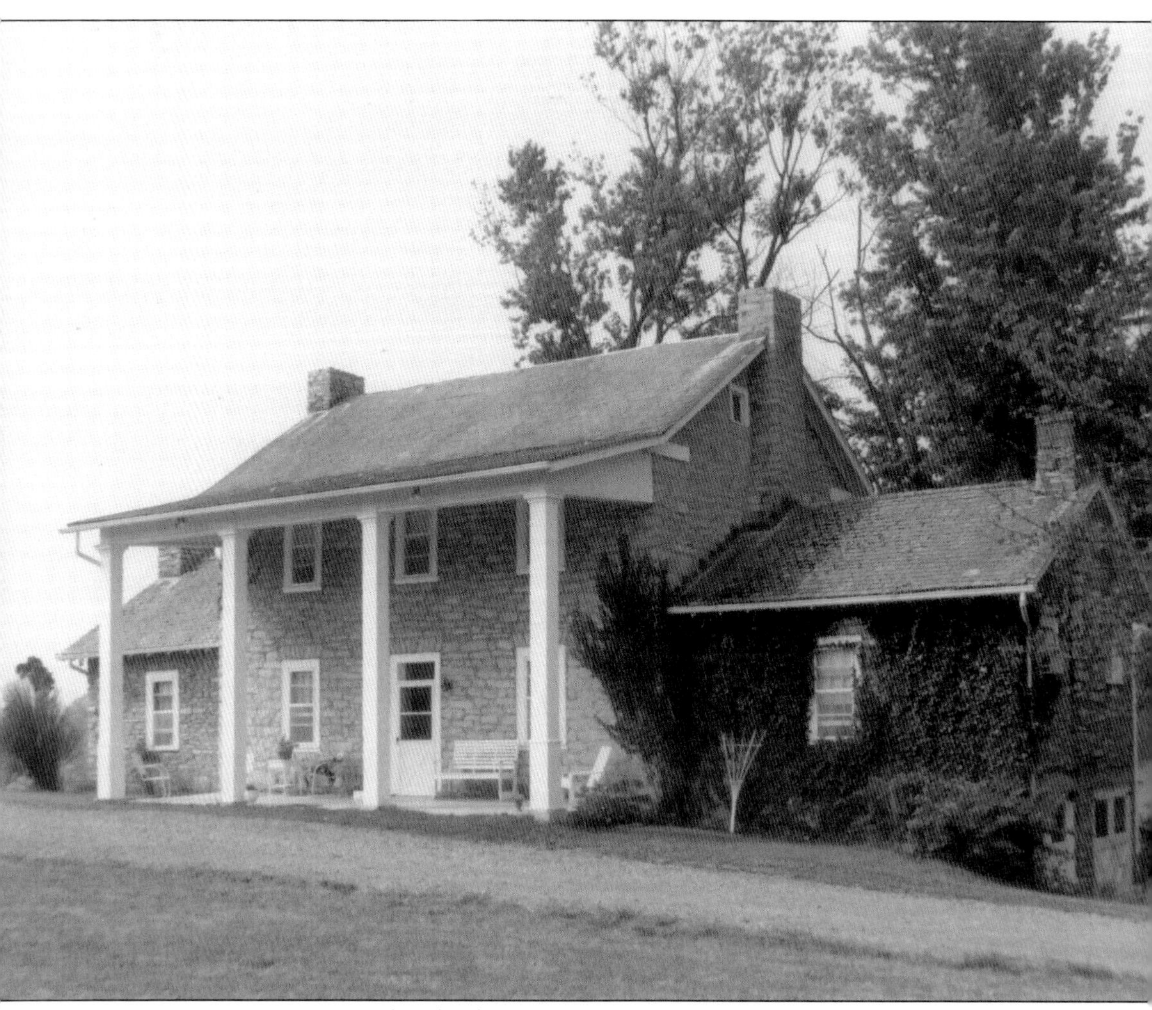

Henson Hunt House. With only a handful remaining today, limestone homes are exceptionally rare in Northeast Tennessee. During the late 18th and early 19th centuries, building a home with stone was fairly expensive and difficult. In 1812, however, Henson Hunt, a plantation owner in the Buffalo and Sinking Creek area of western Carter County, constructed a beautiful stone house. Built of limestone, the home currently sits on a property at the end of Brookdale Drive in the Pinecrest community. The Hunt family lived here for nearly a century, according to a listing in the National Register of Historic Places. The Reba Ottinger family purchased the home and restored the square-shaped house. They put on a new roof, added two wings of limestone, a columned front porch and terraced rear. This home is featured in the May 1929 issue of *American Home* magazine. In 1974, J.W. Street purchased the old Hunt property. Hunt and his wife, Mary Magdalene Pope, are buried in the nearby family cemetery. (Courtesy of the Tennessee Historical Commission.)

TAYLOR-PHILLIPS HOUSE. The Taylor-Phillips House, located on the Milligan College campus, dates back to the 1700s. Two prominent families—the Williamses and Taylors—later lived in the home. Former Tennessee governor Alf Taylor, who is most famous for his campaign for governor against his brother, Robert, also lived here. (Courtesy of the Milligan College Archives.)

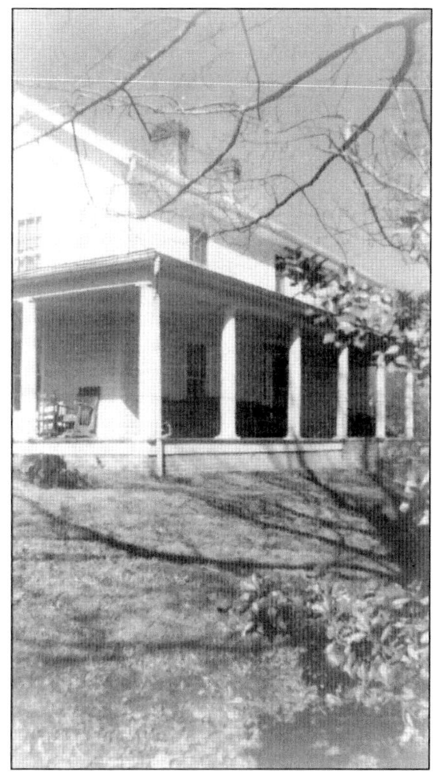

MCCOWN COTTAGE. Built in 1913 as a home for the Milligan College president and his family, McCown Cottage was originally designed by Mary Hardin McCown. By 1976, the college built a new president's home, and McCown Cottage was then used as a guesthouse and later as an administrative building. (Courtesy of the Milligan College Archives.)

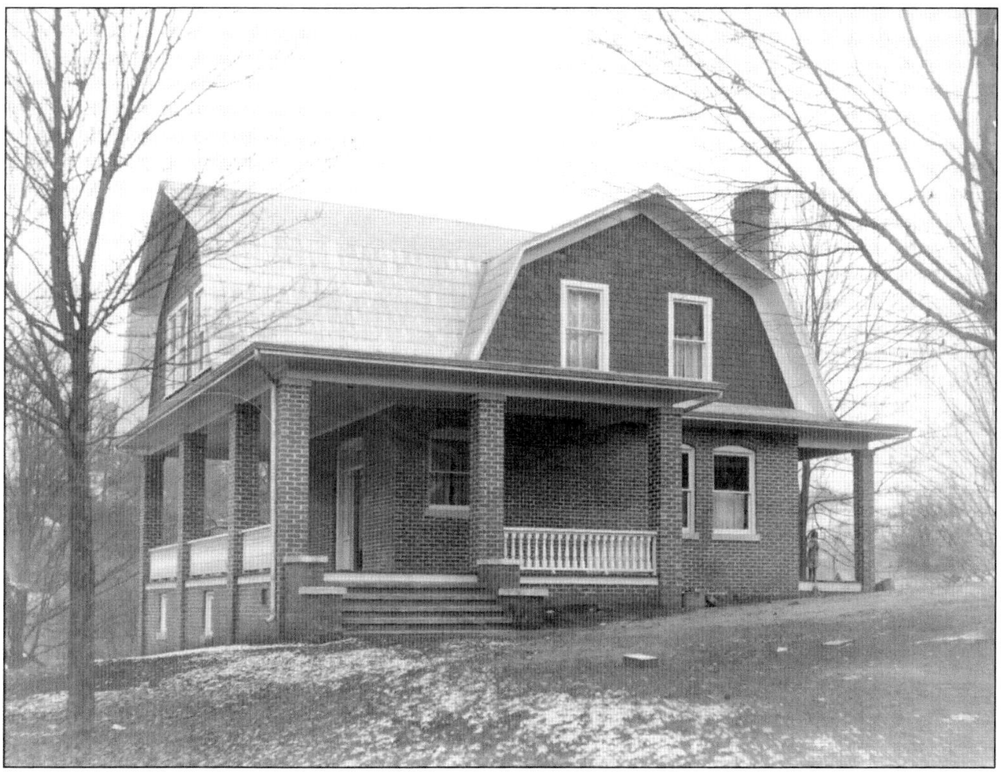

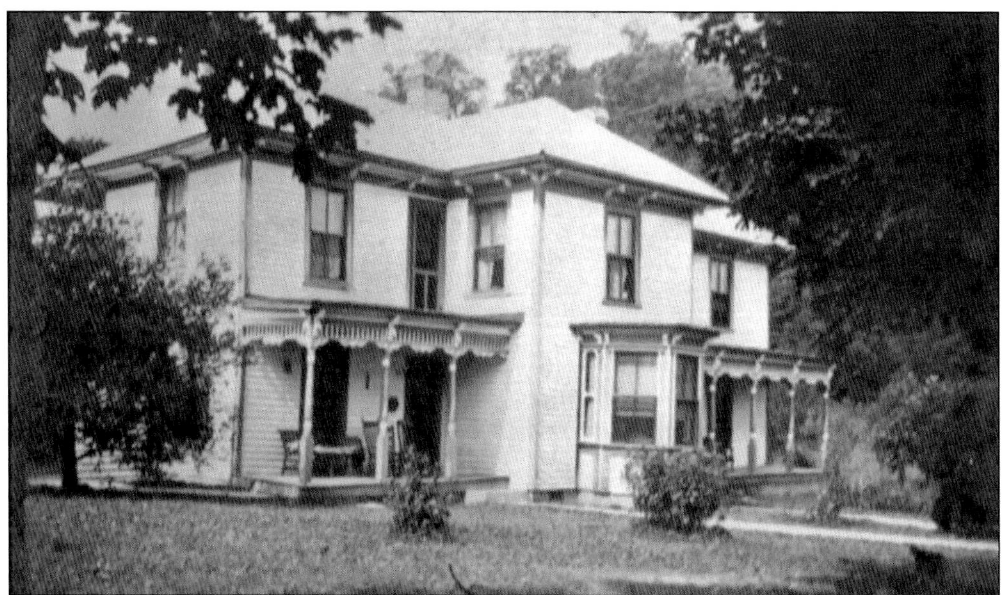

SMALLING FARMHOUSE. The J.H. Smalling Farmhouse is located in western Carter County. According to the state archives, the structure was moved to its current location after the flood of 1901. It was placed on logs and rolled across the land. The family had a sand yard business. (Courtesy of the Tennessee State Library and Archives.)

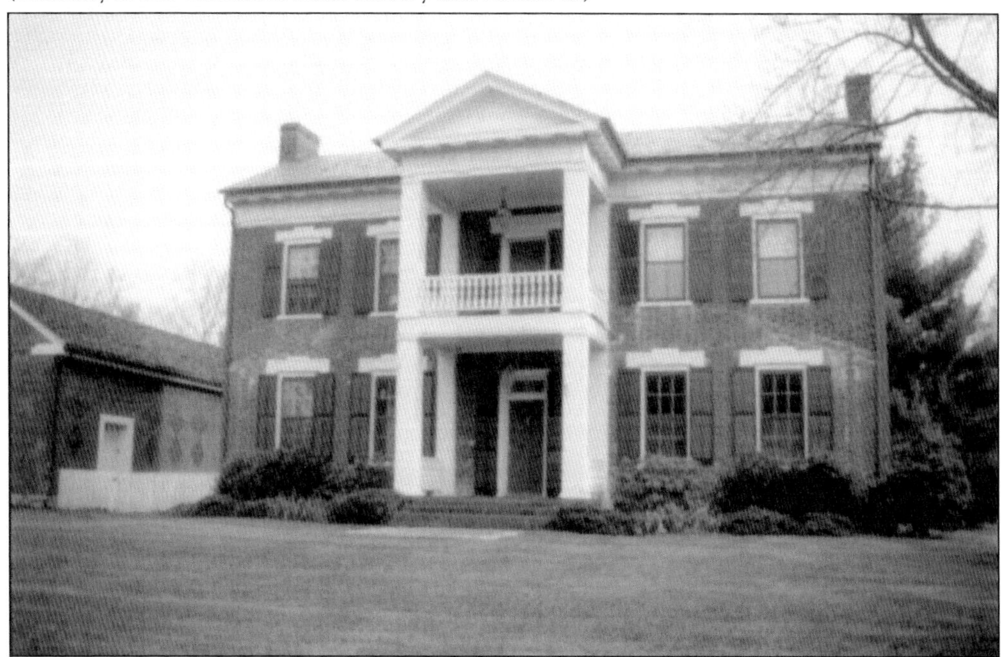

BROOKS MANSION. Reuben Brooks Sr. built his plantation home in 1820 on property in the Blue Springs section of Carter County. It was a center of local Confederate efforts during the Civil War. One family member, William Brooks, was shot and killed by Union supporters as he was recruiting along Stoney Creek. The property, which includes a rare brick slave house, weave house, and smokehouse, stayed in the Brooks family until 1906. The historic Stover House, in which Pres. Andrew Johnson died, is also located on the Brooks farm. (Author's collection.)

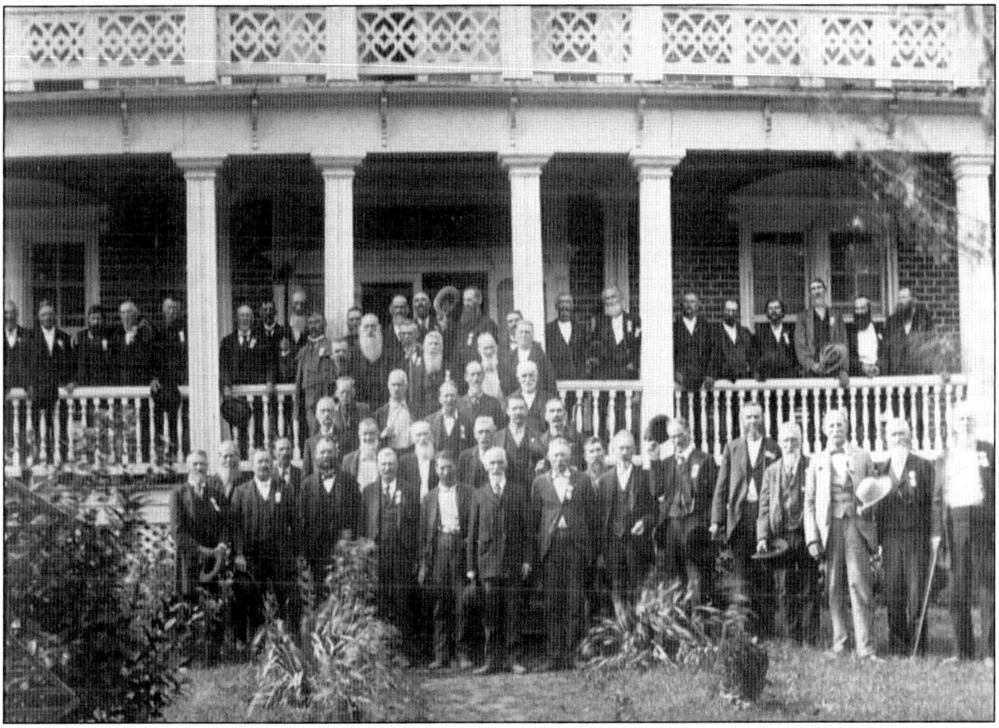

Simerly-Butler Mansion. The Simerly-Butler Mansion rises above Main Street in the town of Hampton. The 20-room mansion was constructed after the Civil War in 1867 by Elijah Simerly. It features 18-inch-thick exterior walls and 12-inch-thick interior walls. It also has a rare widow's walk, a walking area on the roof of the house, probably used to look out over the town of Hampton and farmland. Simerly was a wealthy investor, railroad president, state legislator, and a lead developer in the design and layout of Hampton. A.H. Robinson purchased the home in 1907 and in turn sold it to Nat E. Harris in 1910. Harris was Georgia's governor. He died in 1929, and his wife, Hattie Jobe Harris, lived in the mansion until 1939. The Butler and Matheson families later owned the home. (Both, courtesy of the Library of Congress.)

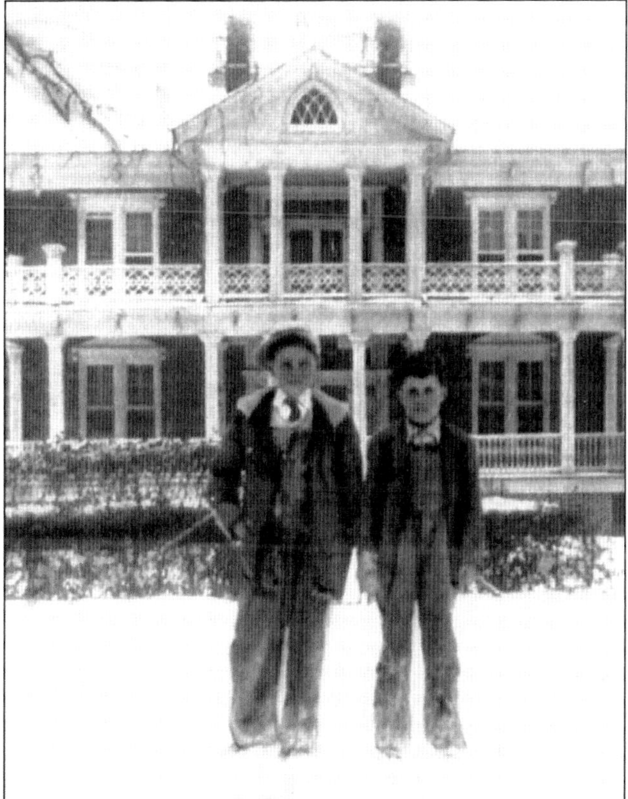

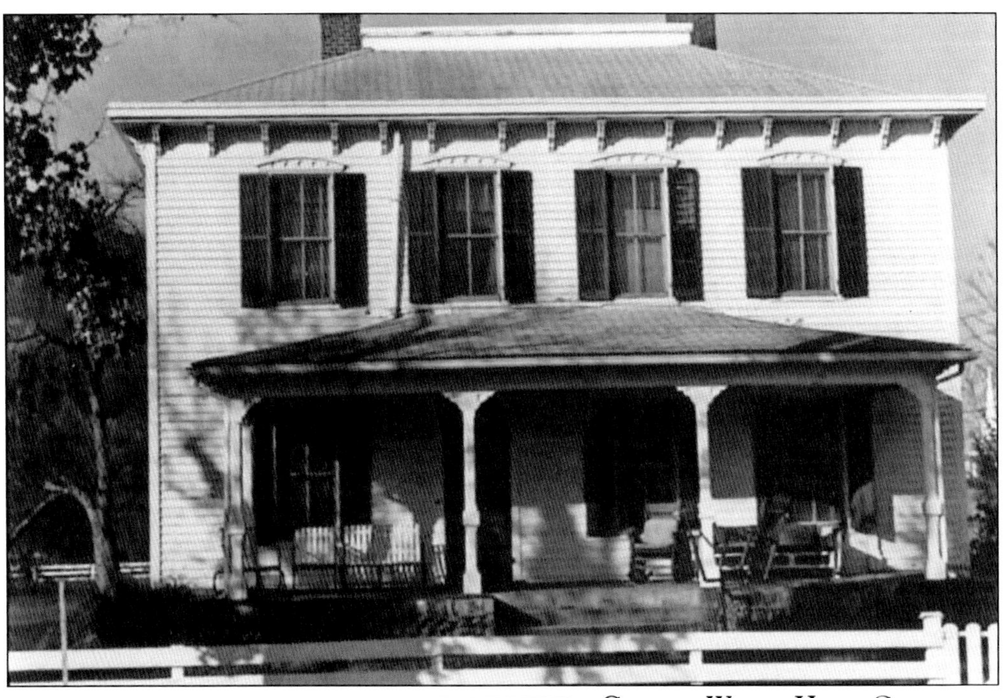

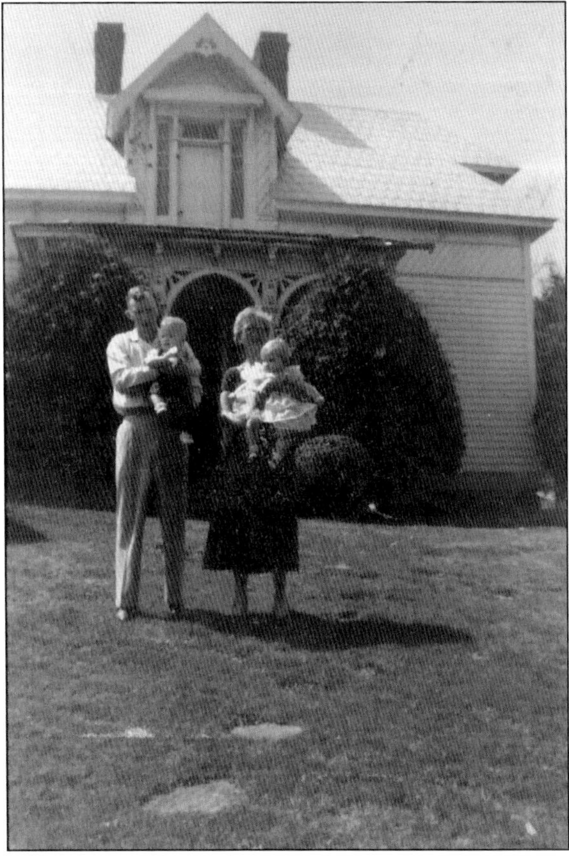

General Wilder Home. Gen. John Wilder built an Italianate residence in Roan Mountain in 1884. The L-shaped home, covered in weatherboard, has had few alterations over the years. Wilder, who developed two Roan Mountain hotels, had moved from Roan Mountain to Johnson City by 1890. In the 1900s, the Graybeal family lived on the property, which includes a smokehouse and a privy. (Courtesy of the Tennessee Historical Commission.)

Pippin House. Tennessee railroad engineer Sherman Pippin owned a beautiful home in Roan Mountain along present-day US Highway 19E. The railroad legend and former hack line driver purchased the farm in 1912. It featured a small outbuilding at the rear where Pippin liked to work. (Courtesy of Joanna Miller.)

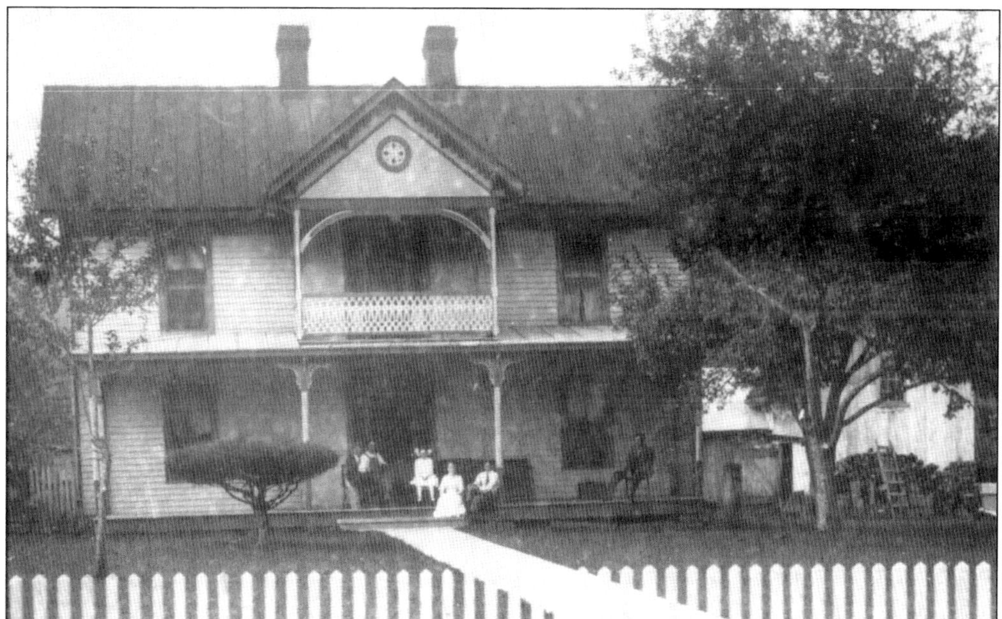

Church House. The beautiful Church House is located at the corner of US Highway 19E and Shell Creek in the Roan Mountain community. It was built by William Church and his wife, Lula Cornelia Hardin, in 1882. After Church died in 1889, Lula Hardin married John Snider. The Churches also constructed a store in front of the home, which still stands at the intersection. (Courtesy of Linda Brinkley Morgan.)

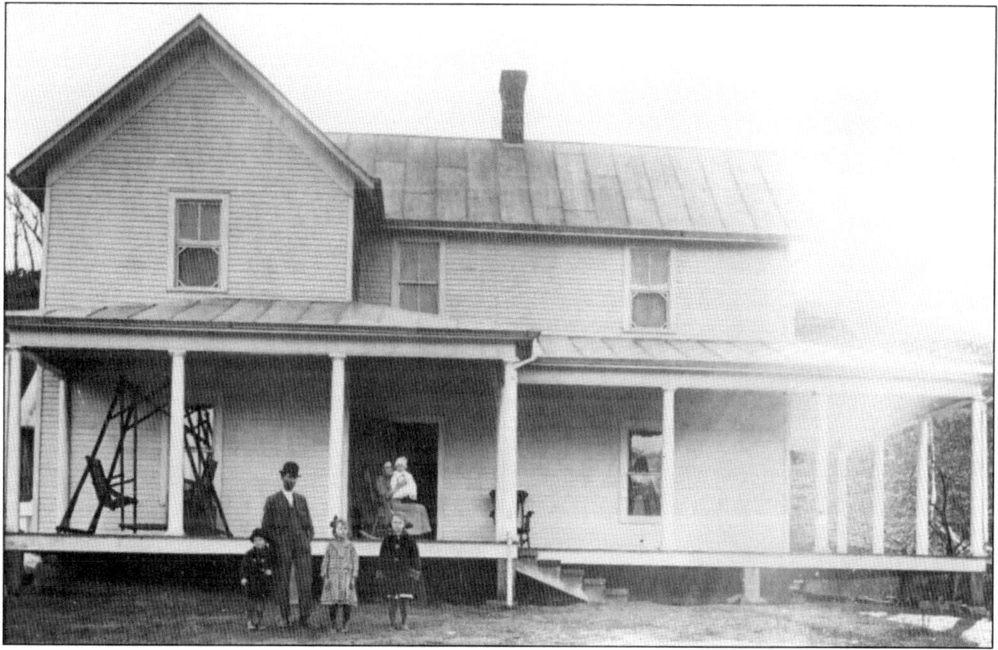

Brinkley House. The Brinkley family of Roan Mountain constructed a large residence in the present-day Shell Creek community in the 19th century. James Walter Brinkley Sr., who built the home, and his wife were in the retail business. The family owned stores in Tennessee and nearby Elk Park, North Carolina. (Courtesy of Linda Brinkley Morgan.)

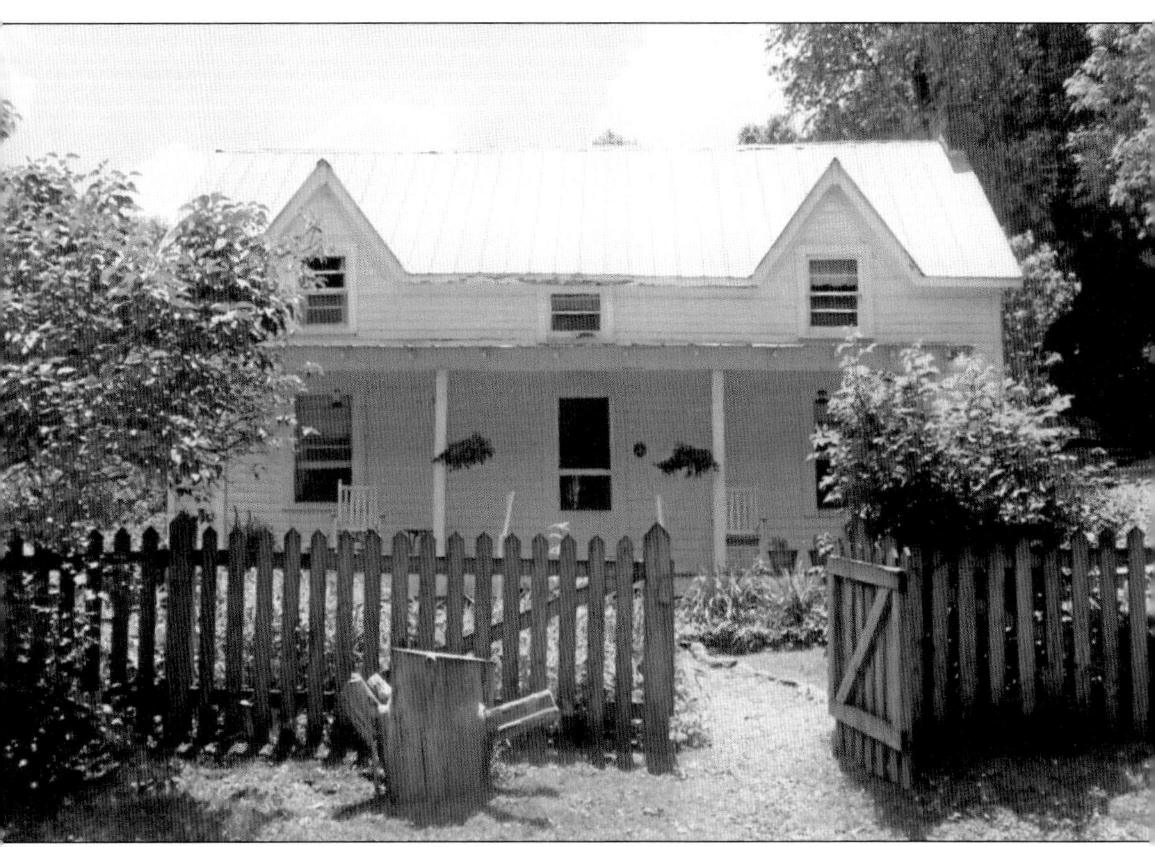

David Miller Homestead. David Miller came to Roan Mountain in the early 1870s and built a log cabin. The home eventually rotted away, but by 1908, his son Nathaniel had built a new house. Descendants owned the property until the state purchased it in 1969. The David Miller Homestead is now part of Roan Mountain State Park. John Frank Miller was Roan Mountain State Park's first interpreter to work at the farm. The farmhouse was added to the National Register of Historic Places in 2014. The Register notes that the home and associated outbuildings reflect the patterns of use of the Appalachian lifestyle of subsistence farming in secluded mountainous regions from the early to mid-20th century and continues to feature many of their original materials and elements with minimal alterations. The field patterns, pasture areas, and the apple orchard were worked in much the same ways they had been since they were planted—with horse and manual labor. (Author's collection.)

Five

Erwin and Unicoi County

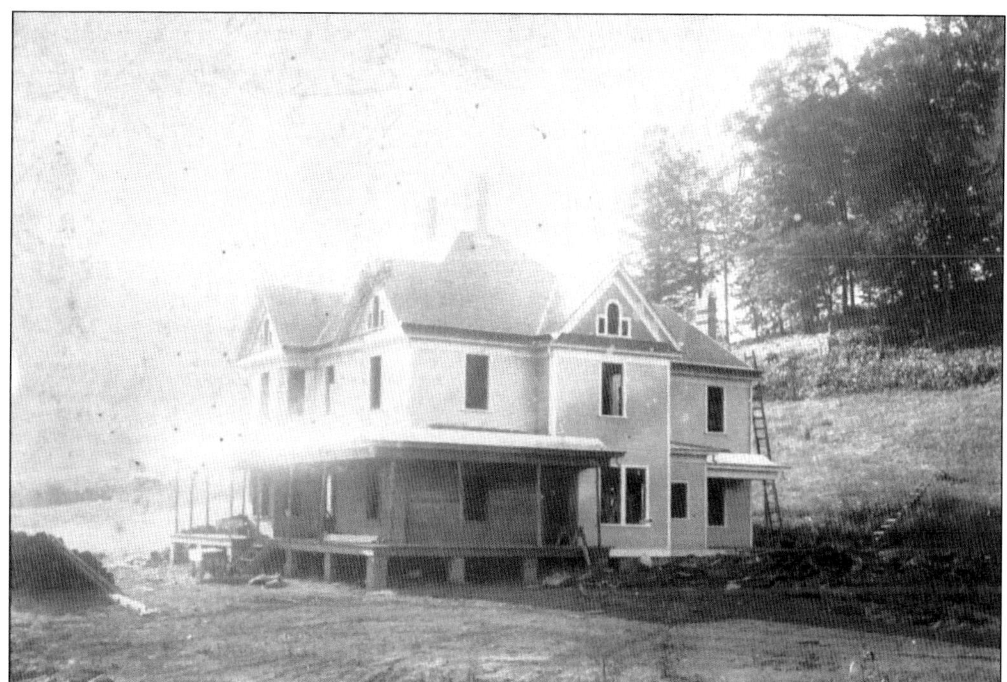

Superintendent's House. The superintendent's house at the Erwin Fish Hatchery was constructed in 1903. G.W.N. Brown built the home, which features 10 rooms on two floors. A.G. Keesecker was the first of six superintendents to reside here. By 1982, the home had deteriorated and was scheduled to be demolished by the federal government. Local residents banded together and transformed it into a museum. (Courtesy of the Tennessee State Library and Archives.)

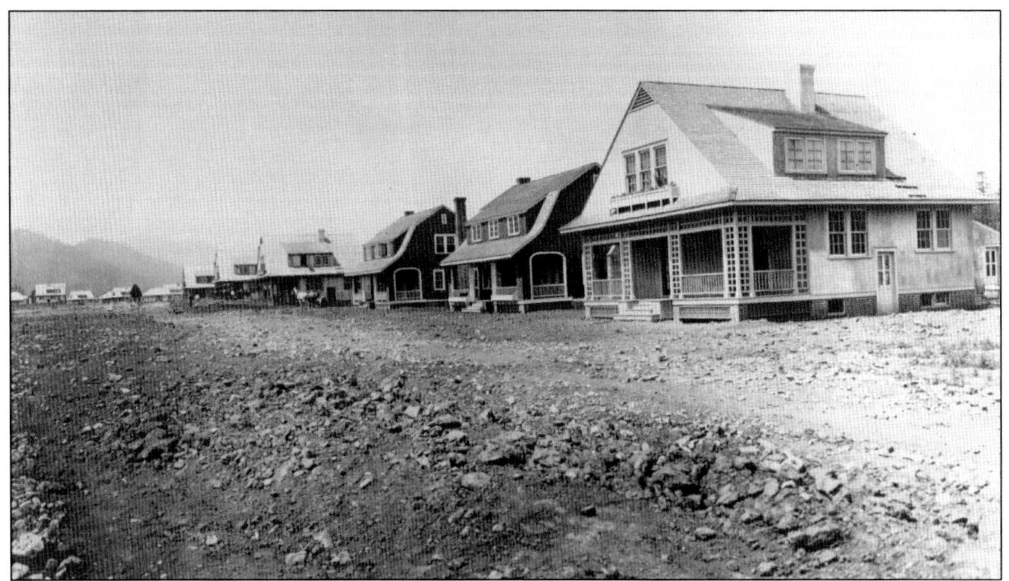

POTTERY HOUSES OF ERWIN. The Pottery Houses of Erwin include dozens of residences covering 135 acres in what has been called the Holston Addition. Built around 1916, the homes lining Ohio Avenue, Holston Place, and Unaka Way were constructed by the Holston Corporation, a division of Erwin's Clinchfield Railroad. The Craftsman homes originally housed employees of Southern Potteries. (Courtesy of the Tennessee State Library and Archives.)

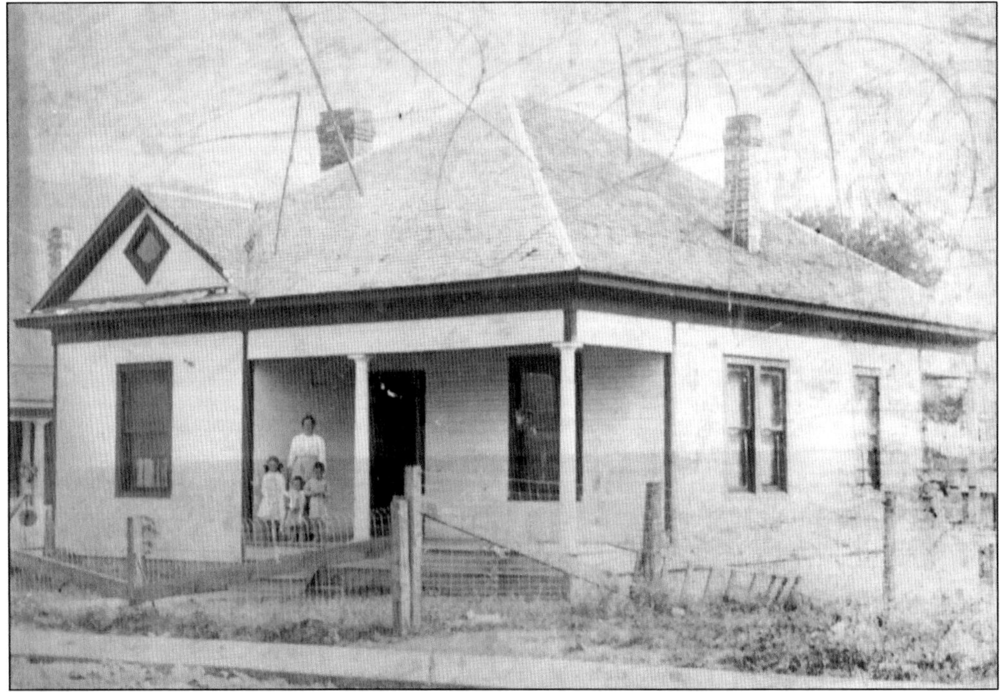

STALLAND HOUSE. The house in this photograph is located on Second Street in the town of Erwin. At the time this photograph was taken in 1911, it was owned by the Stalland family. A woman and three children can be seen on the porch. Several neighboring homes were built about the same time and in a similar design. (Courtesy of the Tennessee State Library and Archives.)

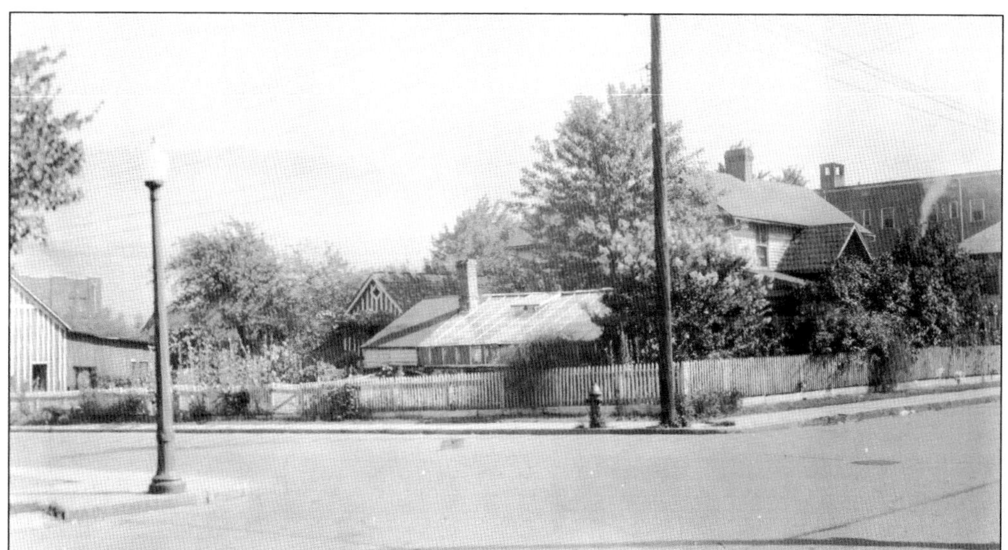

A.R. Brown Home. The A.R. Brown Home sits behind a picket fence on Erwin's Main Avenue. The Folk Victorian home built in 1894 by Nancy Love has been owned by the prominent Brown family since its construction. Although Love built the home, Albert R. Brown moved in shortly after it was completed. Originally, as pictured below, the home had four rooms and few utilities. Brown, a wealthy merchant and community leader, added rooms and utilities as his family grew. The last addition was made in 1916, and the house has remained unchanged and in the Brown family since that time. Brown, Erwin's first mayor and a state representative, owned the town's largest store and was an executive at three Erwin financial institutes. (Both, courtesy of Martha Stromberg.)

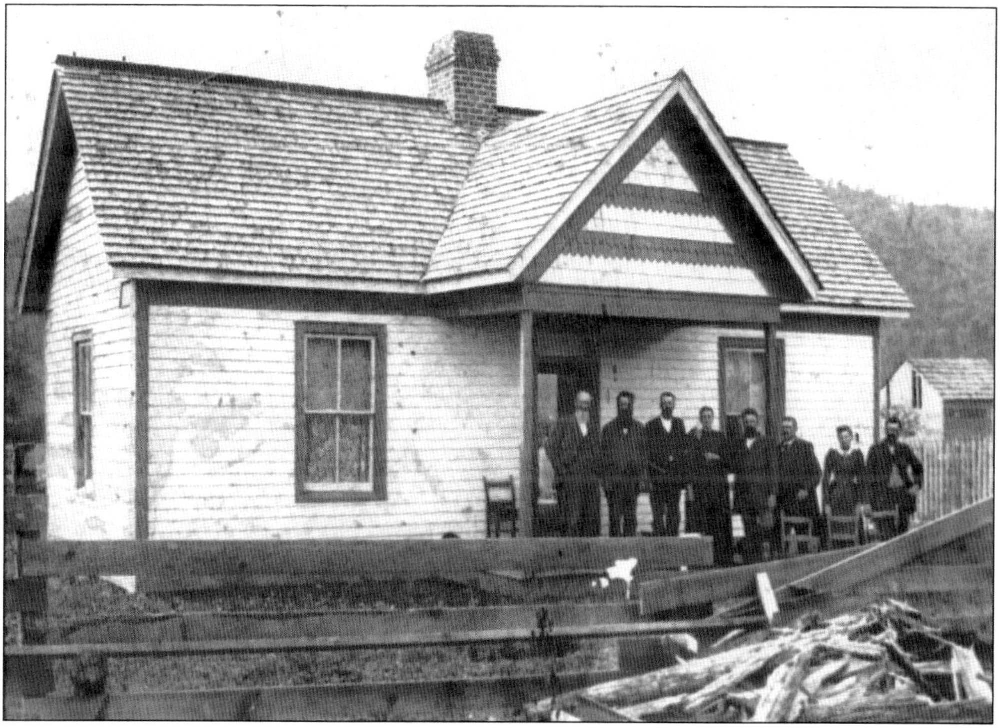

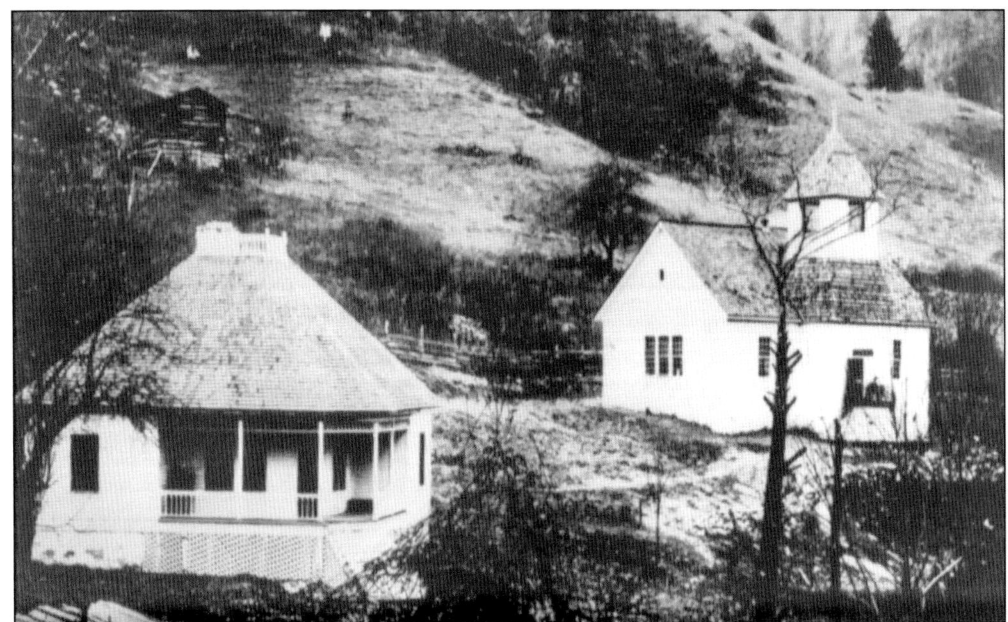

Rocky Fork. Jennie Moore, a Presbyterian missionary, was appointed to work in the Rocky Fork section of southern Unicoi County in 1903. She developed a mission school in the remote mountainous community. She lived in a small cottage, built about 1906, pictured here next to the school. The Jennie Moore Memorial Presbyterian Church was named in her honor. (Courtesy of the Tennessee State Library and Archives.)

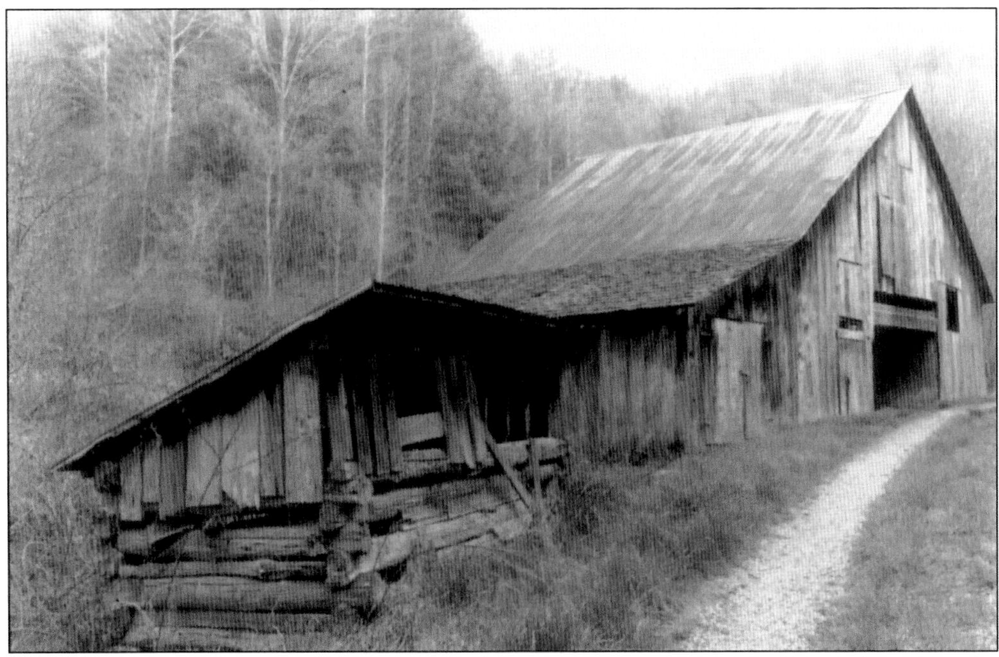

Tilson Farm. The Tilson family came to Flag Pond in Unicoi County in the 1850s, when they purchased land from the Brown family. Their farmstead, located in an isolated mountainous area, is comprised of a pre-1856-era log cabin, an 1890s log cabin, a 1930s frame farmhouse, a 1930s workshop, and a 1940s barn. (Courtesy of the Tennessee Historical Commission.)

Six

Mountain City and Johnson County

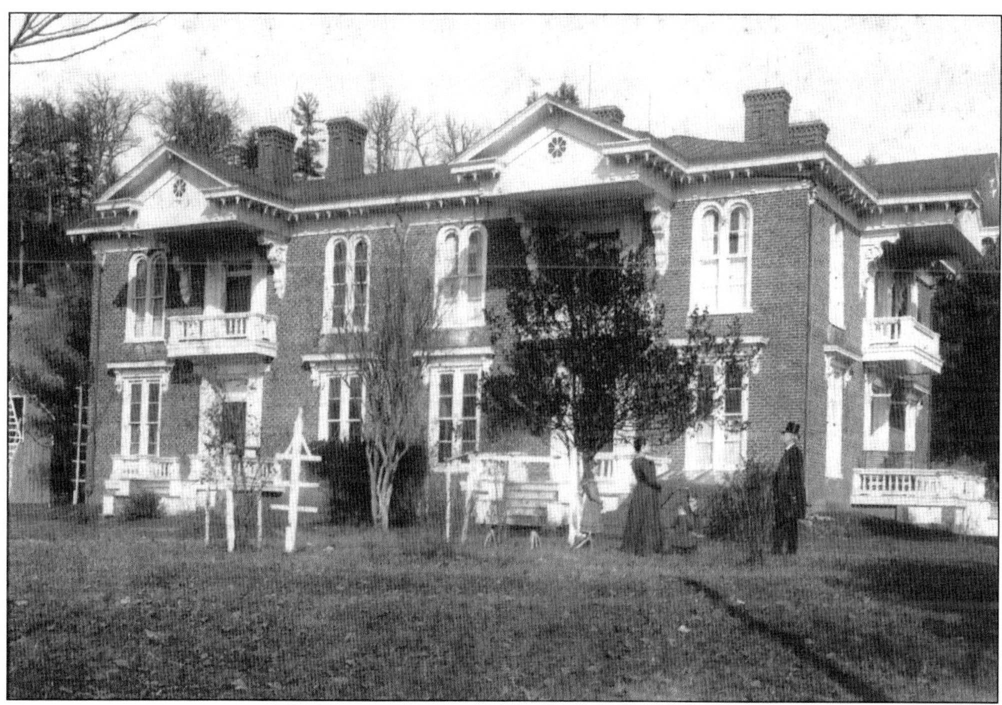

Roderick Butler Mansion. Lt. Col. Roderick Butler built his two-story brick home in 1870 in old Taylorsville, which is now Mountain City. The materials for the home were shipped from Washington. It includes six bedrooms, two porticoed porches, multiple fireplaces and chimneys, a multi-gabled roof, a smokehouse, washhouse, granary, and a barn. Butler became the postmaster of Taylorsville, a judge, and a five-term congressman. (Courtesy of Joan Trathen.)

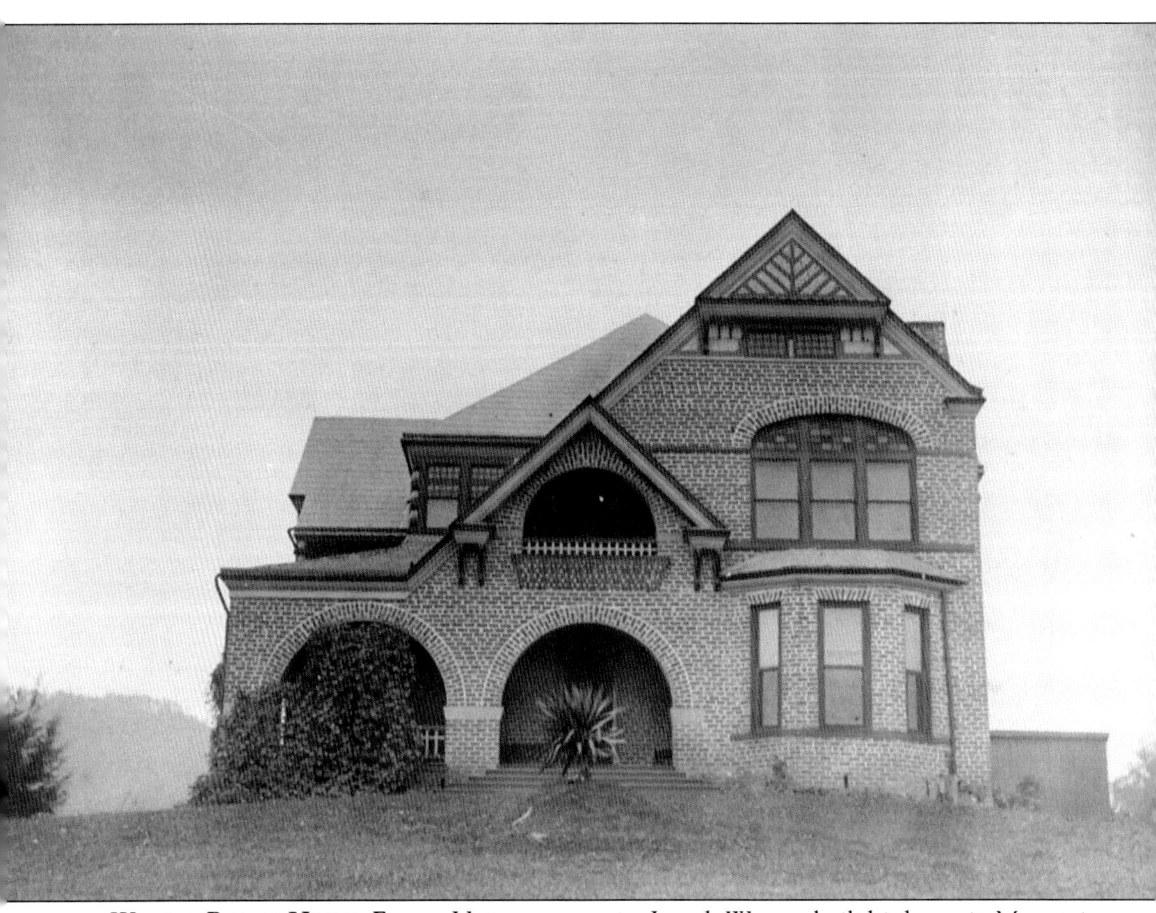

Wagner-Rambo House. Former Union army major Joseph Wagner built his home in Mountain City in 1889 of handmade brick. Wagner had mercantile and mining interests after the war. The Rambo family bought the house, known today as Prospect Hill, in 1910. It is a Victorian residence and sits on a hill. The house, which had 12 rooms and 10 fireplaces, was built on a 30-acre tract. The Rambo family, who owned the home for more than 80 years, modernized the structure, adding electricity, plumbing, and central heat. In 1991, the Rambos sold it to the Cornetts, who in turn sold it to Robert and Judy Hotchkiss, who provided this information. The Hotchkisses, who operate a bed-and-breakfast in the home, have added a few rooms to the rear of the house. (Courtesy of the Tennessee State Library and Archives.)

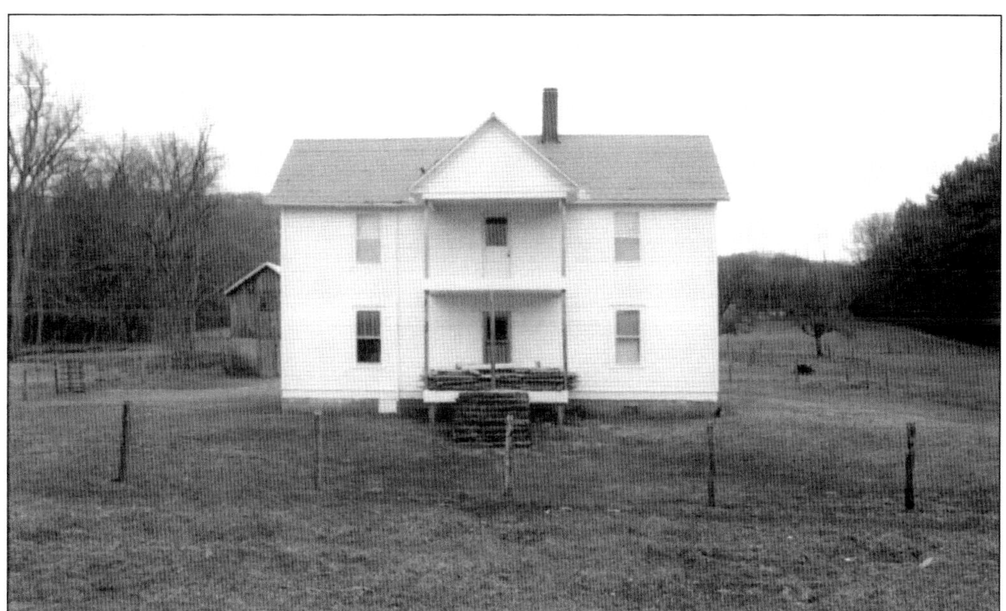

A.J. Wright House. The A.J. Wright House was constructed in 1907 in rural Shady Valley. Its current driveway is on the bed of a turn-of-the-century standard-gauge railroad spur that was removed in 1918. The farmhouse is a typical two-story I-house, with a central hall and one room on each side. It was a successful farm and became a gathering place for residents. (Courtesy of the Tennessee Historical Commission.)

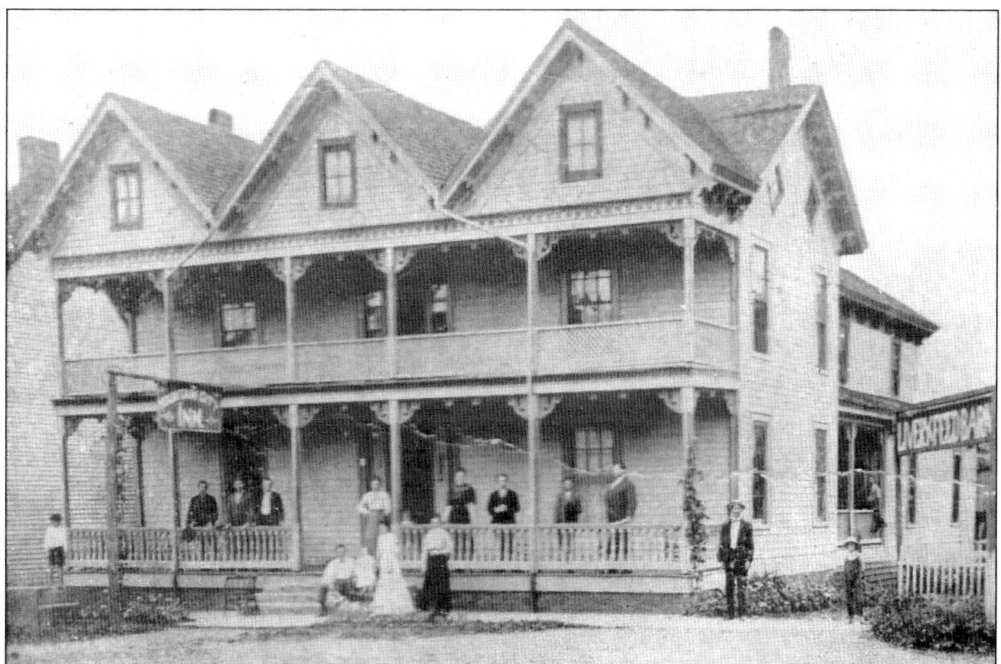

Mountain City Inn. The Mountain City Inn was located along the town's Main Street at the present site of the Johnson County Bank, according to the Tennessee State Library and Archives. J.L. Loyd was the proprietor of the inn, which existed from the 1880s to 1920s. It was torn down in the 1920s. The Taylor movie theater also stood here. (Courtesy of Patsy Green.)

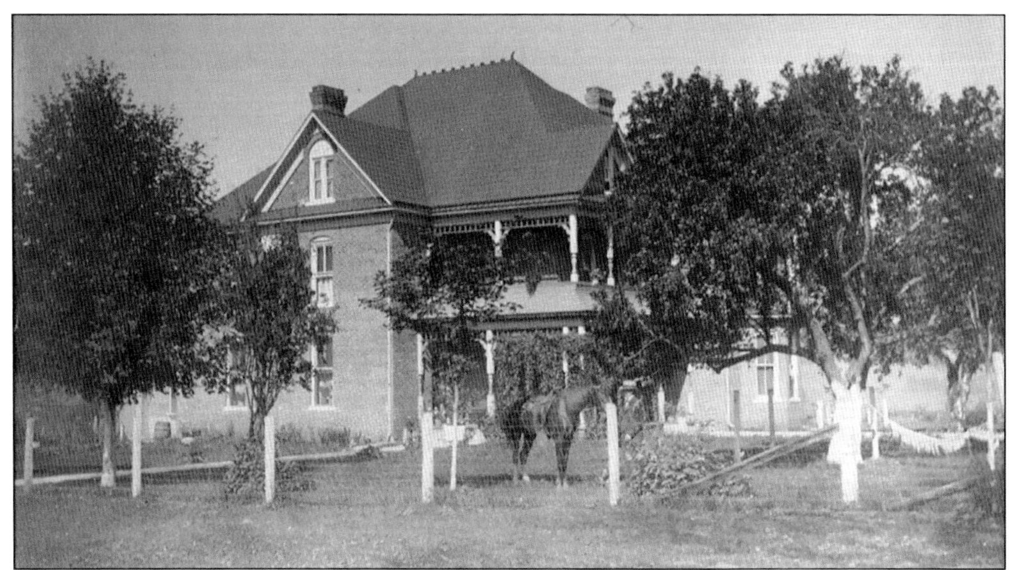

Valverda. Valverda, a large 10-room brick Victorian farmhouse on Dry Stone Branch Road, was constructed in 1890 by James Newton Wills. It was one of the finest homes in Johnson County. The Wills family was responsible for the development of Methodism in the area, and the first Methodist congregation met on the Wills farm. (Courtesy of the Tennessee State Library and Archives.)

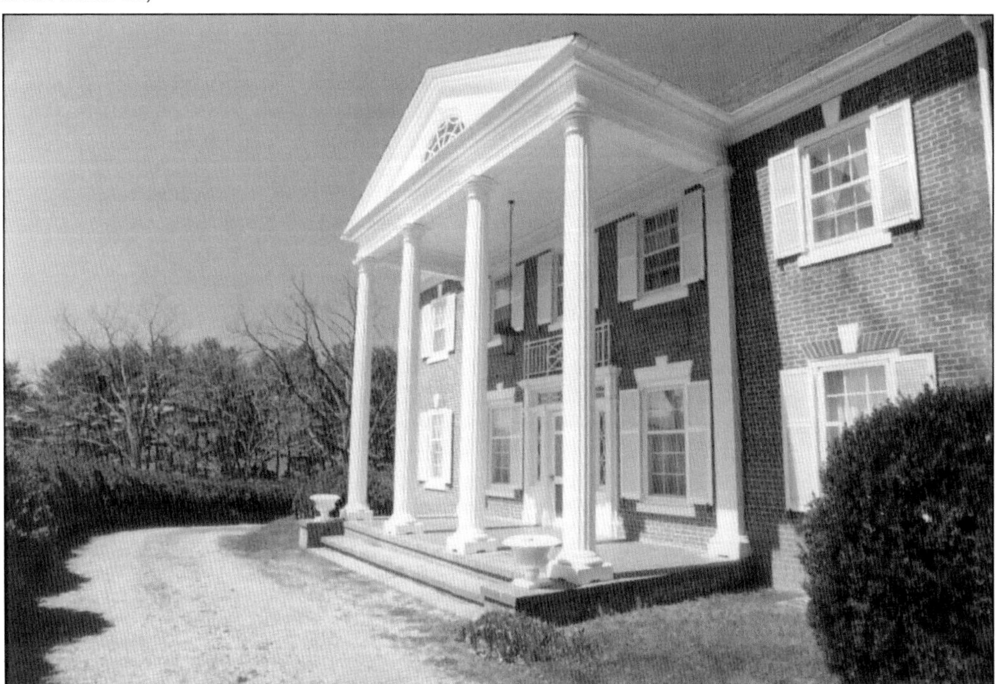

Maymead Farm. Founded in the 18th century, Maymead Farm is one of the oldest farms in Johnson County. The National Register of Historic Places listing includes about 1,000 acres of land, 26 buildings, and a family cemetery. Two houses on the property—the Barton Roby Brown House, built in 1905, and Maywood, built in 1930—are also listed. Maywood is pictured here. (Courtesy of the Tennessee Historical Commission.)

Seven

Greeneville and Greene County

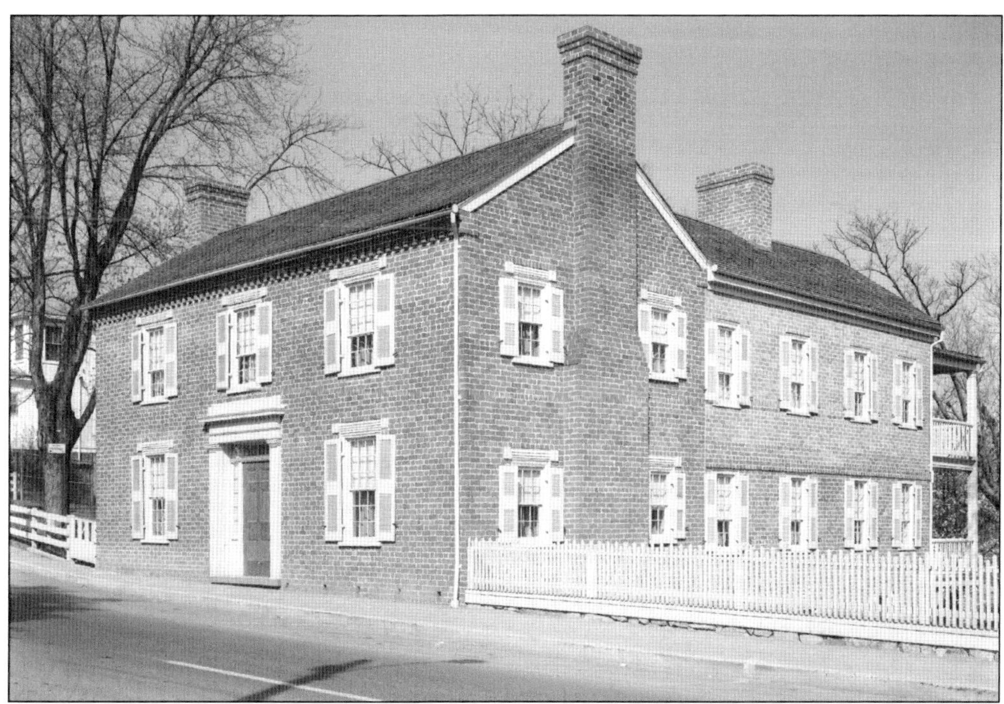

Andrew Johnson House. Pres. Andrew Johnson owned two homes in Greeneville, including the homestead along Main Street. The home was built shortly before the politician purchased the property in 1851. He became president in 1865 after Abraham Lincoln was assassinated. Johnson's presidency lasted until 1869. (Courtesy of the Library of Congress.)

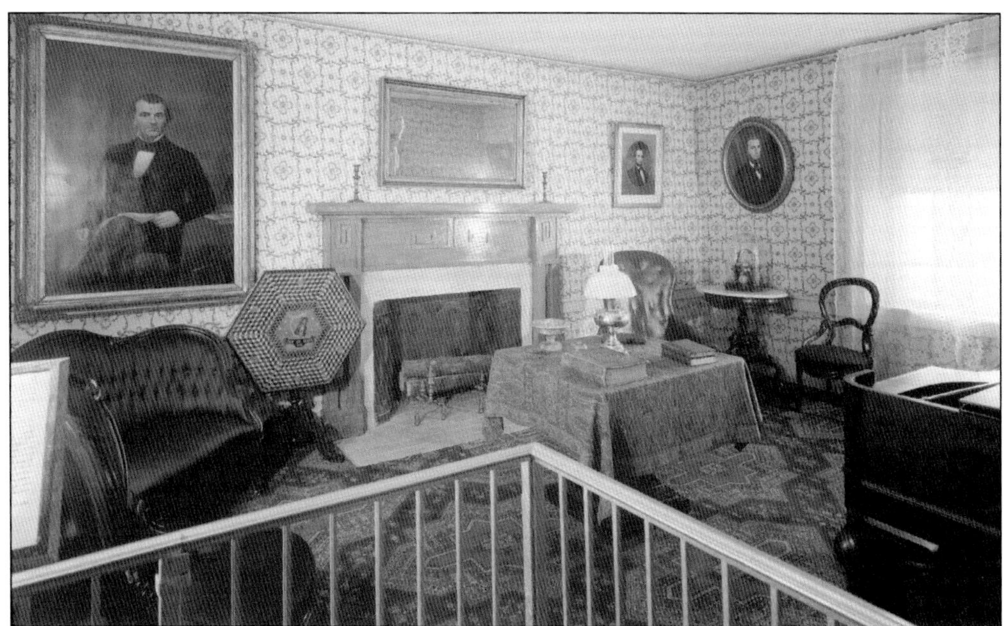

Inside the Andrew Johnson House. President Johnson did not move into his beautiful Greek Revival home on South Main Street in Greeneville until 1869, after he left the White House. He had purchased the home in 1851, but instead lived in Nashville and Washington, DC. The home is now filled with Johnson's personal items. This photograph shows the interior of the first-floor parlor room. (Courtesy of the Library of Congress.)

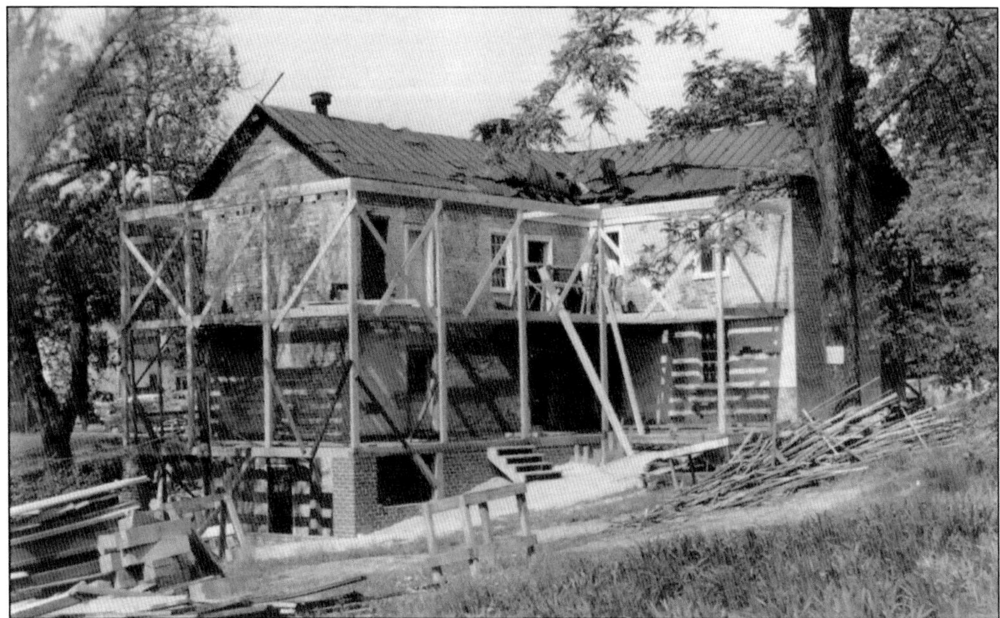

Andrew Johnson Home Renovations. After President Johnson's death in 1875, the family kept his home in Greeneville until 1944, when the federal government purchased the property. The government restored the property and opened it up to the public. The rear of the home can be seen in this photograph during renovations. (Courtesy of the Andrew Johnson National Historic Site.)

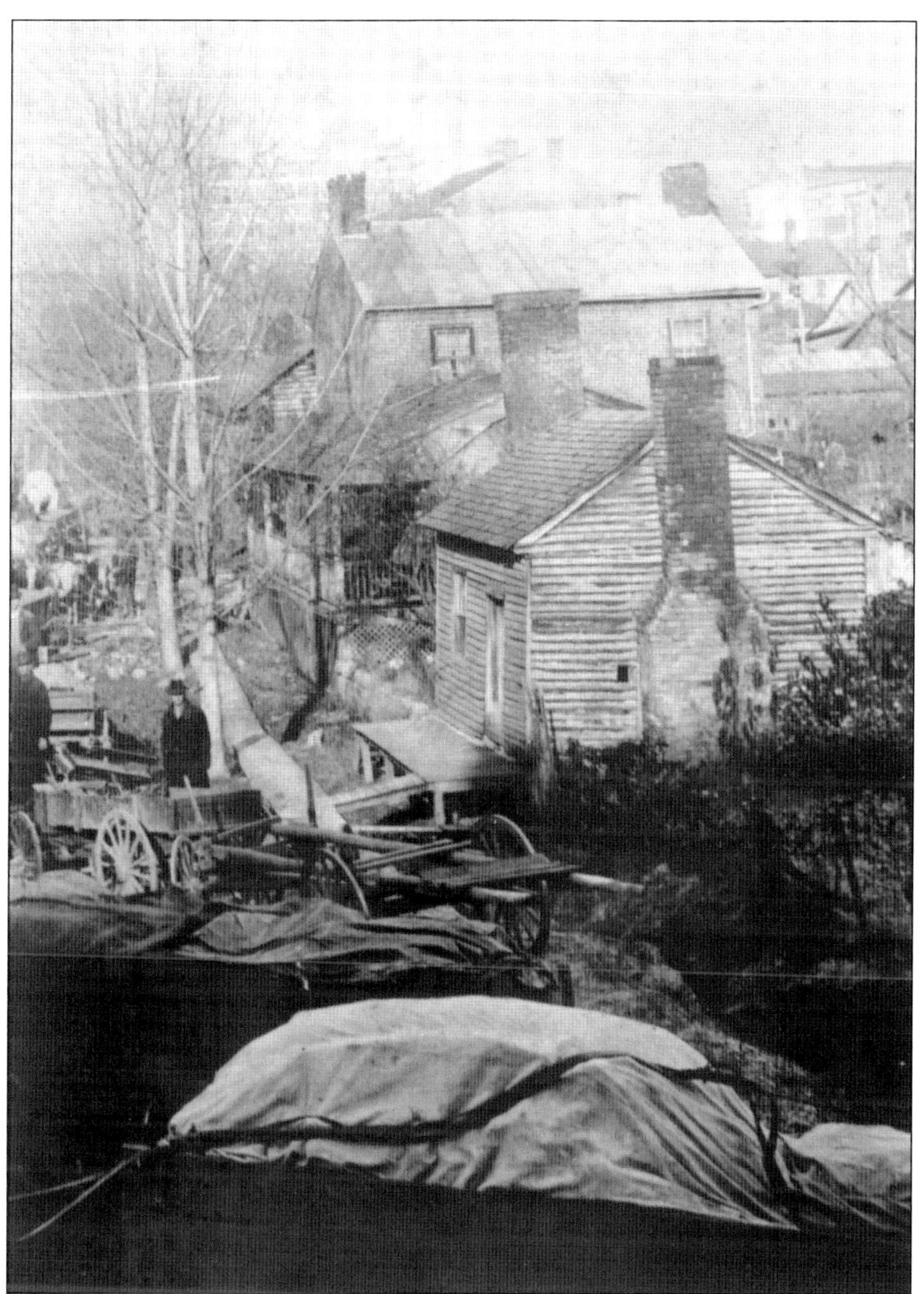

Andrew Johnson's Early House and Tailor Shop. Andrew Johnson arrived in Greeneville from North Carolina in 1826 as a tailor's apprentice. In 1827, he married Eliza McCardle. By 1830, he moved his family into a two-story brick home, which is now standing at College and Depot Streets. Johnson also bought a small building to be used for his tailor shop and moved it near his new house. Johnson lived in the home until 1851, when he purchased a new home on Main Street. During his early days in Greeneville, Johnson became interested in politics. He was elected alderman, mayor, state legislator, and US representative. Eventually, in 1865, Johnson moved into the White House. The back of his early Greeneville home can be seen in this old photograph. (Courtesy of the Library of Congress.)

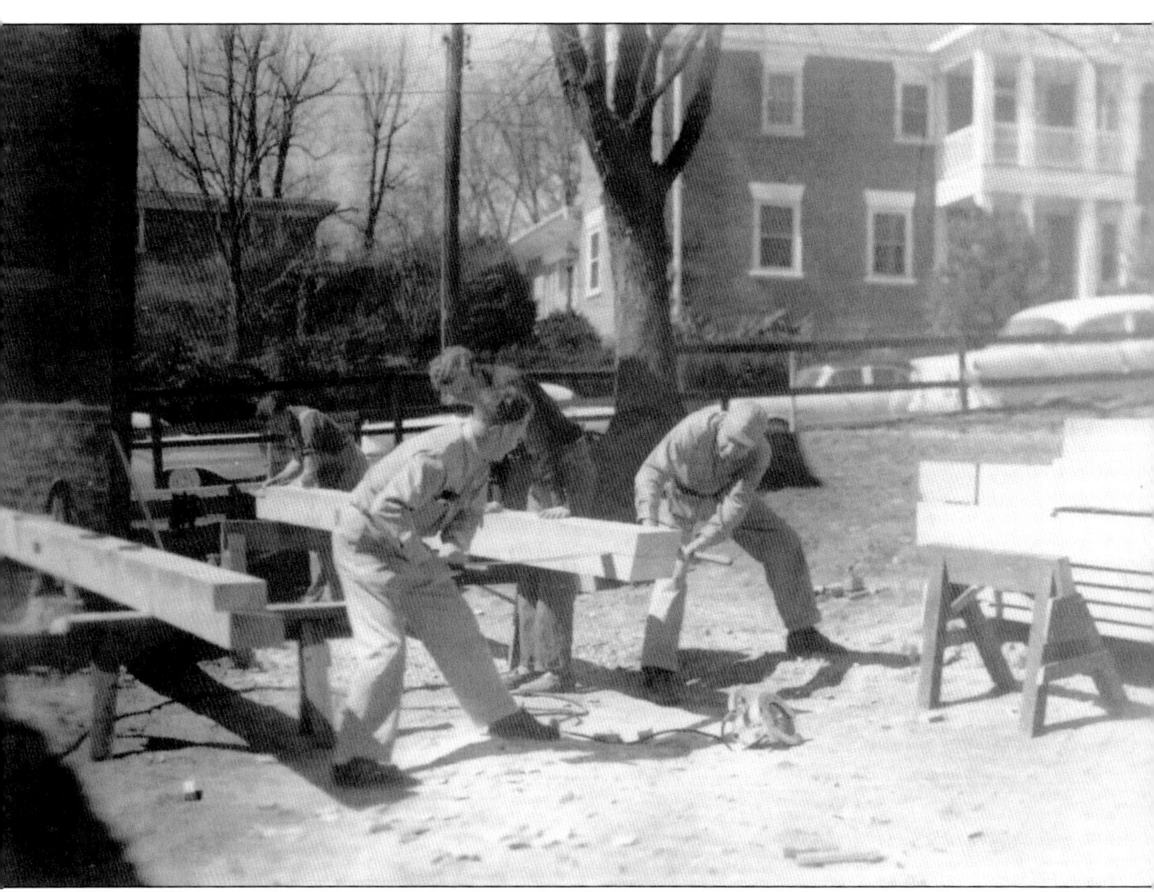

GREENWOOD. Contractors can be seen working along Main Street in downtown Greeneville during the mid-20th century in this photograph. They are working in front of Andrew Johnson's Homestead, which is not visible here. Instead, the Federal brick home known as Greenwood can be seen in the background of this photograph. Greenwood, one of the town's oldest structures, was constructed about 1810 by Dr. Josiah Clawson and was later added to by James P. McDowell in the late 1840s. The McDowell family resided in the home until the Civil War, and it then became the residence of William R. Brown. Another historic home, the Sevier-Lowry House, is next to Greenwood. The Sevier-Lowry House is the oldest home in Greeneville. It was originally a log structure, but it now has clapboard siding. (Courtesy of the Andrew Johnson National Historic Site.)

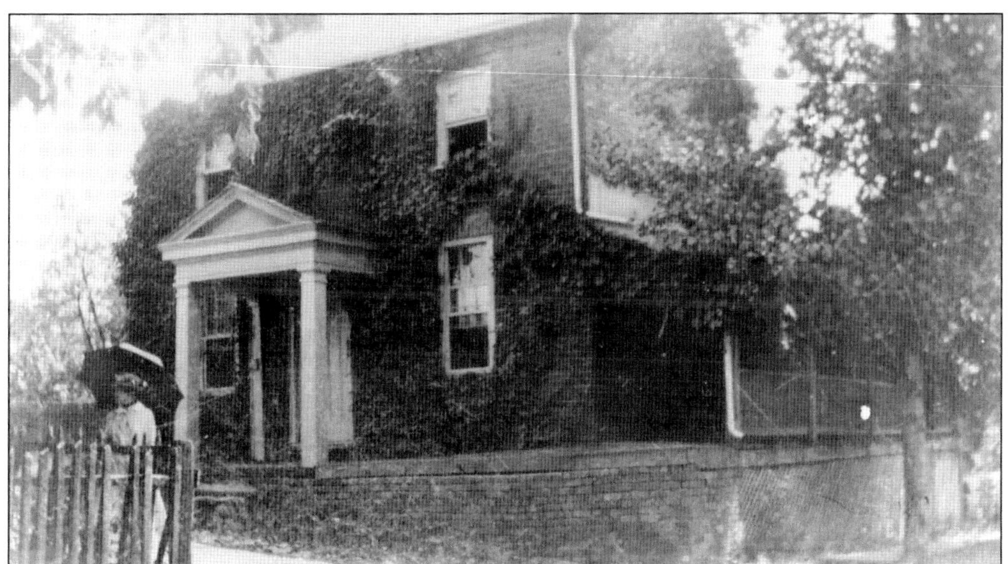

Kerbaugh House. Andrew Johnson's early home, also known as the Kerbaugh House, was a small two-story structure with a one-story ell in the rear. The interior woodwork is a good example of early-19th-century pre–Greek Revival styling, according to the National Park Service, which now owns the property. The Kerbaugh family was the last to reside in the home before it was opened to the public. (Courtesy of the Library of Congress.)

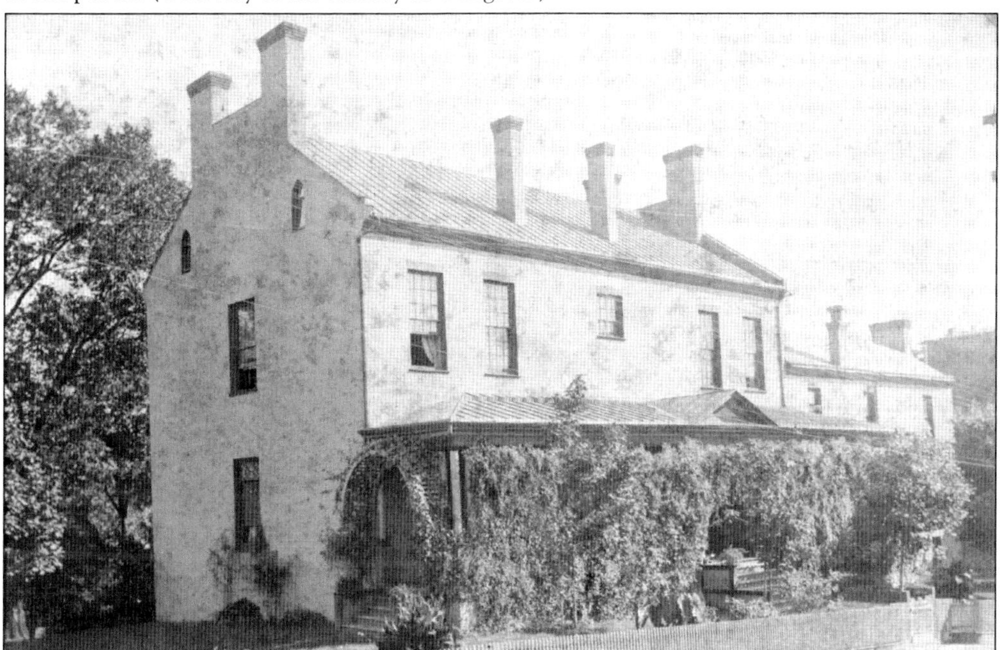

Dickson-Williams Mansion. The stately Dickson-Williams Mansion was built by William Dickson for his daughter Catharine, the wife of Alexander Williams. Dickson was Greeneville's first postmaster. Built atop a small hill overlooking Main Street, the mansion was designed and constructed by Thomas Battersby and John Hoy from 1815 to 1820. The mansion's property once spread for an entire block and featured beautiful terraced gardens. (Courtesy of the Tennessee State Library and Archives.)

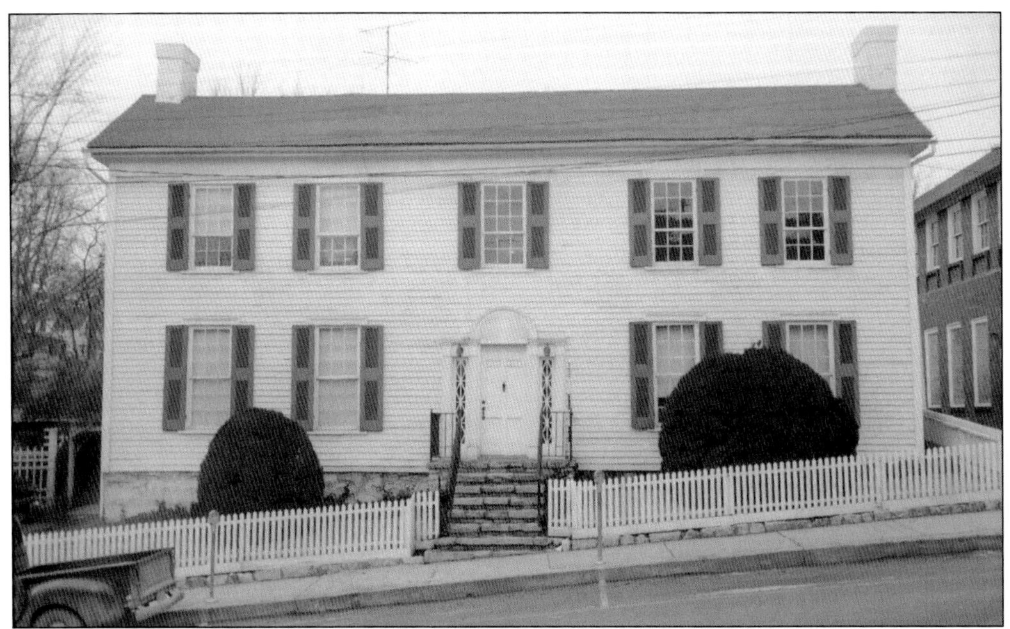

Sevier-Lowry House. The Sevier-Lowry House, located on Main Street, may be Greeneville's oldest home. It is one of two homes built by Valentine Sevier, a nephew of prominent Tennessee pioneer and politician John Sevier. Built in 1790, the structure is actually a log home covered in white clapboard. The mantel in the drawing room comes from the office of Gen. Thomas P. Arnold, a local attorney and congressman. Besides Valentine Sevier, several prominent Greeneville residents have lived here, including William Dickson, William M. Lowry, Martha Washington Arnold Marshall, W.H. O'Keefe, and Edith Susong. Greenwood, the town's oldest brick residence, is next door. (Both, courtesy of the Library of Congress.)

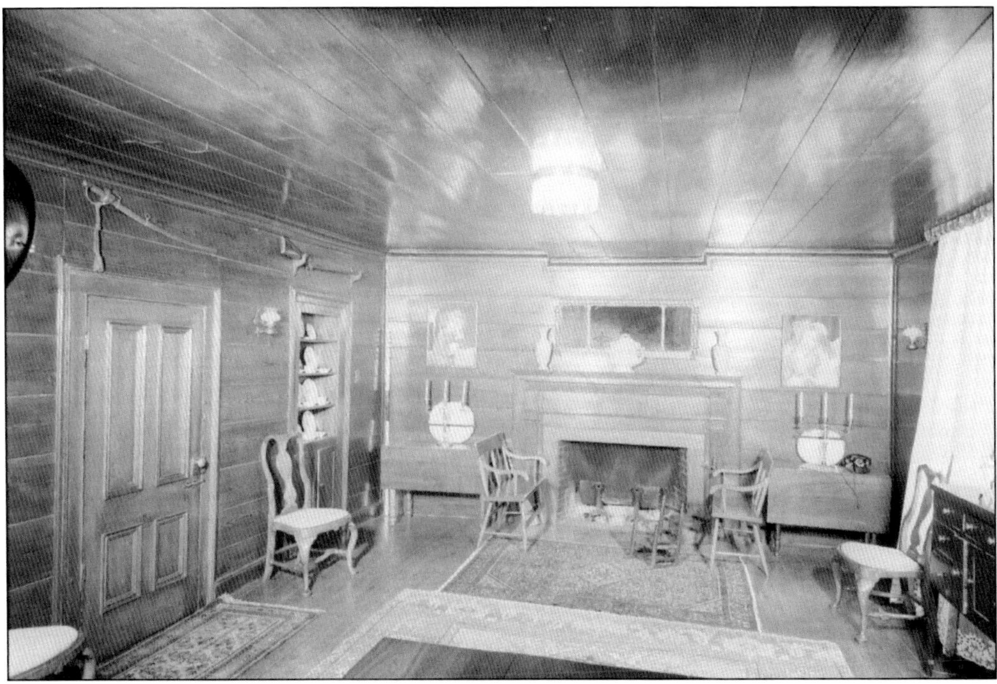

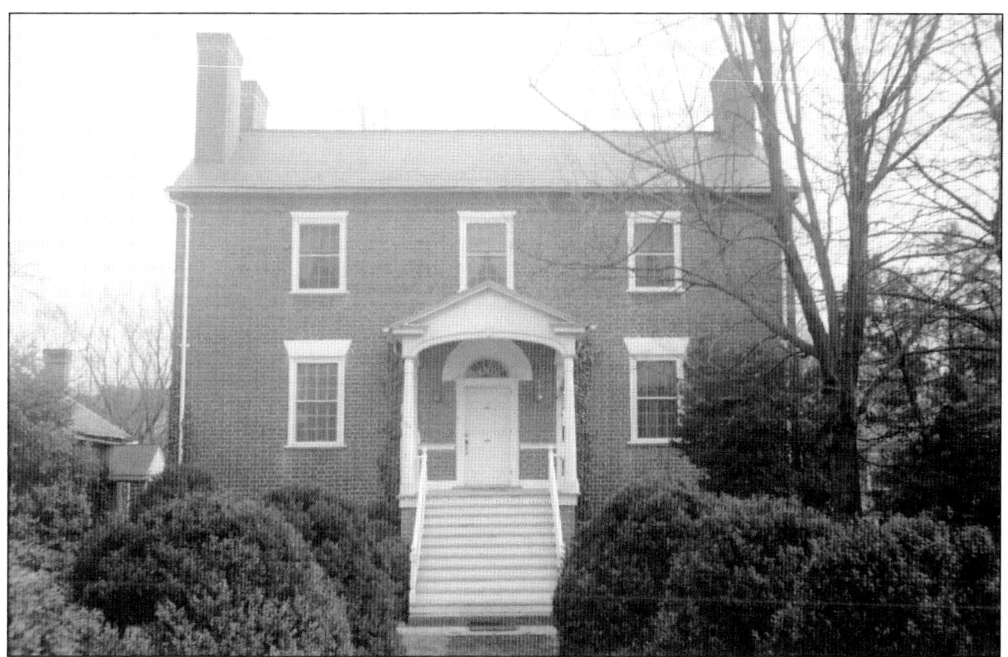

VALENTINE SEVIER HOME. Valentine Sevier's second home in Greeneville was constructed at the Big Spring in 1820. Sevier was a community leader, establishing businesses and infrastructure in town. The property on Main Street, next to the library, features an impressive brick Federal-style home and office. Large bushes line the sidewalk leading to the front entrance of the home. Slave labor is believed to have been used to make bricks on the property. All of the hand-carved woodwork may have been done by Irish craftsmen. The original three-story home can be seen in the above photograph. The smokehouse and brick law office remain, and can be seen in the photograph below. (Both, courtesy of the Library of Congress.)

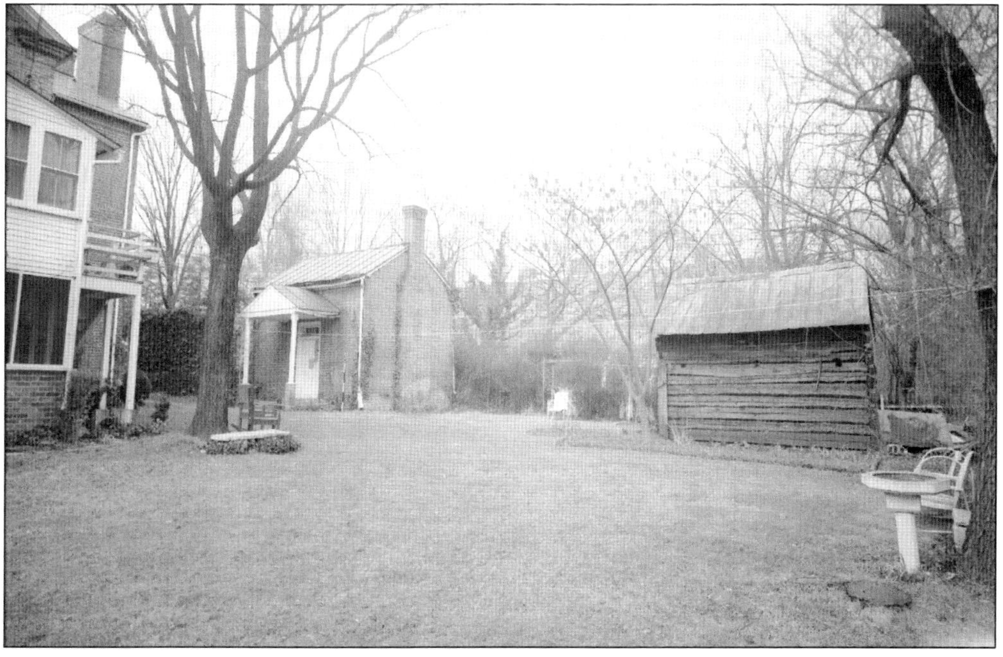

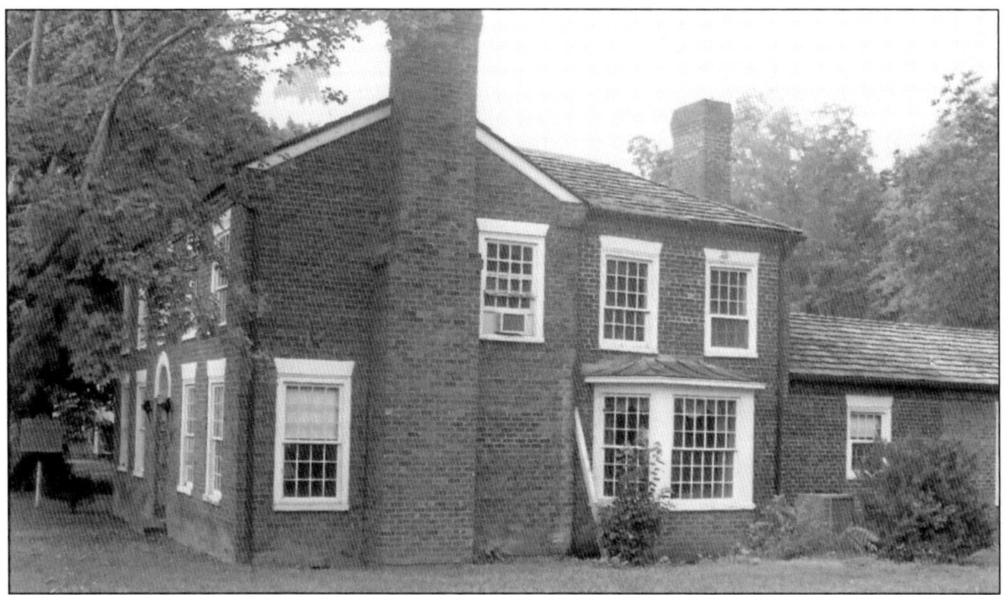

Harmony House. The Harmony House, a brick two-story Federal-style home, standing along Main Street in Greeneville, was built in 1851 by Dr. William A. Harmon. Harmon was a builder, lawyer, physician, and teacher. During the Civil War, soldiers camped on the property. Residents stayed here for protection, and food was stored in a hole in the home's living room, according to historians. More recently, local historian and community leader Richard Doughty lived here until he died. Doughty also relocated the Antrim log cabin, pictured below, to the property. Originally, the cabin was constructed by Thomas Alexander in 1793 on Buckingham Road, southeast of Greeneville. Built of walnut logs, the cabin was relocated to Greeneville in 1965. The home was first a one-room log home but has been significantly altered. (Both, author's collection.)

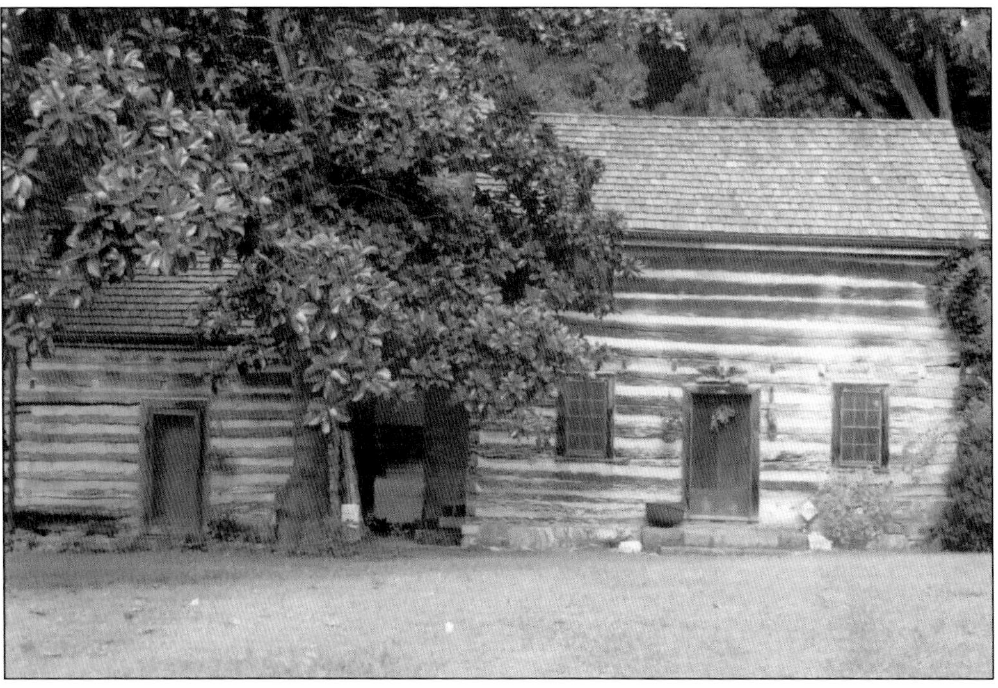

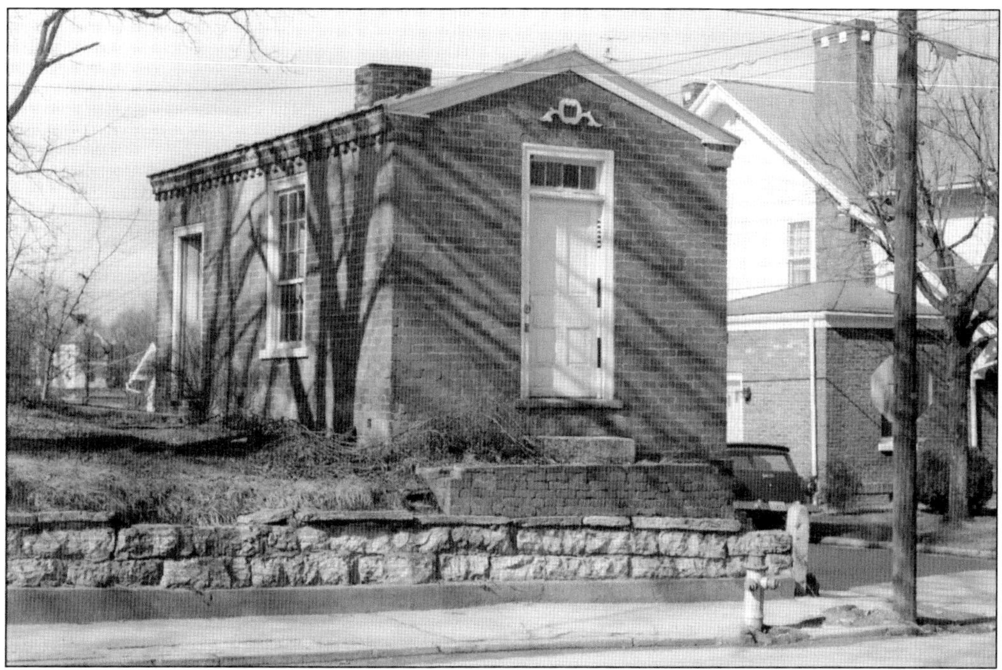

McKee Home and Law Office. The McKee home and office sit at the intersection of Irish and McKee Streets in Greeneville. The McKee home, a small structure of batten construction, was built around 1860. McKee's office is a small brick one-story structure built in 1860. It was once used as the offices of Armitage and McKee attorneys during the late 19th century. (Courtesy of the Library of Congress.)

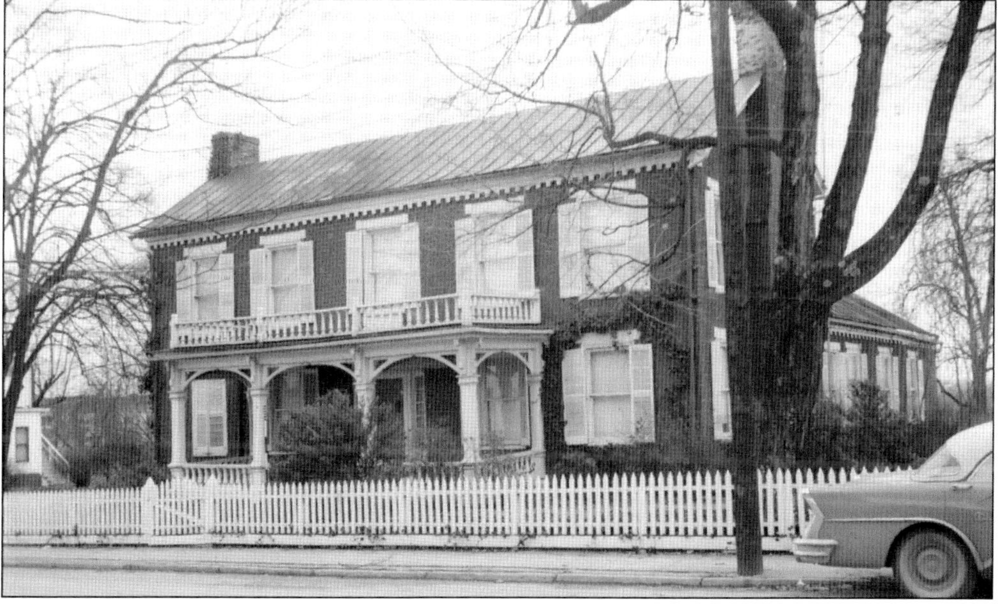

Rumbaugh-Hacker Home. The Rumbaugh-Hacker Home was built in the 1840s and purchased by Col. James Rumbaugh in 1858. It is located on Irish Street and is similar in design to the nearby Samuel Snapp Home, which is across the street. A frame slave house with a brick chimney is behind the home. Joseph Hacker and his family later lived here. (Courtesy of the Library of Congress.)

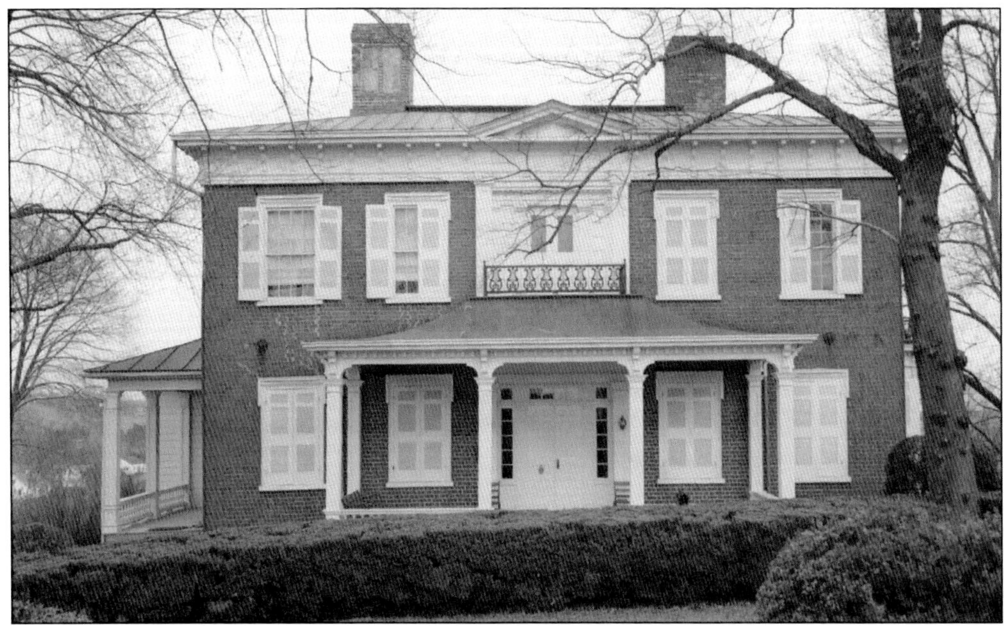

Brown-Milligan Home. The Brown-Milligan Home, also known as Boxwood Manor, was constructed just prior to the Civil War. The Greek Revival home, located on South Main Street, was built for Joseph R. Brown. Boxwood Manor features massive boxwoods that were grown along the Nolichucky River. Unique elements inside include a stately staircase and a dumbwaiter. (Courtesy of the Library of Congress.)

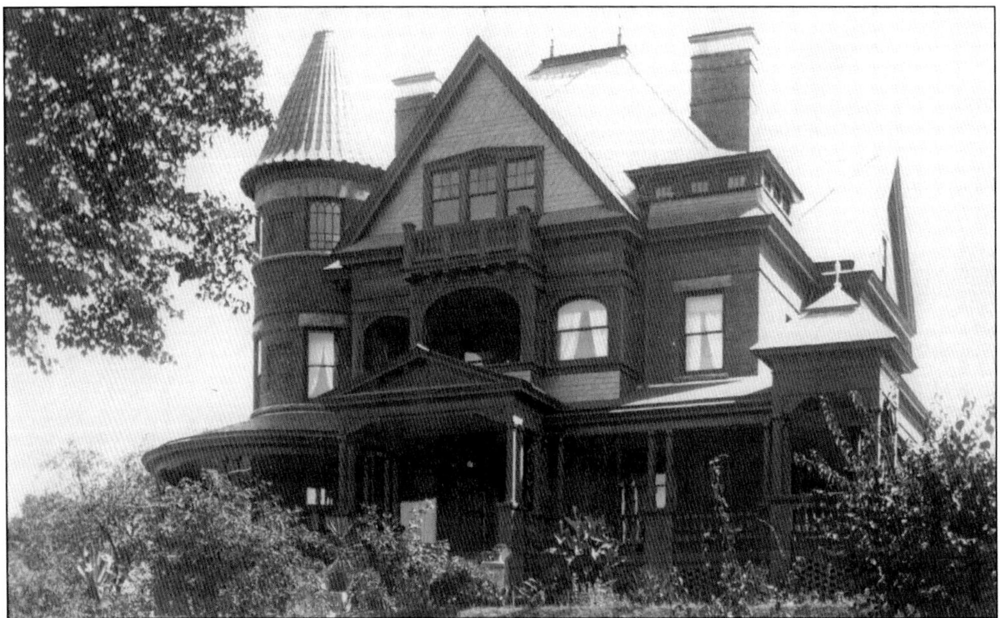

Reeve House. Knoxville architect George F. Barber designed some of the country's most impressive Victorian homes, including Melville P. Reeve's residence on College Street in Greeneville. The home, most recently owned by Jeffers Mortuary, was built in 1890. In addition to a private home and a funeral home, the structure has also hosted a school, a teen recreation center, and Golden Gloves boxing. (Courtesy of the Greeneville Greene County History Museum.)

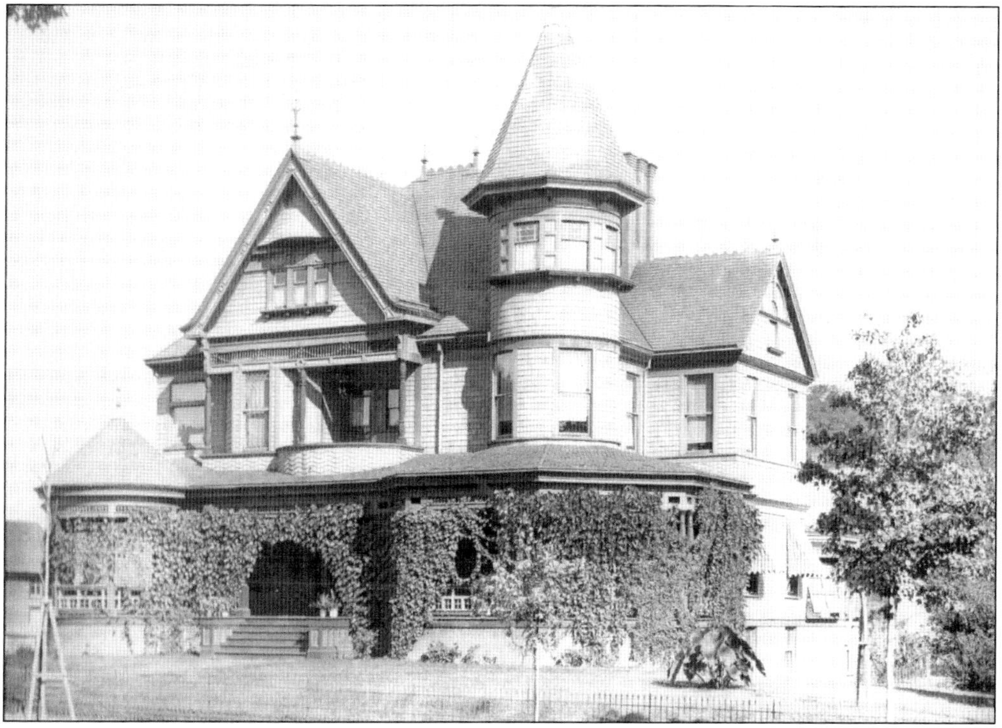

SNAPP HOUSE. A large Victorian mansion once stood along Main Street at the corner of Church Street near the present-day Andrew Johnson Bank. It was known as the Snapp House, but has long since been torn down. It had many Victorian features, including large towers. (Courtesy of the Greeneville Greene County History Museum.)

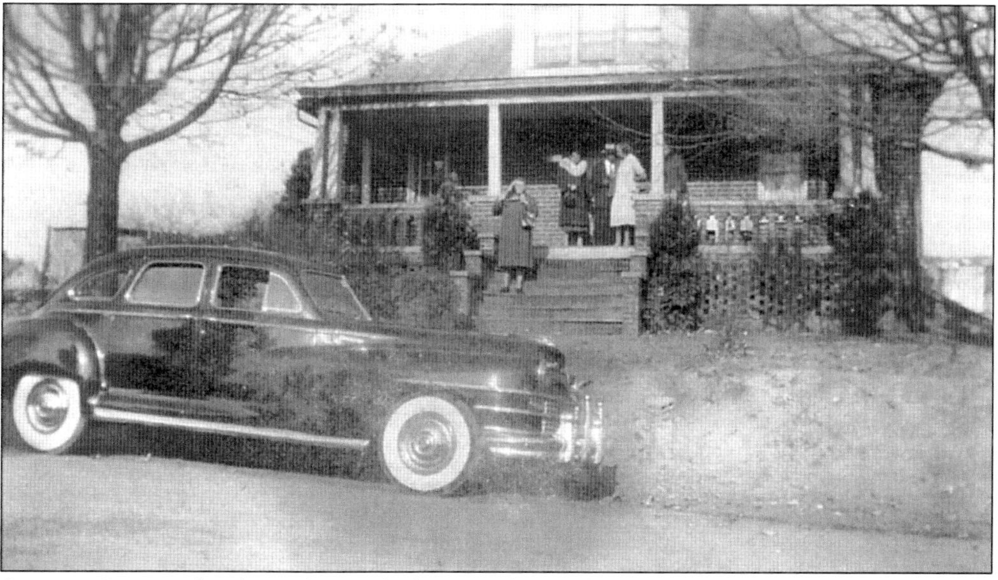

GEORGE CLEM. This bungalow-style home is located in Greeneville's African American neighborhood, near the historic George Clem School. Teachers and professors are believed to have stayed in this home. The school was in use from 1887 to 1965. Clem was a school principal. (Courtesy of the Greeneville Greene County History Museum.)

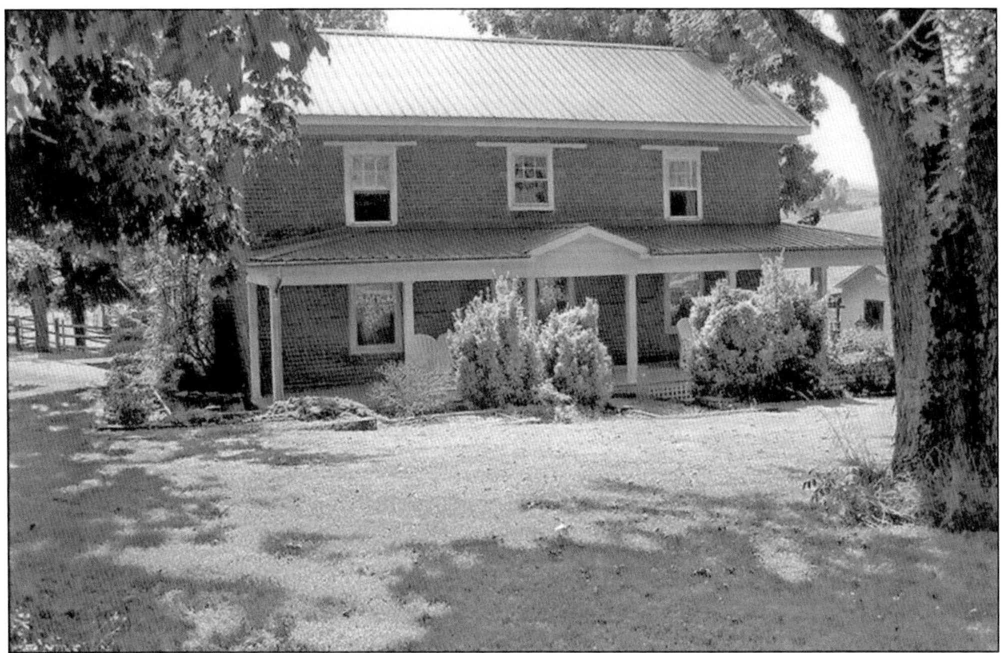

Hull House. The Hull House, a home with three-foot-thick brick walls, is located on Brown Springs Road in Mosheim. The Brown family built the home, but it is named after the Hull family, who lived here the longest. There are seven springs on the property, which led it to become a health resort in the late 1800s and early 1900s. (Courtesy of Sylvia Bright.)

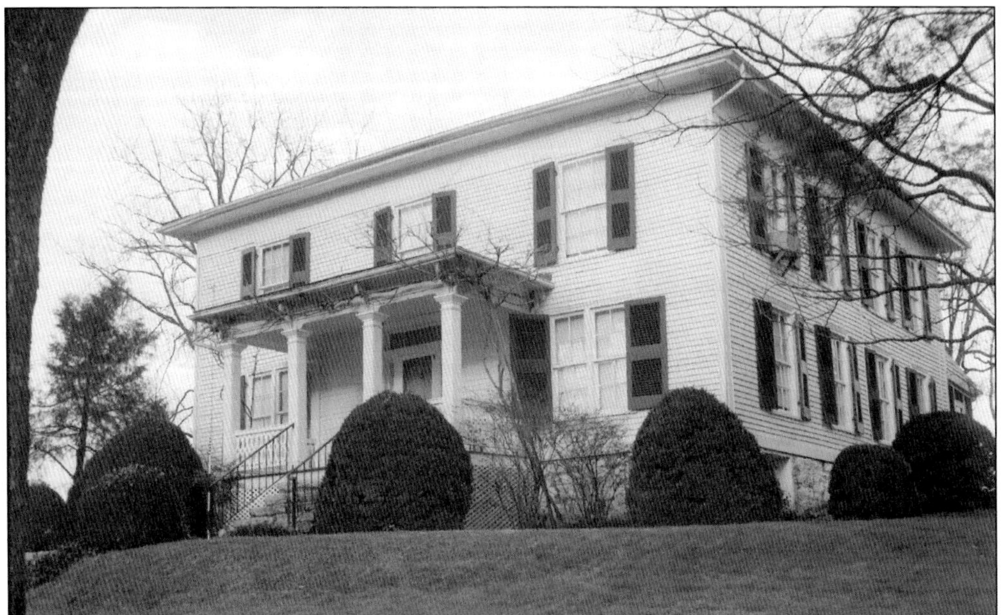

Reaves-Crisplin House. The Walnut Lawn Farm manor house was constructed in 1855 by Maj. James G. Reaves. The ten-room house, with five on each floor, once faced the old stage route which led travelers to North Carolina. The Reaveses entertained guests on the first floor, where there are two parlors, a kitchen, a sitting room, and a dining room. (Courtesy of the Library of Congress.)

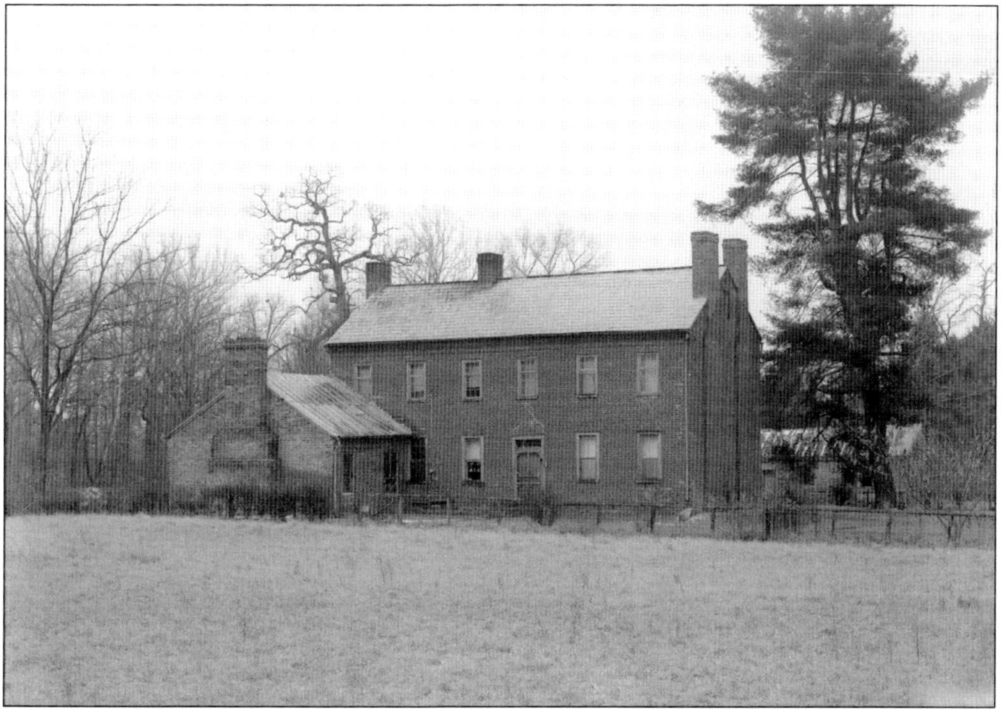

DOAK HOUSE. The Doak House, a museum since the 1970s, was built around 1830 near Greeneville, Tennessee. The Rev. Samuel Witherspoon Doak constructed the home. He and his father, Rev. Samuel Doak, started Tusculum Academy in 1818. The academy was later named Tusculum College, which it remains today. (Both, courtesy of the Library of Congress.)

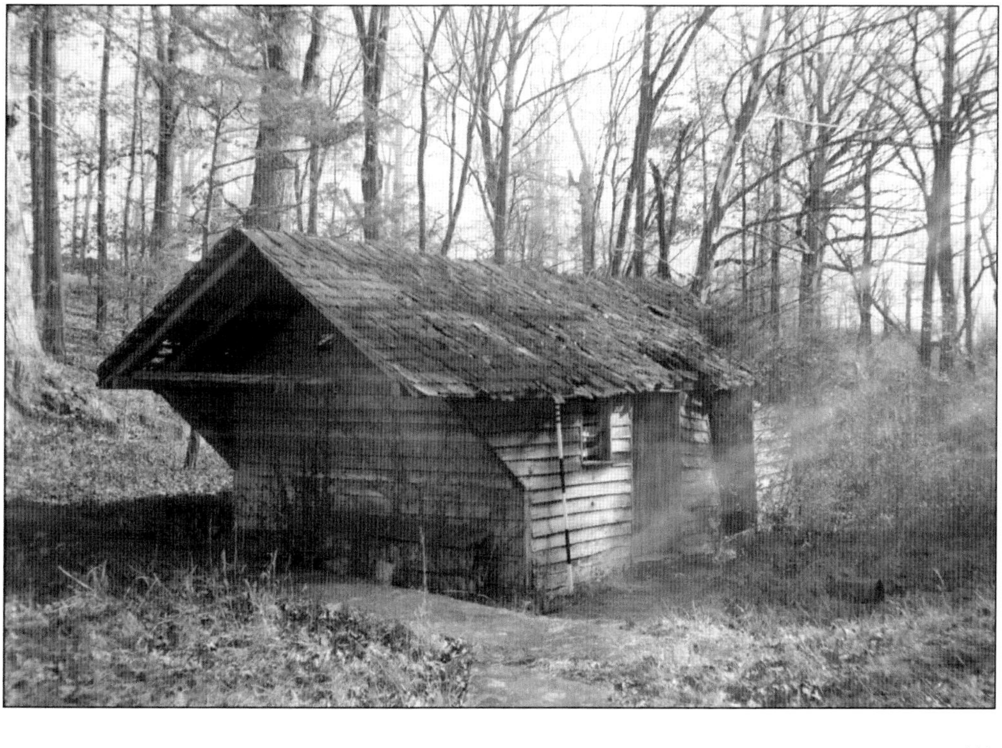

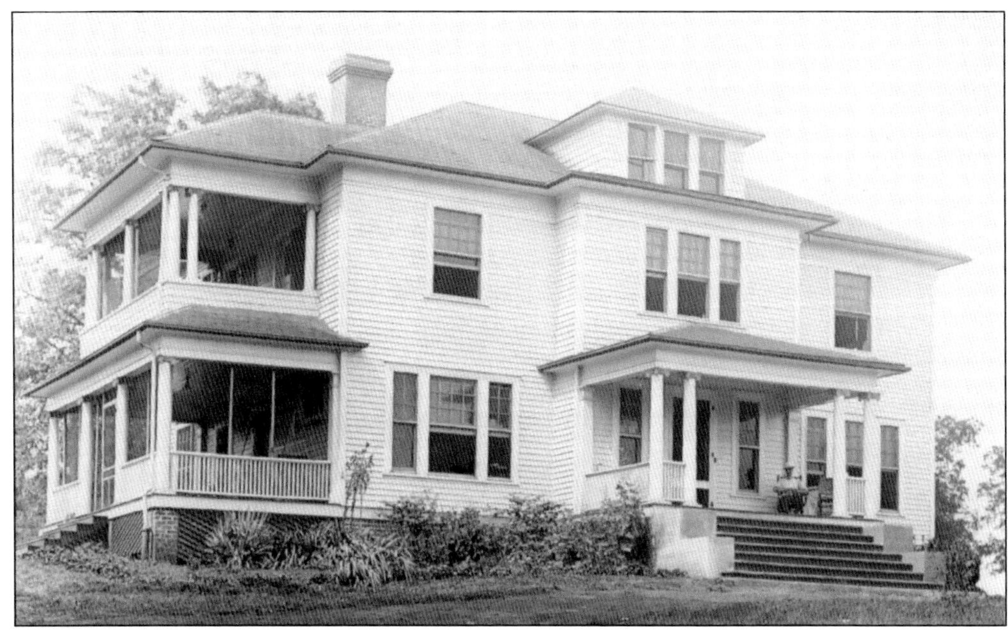

Tusculum College President's Home. Presidents at Tusculum College, Tennessee's oldest higher education institute, did not have a proper place to live until about 1909. At the time, Nettie McCormick, a philanthropist, purchased land and paid for the president's home to be built. Pres. Charles Oliver Gray was the first to reside in the home, which is located directly across from the college campus. (Courtesy of the Tusculum College Archives.)

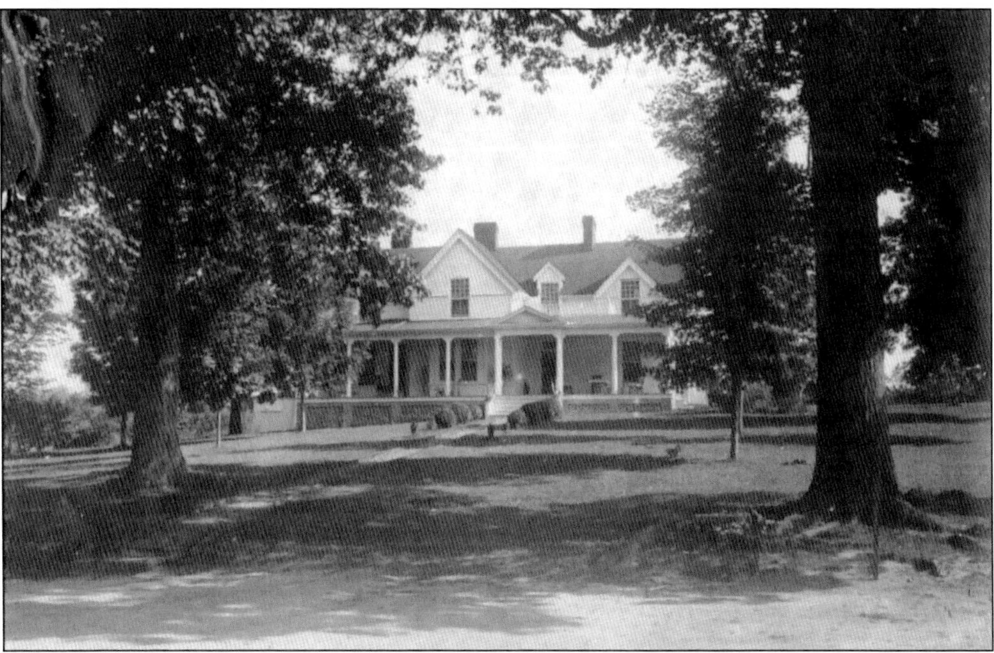

Rankin House. The Thomas Samuel Rankin House is located on the Erwin Highway, across from Tusculum College. It is next door to the college president's home. Rankin, who began working at the college after he graduated in 1885, was a professor, bursar, and treasurer. (Courtesy of the Tusculum College Archives.)

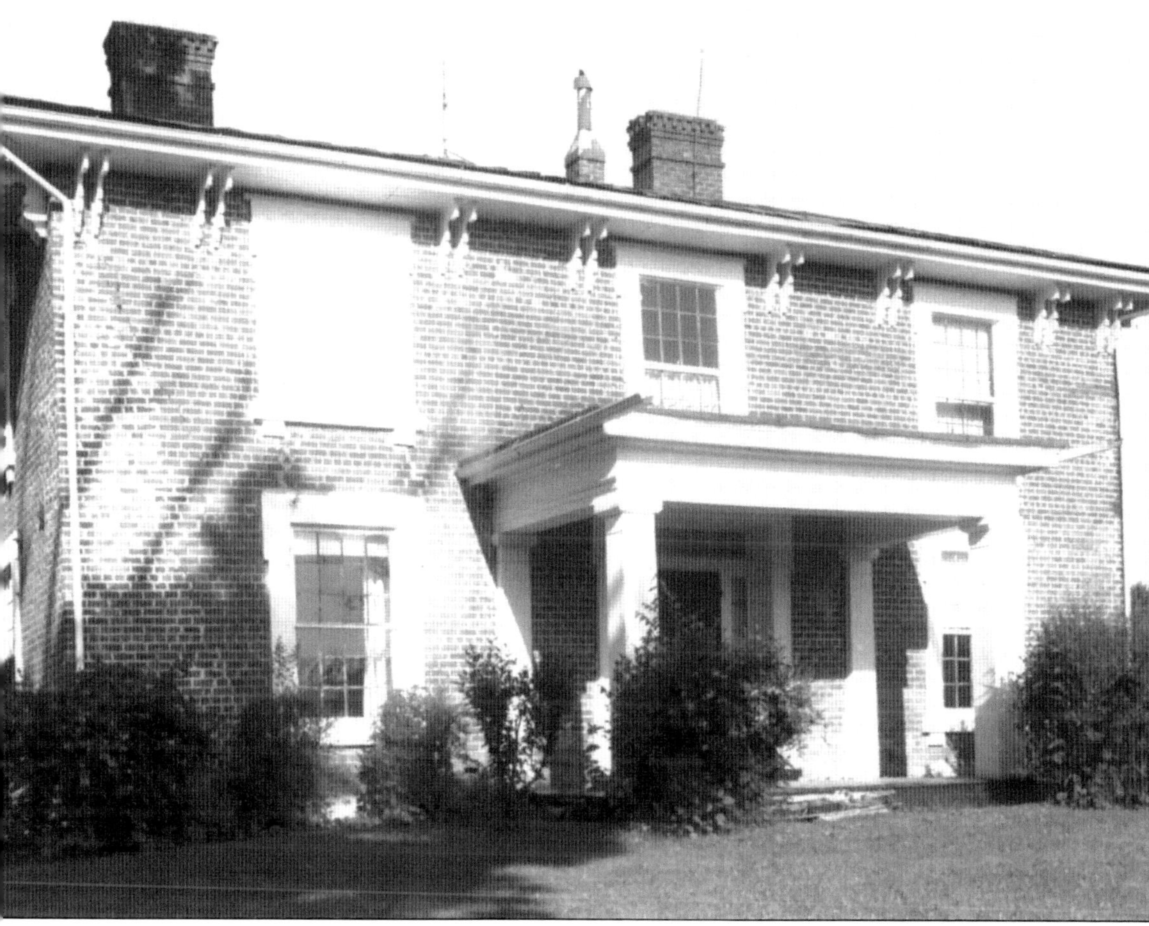

James Lowry House. The James Lowry House was constructed around 1850–1865 along the Asheville Highway. Prominent resident Daniel Allen built the Greek Revival home for his daughter Nancy and her husband, James Lowry. Allen was a prosperous farmer and landowner who accumulated thousands of acres in Greene County during his lifetime. The Allen family also built the Allen-Birdwell House on Allen's Bridge Road. Little is known about Lowry, except that he was a farmer. Stylistically, the home presents itself as a rural conception of Greek Revival architecture with austere lines and rather formidable details, according to a listing in the National Register of Historic Places. The brick house consists of a square, two-story main block with a two-story ell. The main block is accentuated on the facade with a central one-story portico supported by wooden pillars. The Register notes that the home possesses many of its original interior decorative finishes, including three different types of marble. (Courtesy of the Tennessee Historical Commission.)

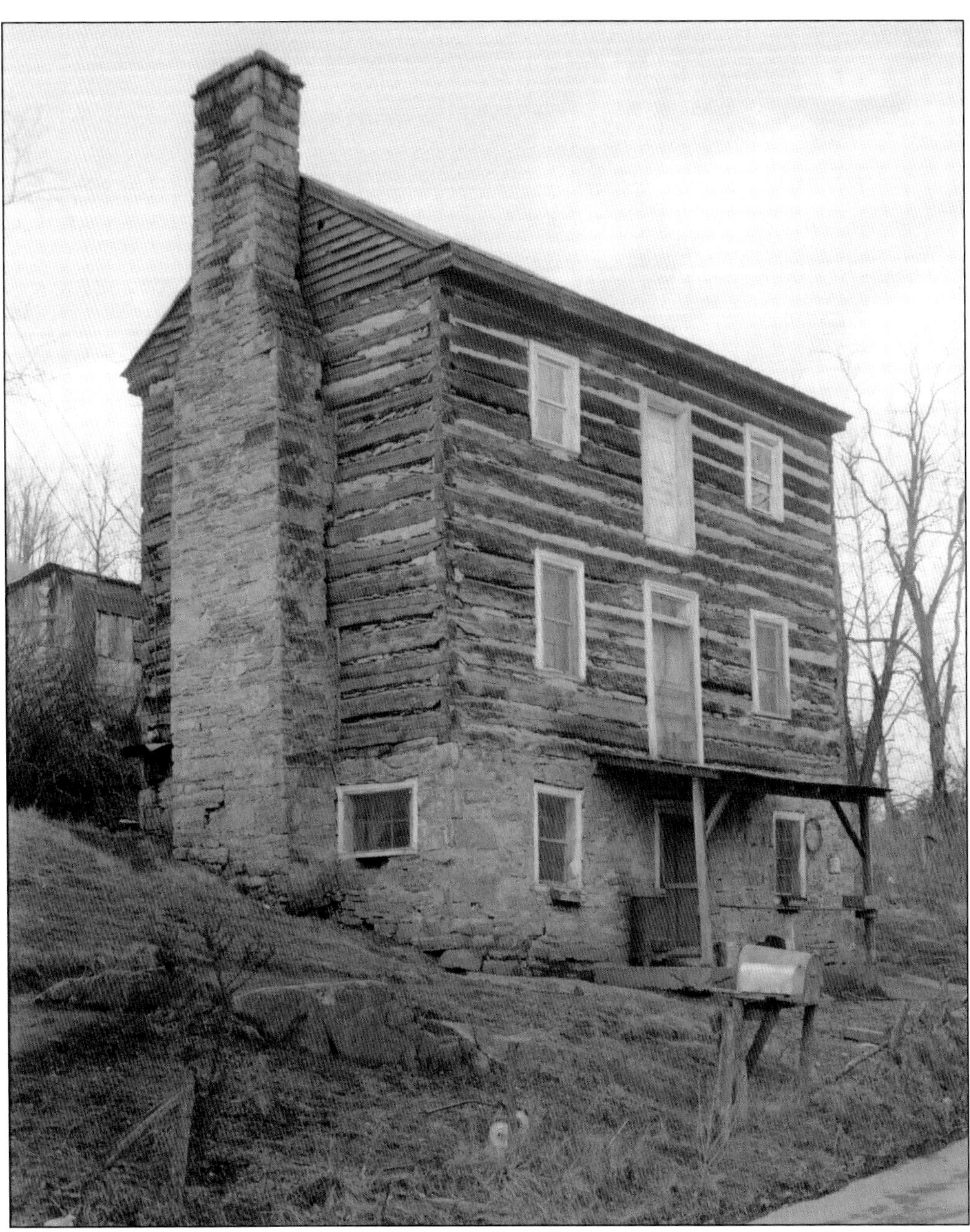

Mauris-Earnest Fort House. One of Tennessee's oldest homes stands protectively overlooking the Nolichucky River in Chuckey. The Mauris-Earnest Fort House is also the oldest building in the Earnest Farms Historic District. It was built on the original parcel of land deeded to Henry Earnest in 1782. Built into the side of a hill, the first floor of the fort house is made of solid limestone. The upper two floors are made of V-notched logs. It also features an exterior stone chimney. The front elevation of the structure contains nine symmetrical openings, according to the National Register of Historic Places. During its early days, local settlers stayed protected in the home against Cherokee attacks. Once the residents felt more comfortable, they eventually crossed the river and built a new house. Historian Carroll Van West said the home reflects traditional log construction traditions. (Courtesy of the Tennessee State Library and Archives.)

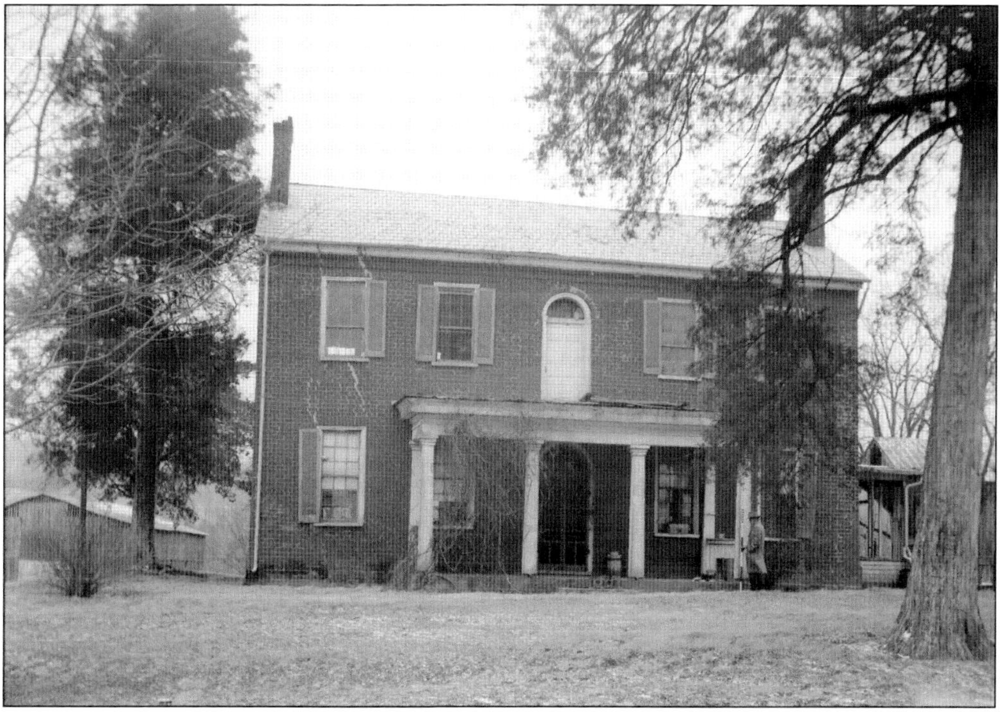

Earnest House. Henry Earnest built a home along the Nolichucky River in 1800. The house was located on the south side of the river, across from the historic fort house. After he died in 1809, his son Peter Earnest decided to expand the home. He added a Federal-style front in 1820. He also constructed a smokehouse and slave quarters. The home features some of the area's finest woodwork. It was done by an English carver who lived here for one year to do the work. The Earnest farmhouse, a nearby Methodist church, and three other nearby farms comprise the Earnest Farms Historic District. (Both, courtesy of the Tennessee State Library and Archives.)

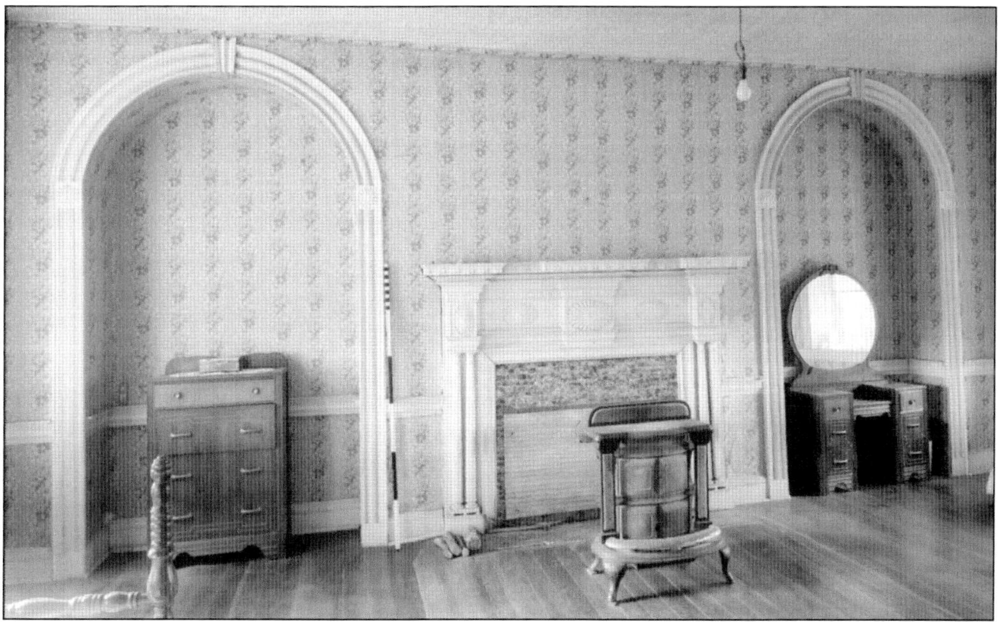

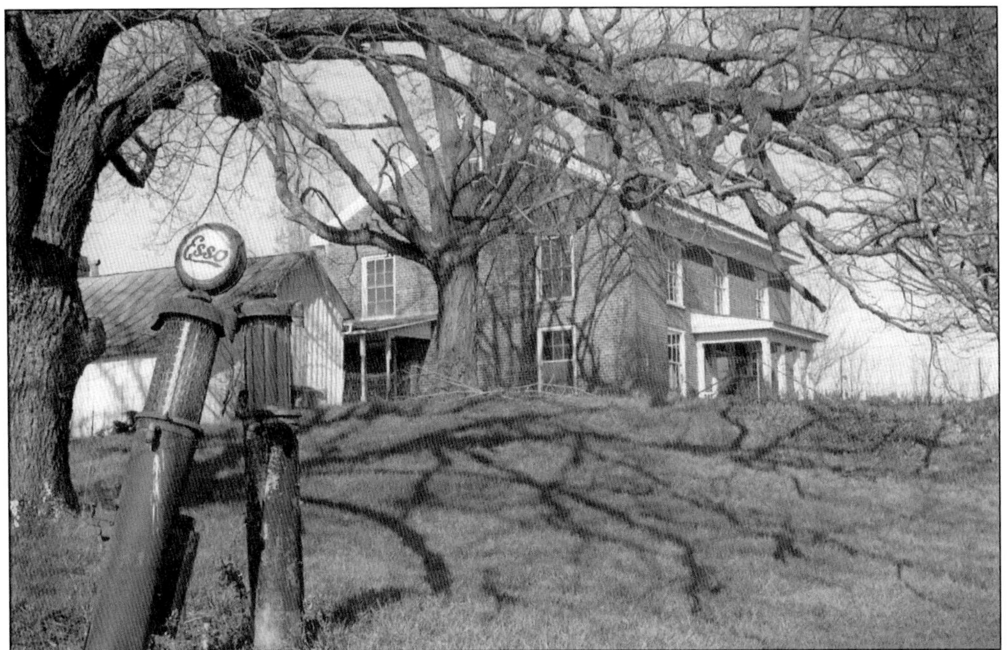

Johnson Homestead. The Johnson Homestead is a large brick, Federal-style farmhouse in the Chuckey community of Greene County. It is part of old Earnestville, named after the Earnest family, early pioneers along the Nolichucky River. The Johnson house was built before the Civil War. (Courtesy of the Greeneville Greene County History Museum.)

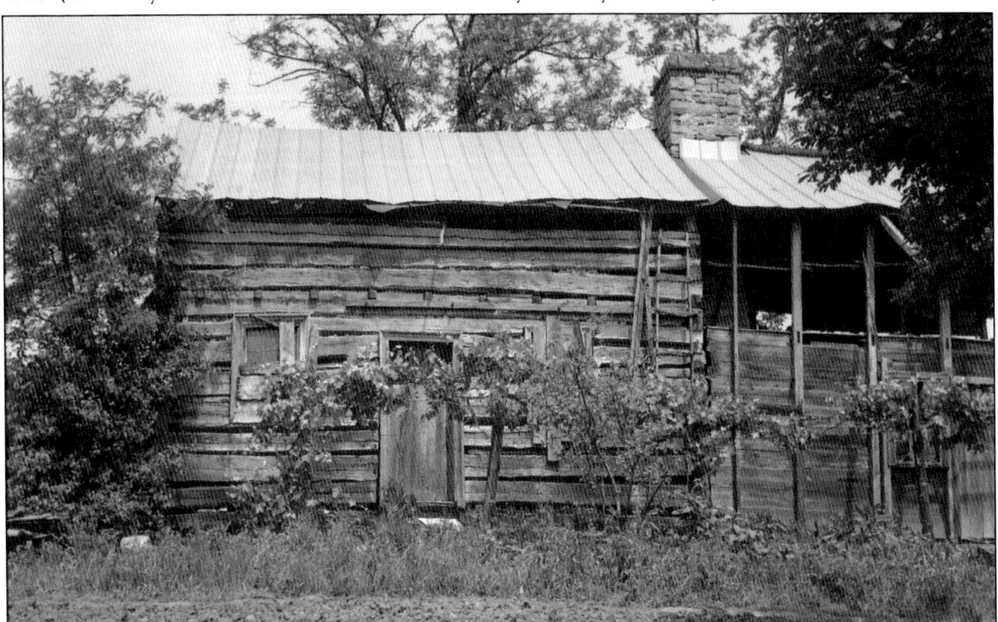

Davy Crockett Birthplace. Legendary frontiersman, soldier, and politician David "Davy" Crockett was born in 1786 along the Nolichucky River near the mouth of Big Limestone Creek. His father built a small log cabin, which the Stonecypher family is believed to have dismantled in the 1800s. Davy Crockett Birthplace State Park now includes a replica of the cabin, a museum, and a large campground. (Courtesy of the Tennessee State Library and Archives.)

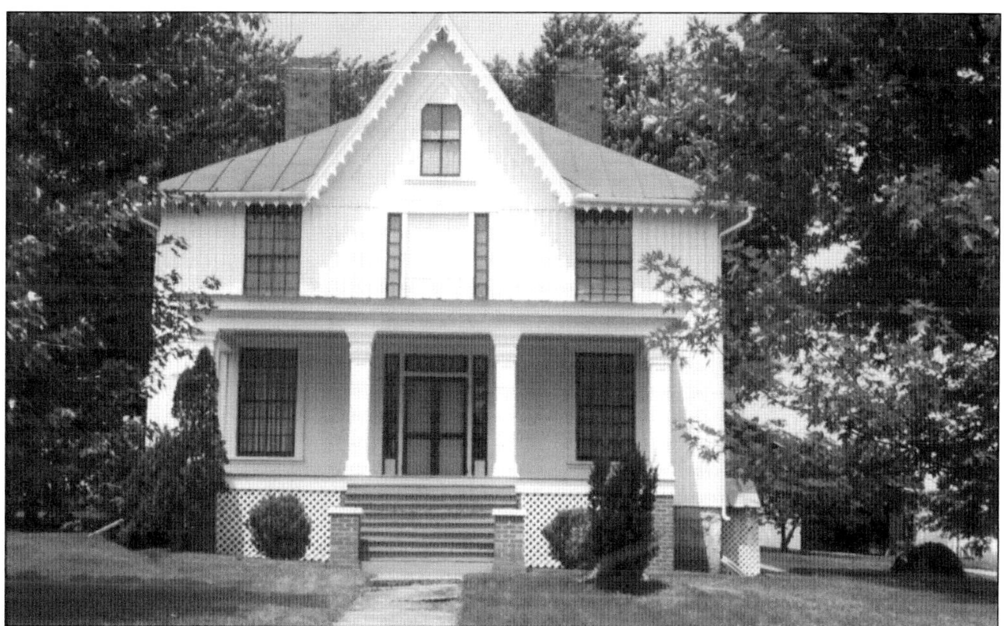

BROWN-NEAS HOUSE. The Brown-Neas House was constructed about 1868 in the Afton community. The white, two-story, board-and-batten structure is one of the finest examples of Gothic Revival style in the region, according to a listing in the National Register of Historic Places. The house was built for John Brown, a local farmer and miller. The Neas family later lived here. (Courtesy of the Tennessee Historical Commission.)

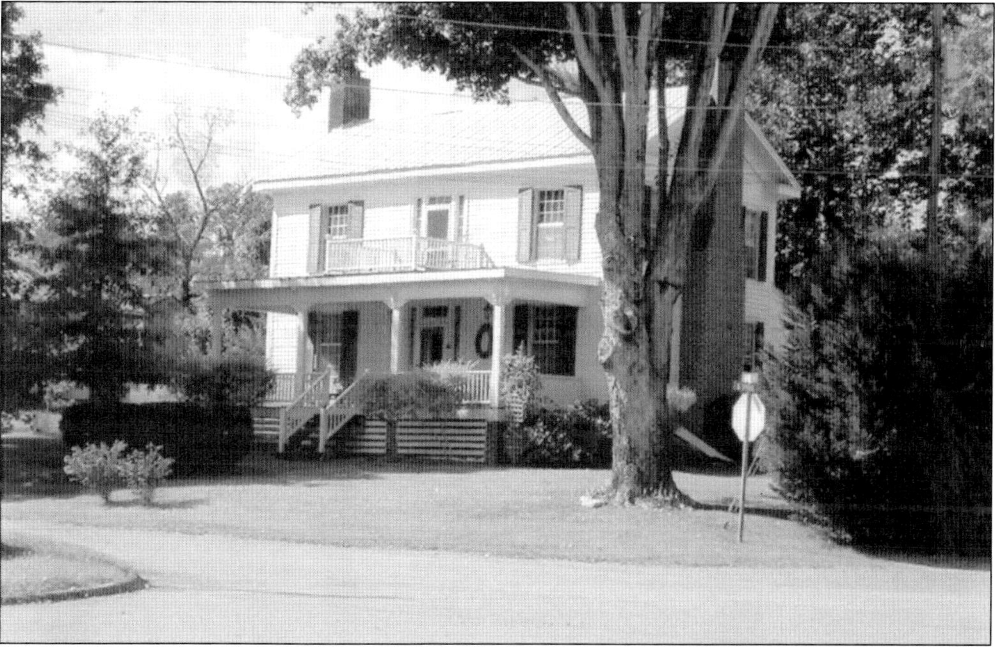

MOSHEIM. This historic home is located in the town of Mosheim in Greene County. According to local historian Sylvia Bright, it was used as the general's headquarters and a hospital during the Civil War. When a bank was constructed across the street, the contractors found bones from limbs of bodies. The home was built in the early 1800s. (Courtesy of Sylvia Bright.)

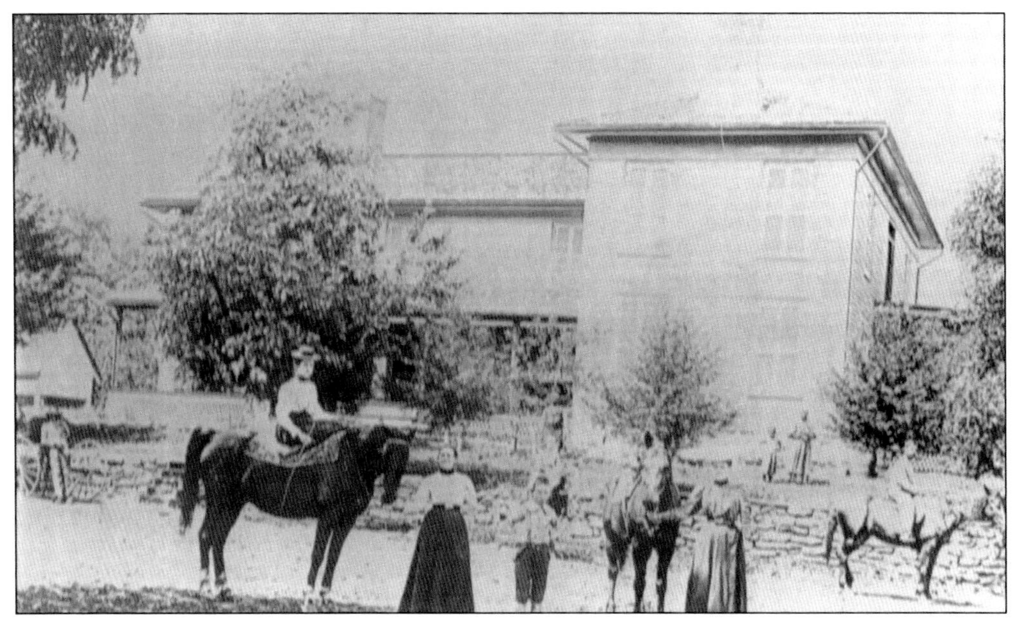

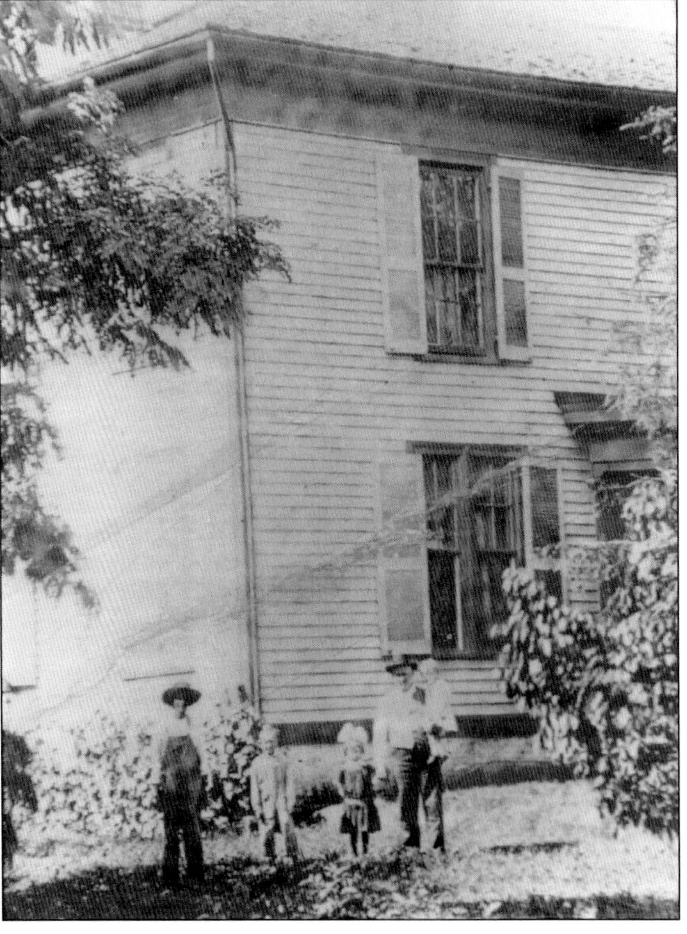

Allen-Birdwell House. Still Hollow Farm, which features the Allen-Birdwell House, was founded in 1857 by James Allen along the Nolichucky River. Allen was the son of Daniel Allen, a friend of Pres. Andrew Johnson. The white farmhouse was built in 1865 and serves as the center of the 176-acre farm. The domestic complex is comprised of the house, well house, and a smokehouse. James Allen Jr. acquired the farm in 1885, and in 1952, George Leo Birdwell, his wife's nephew, obtained the property. The active farm continues to produce tobacco and cattle, as well as corn and freshwater prawns. During the 21st century, the site has also welcomed visitors for tours and special events. (Both, courtesy of the Greeneville Greene County History Museum.)

Eight

Rogersville and Hawkins County

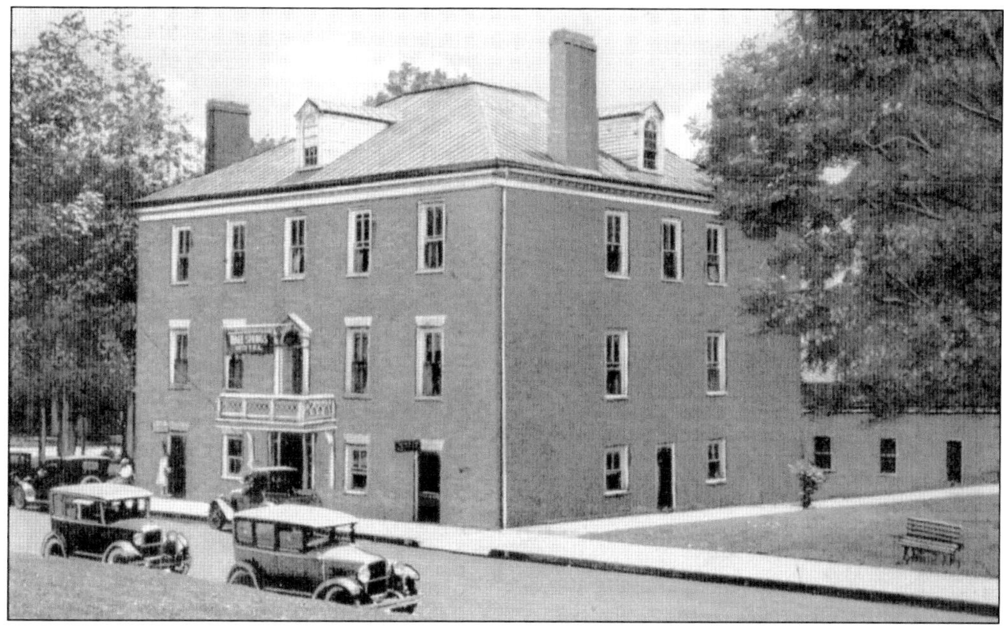

Hale Springs Inn. John A. McKinney built the Hale Springs Inn in 1824. During the 19th century, the inn played host to many famous individuals, including US presidents Andrew Jackson, James K. Polk, and Andrew Johnson. Union soldiers occupied the hotel during the Civil War. Carl and Janet Netherland-Brown purchased and renovated it in 1982, and in 2003, the Rogersville Heritage Association purchased it. (Courtesy of the Rogersville Heritage Association.)

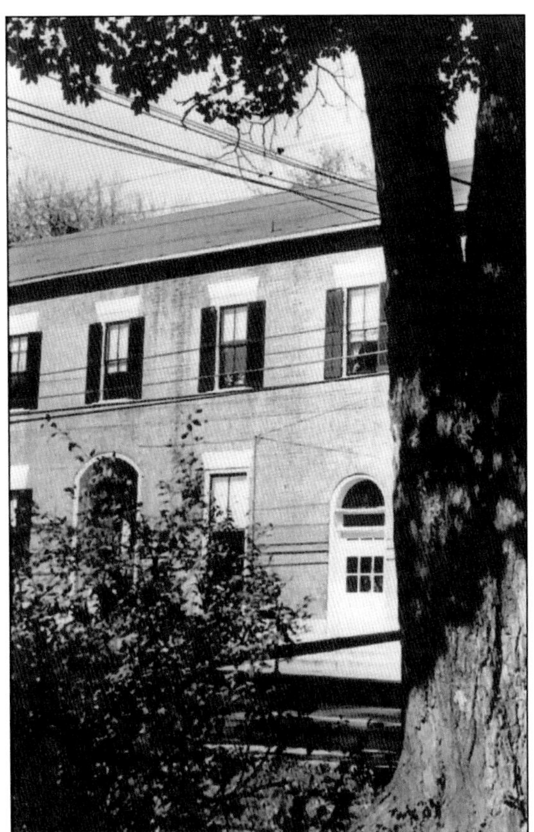

KYLE HOUSE. The Kyle House was originally built as a log structure in the early 19th century on Main Street. Eventually, William Simpson built the brick Federal-style building standing here today. The property, featuring 22 rooms, eventually fell into the hands of Gale P. Kyle, who bought the home in 1905. The building has served as a home, boardinghouse, and various businesses. (Courtesy of the Rogersville Heritage Association.)

SMITH HOUSE. The simple yet elegant Smith House is one of the oldest homes along Rogersville's Main Street. It was built by William Kenner in 1824 and features a large hedge out front. It was an inn on the Great Stage Road that cut through town. Absalom Kyle operated the inn, and the Kyle and Smith families have owned the two-story property ever since. (Courtesy of the Rogersville Heritage Association.)

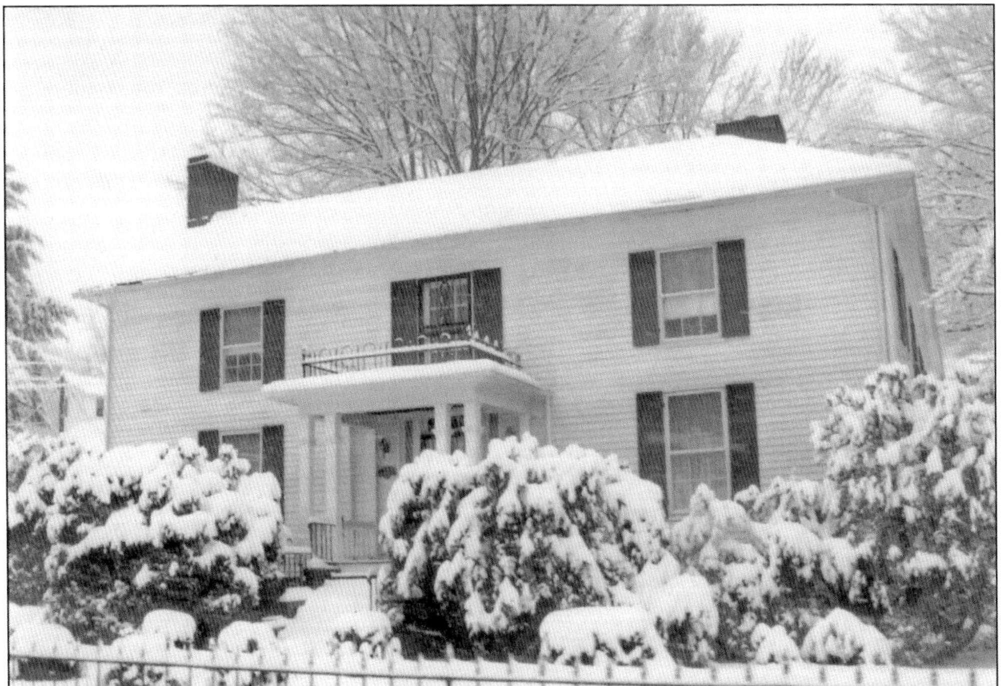

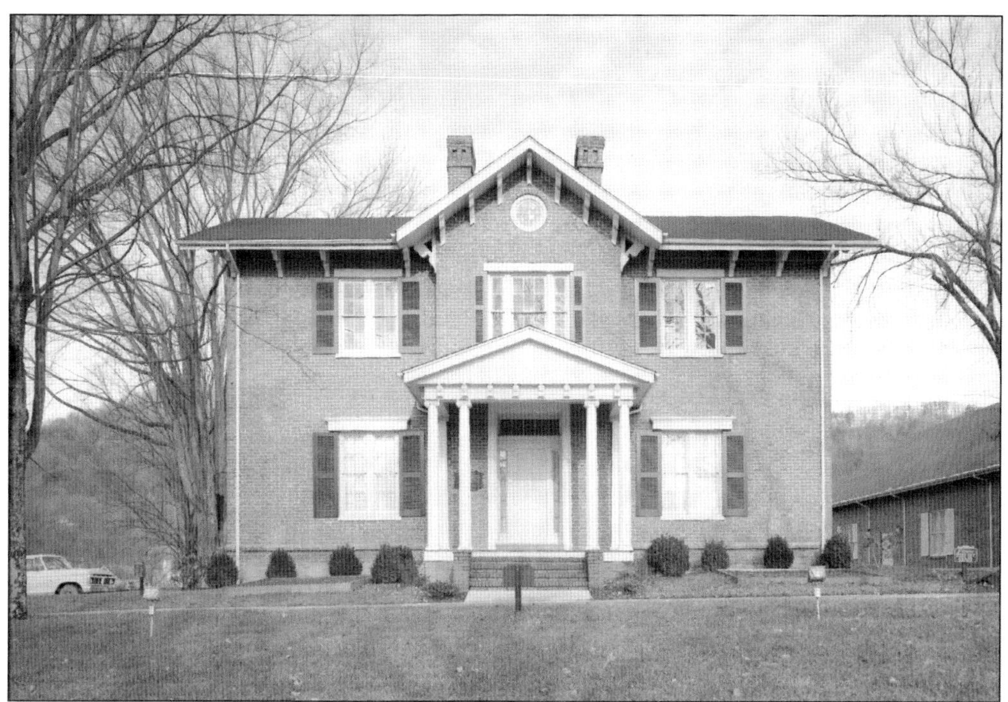

Clay-Kenner House. The impressive Clay-Kenner House was constructed around 1835 along Main Street in Rogersville. It was built on land that once belonged to pioneer Thomas Amis. It passed along to the Mitchell, McKinney, Bynum, Clay, and Kenner families. During the Civil War, the owners stored valuable items in a hidden room in the home. According to the Historic American Buildings Survey, the residence is an excellent example of early Italianate or "bracketed" architecture in Tennessee. The house is noted for its spiral staircase, plaster ceiling moldings, marble and wood mantels, jib windows, spacious rooms, and its elaborate built-in bookcases and cabinets, the survey states. (Both, courtesy of the Library of Congress.)

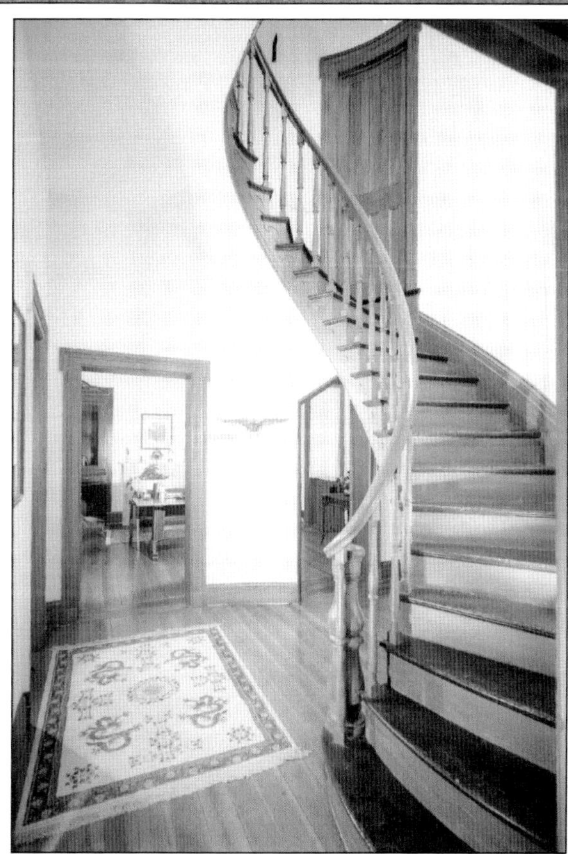

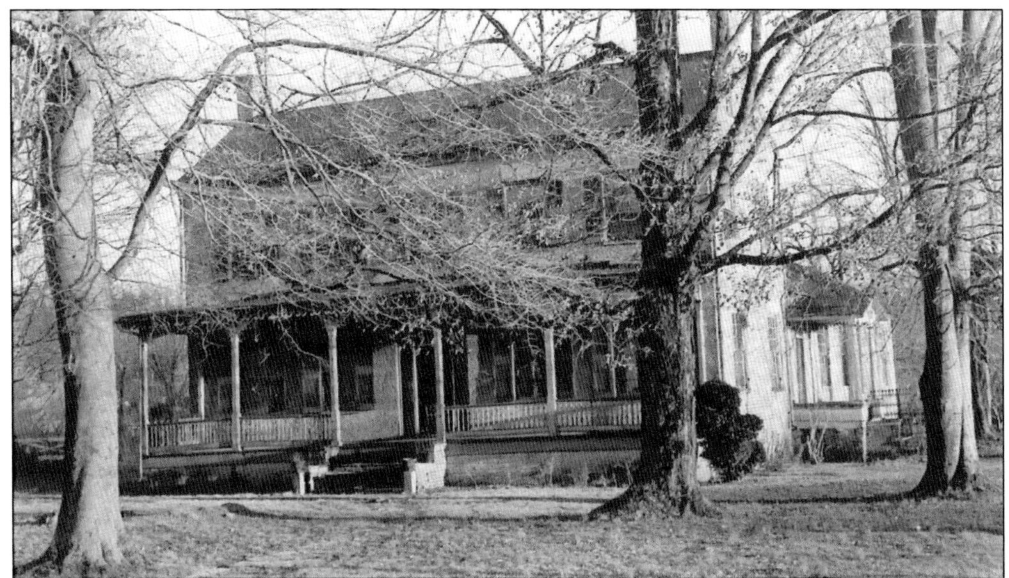

Rosemont. Rosemont is a beautiful two-story brick home sitting far back along Rogersville's Main Street. The home, built in 1842 by John McKinney for his daughter Susan and her husband, John Netherland, features an impressive, ornate one-story porch. According to historians, there have been gardens on the property in the past. Netherland, an attorney and senator, ran unsuccessfully for governor of Tennessee in 1860. (Courtesy of the Rogersville Heritage Association.)

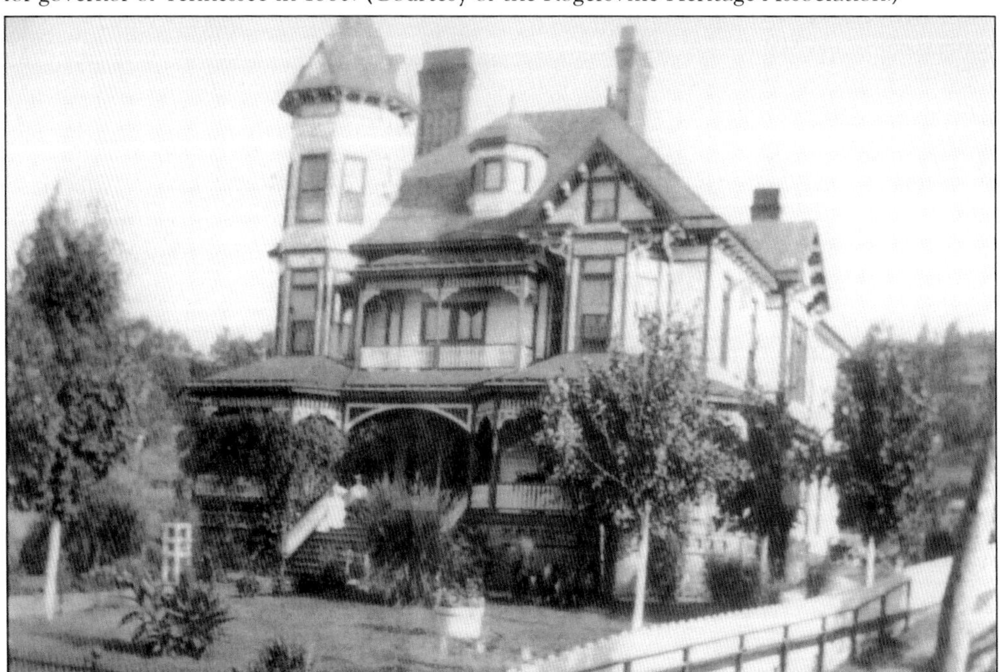

Spears House. The Spears House was built in 1895 on Broadway Street in Rogersville. The family lived in the home while their children attended school. When their education was complete, the family moved. They sold the house to W.D. and Mary Kenner, who lived in it until it burned in 1929. The site was then divided into three lots, on which homes were then constructed. (Courtesy of the Rogersville Heritage Association.)

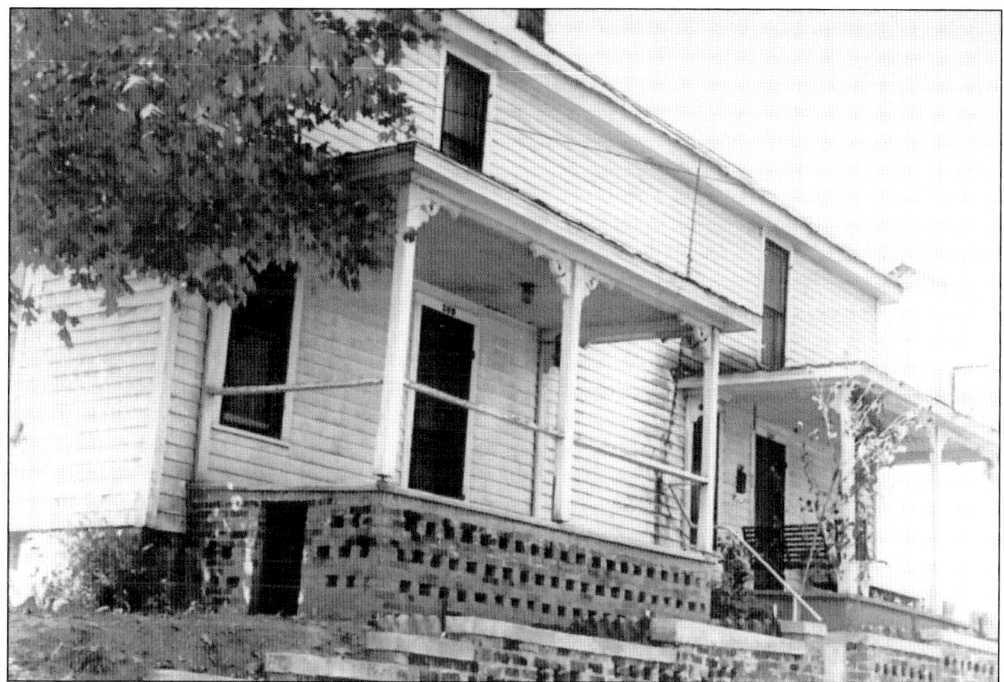

Pettibone Doublehouse. The Pettibone Doublehouse on South Rogers Street in Rogersville is also known as the Old Tavern House. This double house, constructed about 1795, is built of logs under the clapboard exterior and was connected to the original Rogers Tavern. (Courtesy of the Rogersville Heritage Association.)

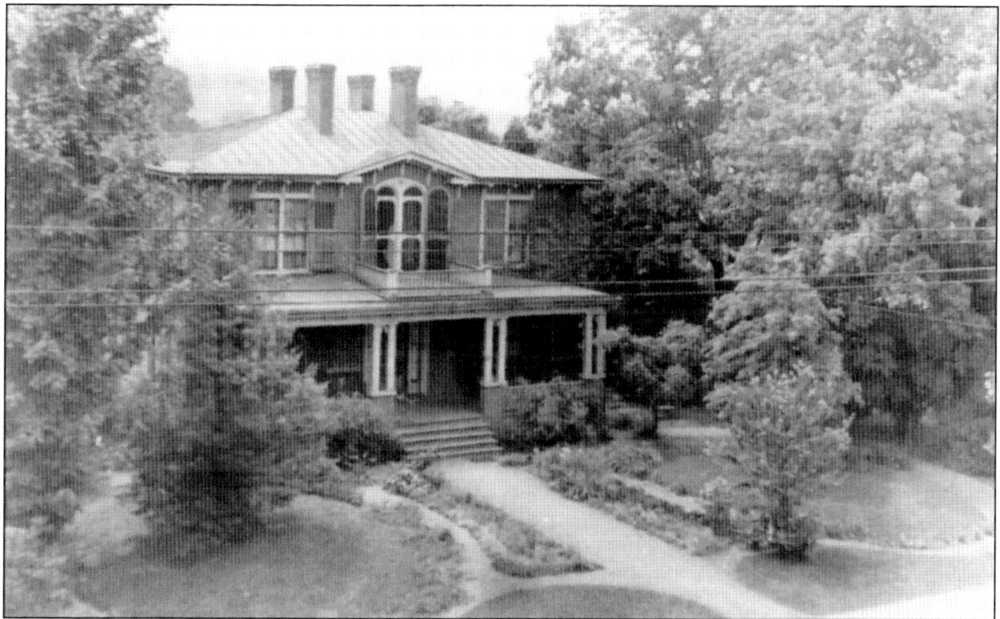

Miller House. The Miller House was built along Main Street in Rogersville during the 19th century. Jacob Eastman Miller, who owned a hospital, bought the home in 1896. He willed the house to Hal E. Portrum, an attorney. He died in 1949, and his wife lived there until her death in 1957. It was sold to a bank in 1957 and torn down. (Courtesy of the Rogersville Heritage Association.)

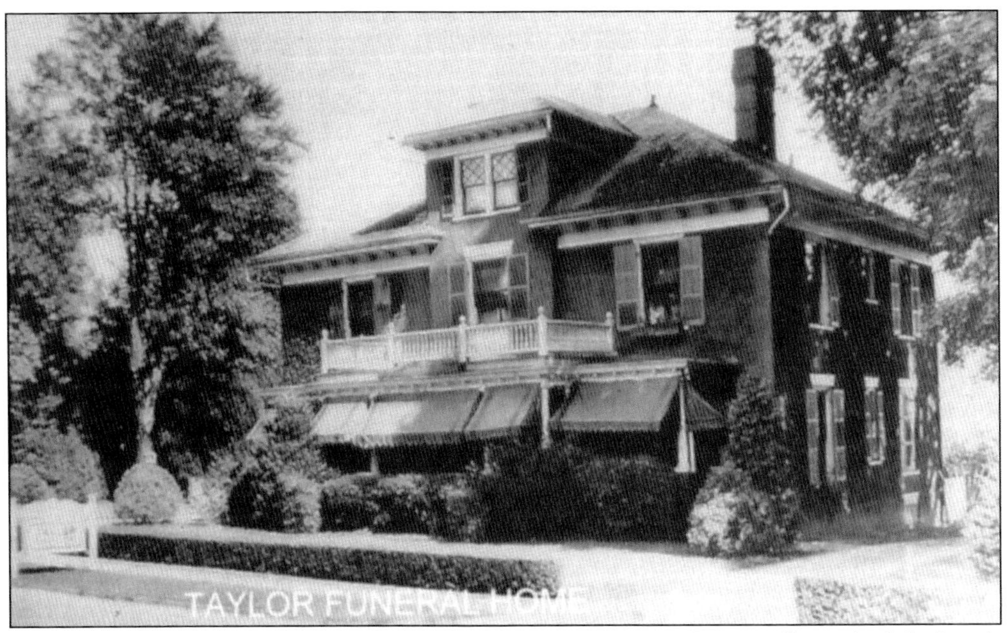

HEISKELL HOME. The grand brick home at 324 West Main Street in Rogersville was built by Joseph Brown Heiskell in 1852. Heiskell was a prominent lawyer, Confederate supporter, and state senator. In 1857, the McKinney family bought the house. By the 20th century, it became a funeral home; today, it is once again a private residence. (Courtesy of the Rogersville Heritage Association.)

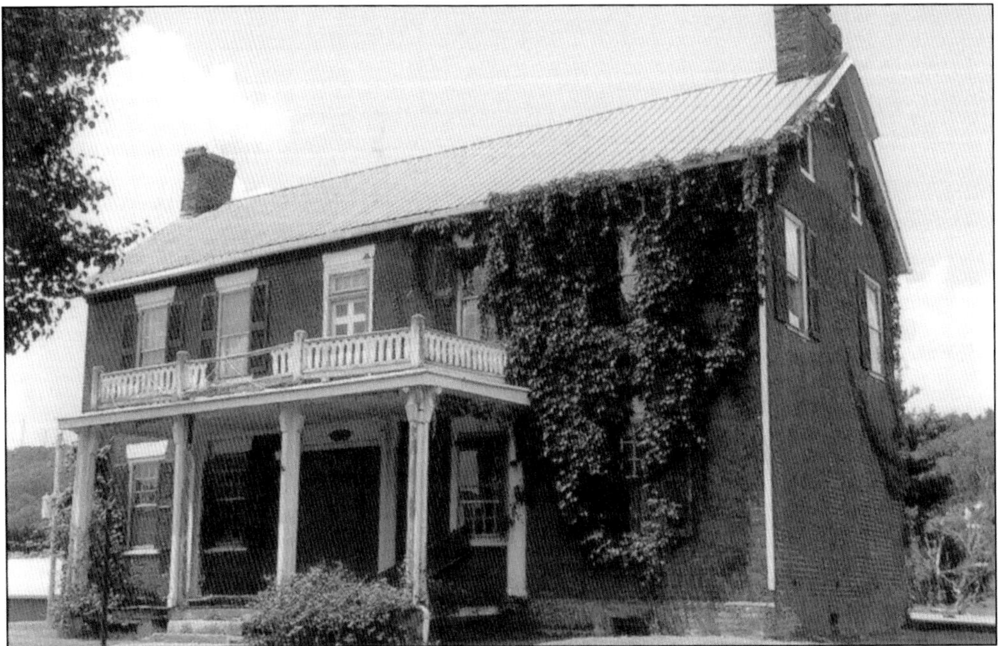

BLUE SPRINGS. The recently abandoned Blue Springs House is located on Main Street in Rogersville. A log home was originally constructed on the property. The brick home now standing was eventually built. The log home was removed in 2008. Few details are available on this home. (Courtesy of the Rogersville Heritage Association.)

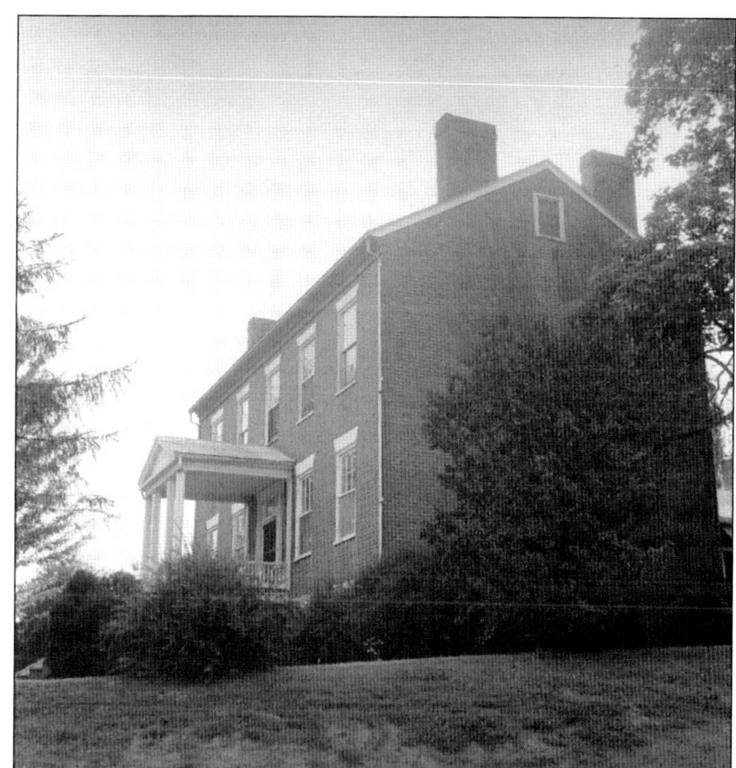

STAGECOACH INN. The Stage Coach Inn was built about 1840 just west of Rogersville along present-day US Highway 11W. It stood for more than 100 years and welcomed guests who traveled by stagecoach. It featured large rooms with fireplaces. The large brick residence was torn down by Burlington Industries to build a plant in the early 1970s. (Courtesy of the Tennessee State Library and Archives.)

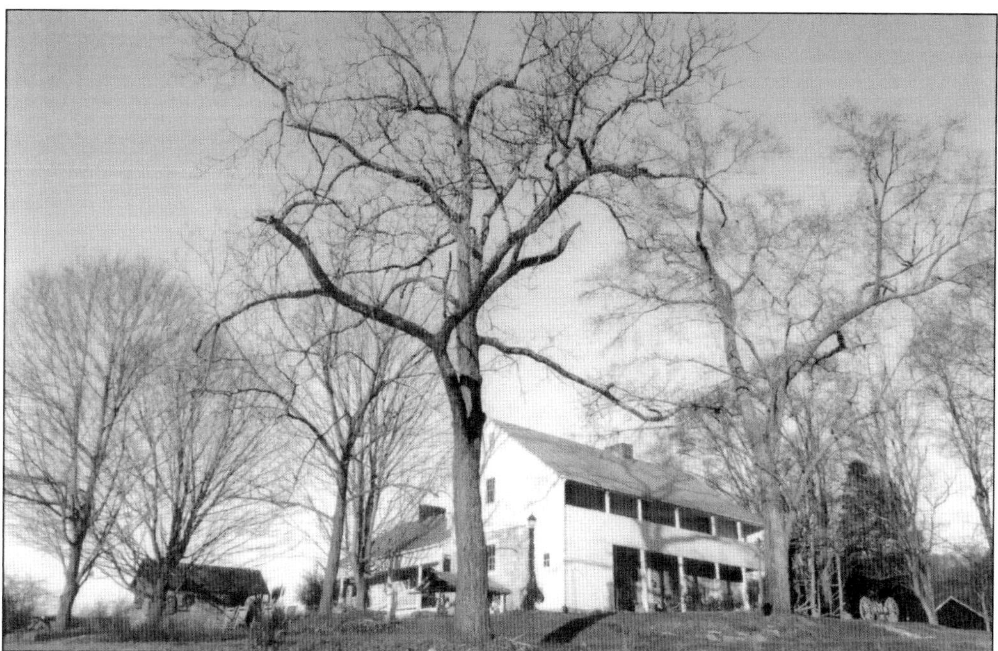

AMIS HOUSE. The Amis House is a pioneer settlement near Rogersville, Tennessee. It was built about 1780 by Thomas Amis, the father-in-law of Rogersville founder Joseph Rogers. In addition to his stone house, Amis developed a tavern, general store, distillery, sawmill, and a gristmill. (Courtesy of Wendy Amis Jacobs.)

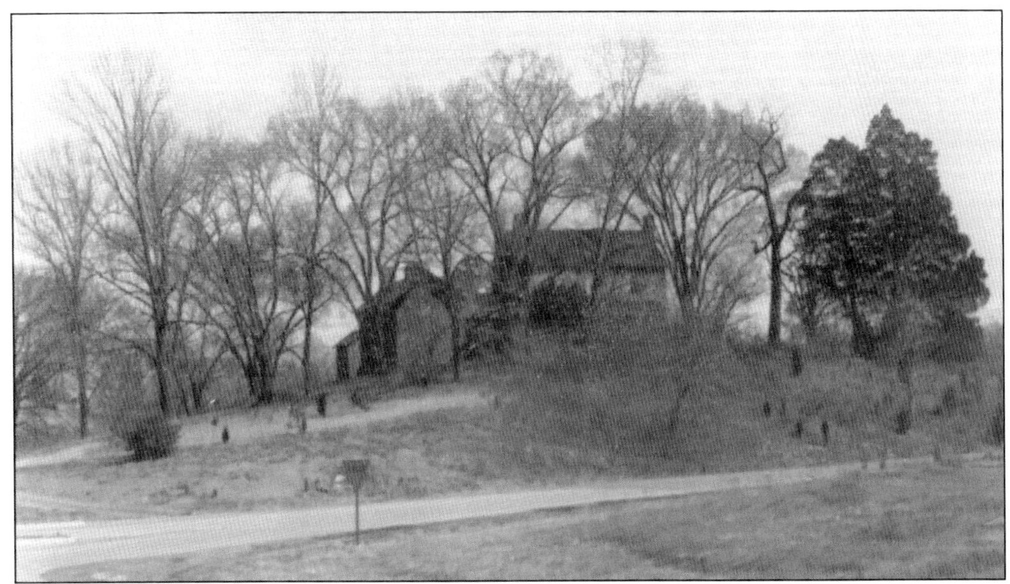

Stony Point. Stony Point mansion near Surgoinsville may be Tennessee's oldest brick house. It was built in 1780 by William Armstrong III. The front of the mansion is of Georgian architecture and originally included five rooms. By 1850, Armstrong built a Federal-style addition on the rear of the home. (Courtesy of the City of Kingsport Archives.)

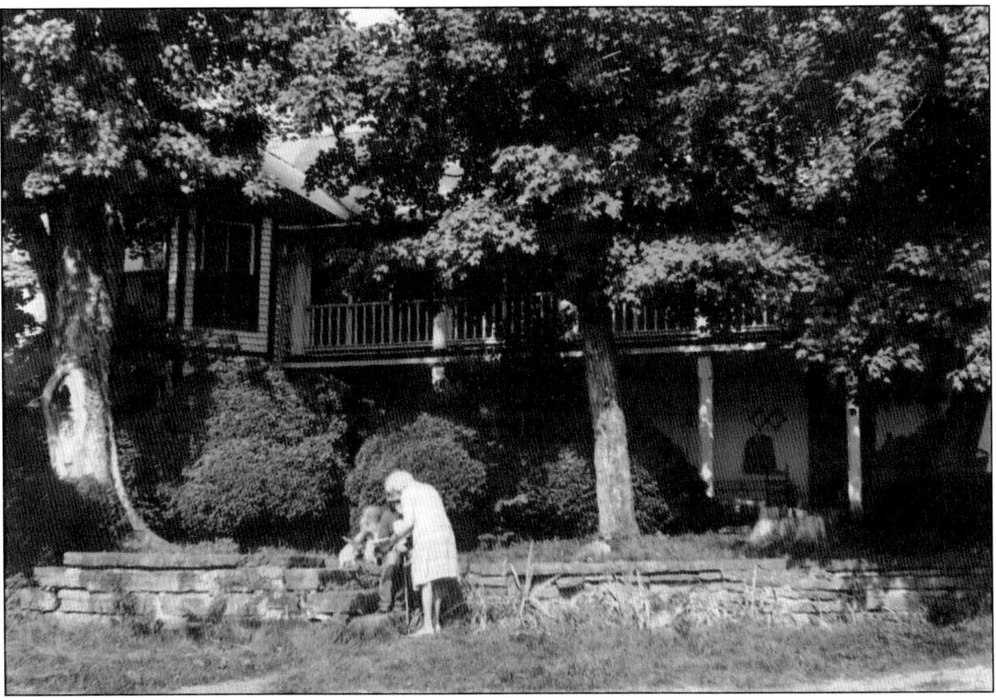

Long Meadow. The Long Meadow Farm is one of the oldest in Tennessee. William Young built a log cabin here in 1763 and named it Long Meadow because of the three-mile-long meadow in front of the home. During its early years, many notable pioneers visited the prominent Young family, including Davy Crockett and John Sevier. The farm now features a beautiful two-story mansion. (Courtesy of the Tennessee Historical Commission.)

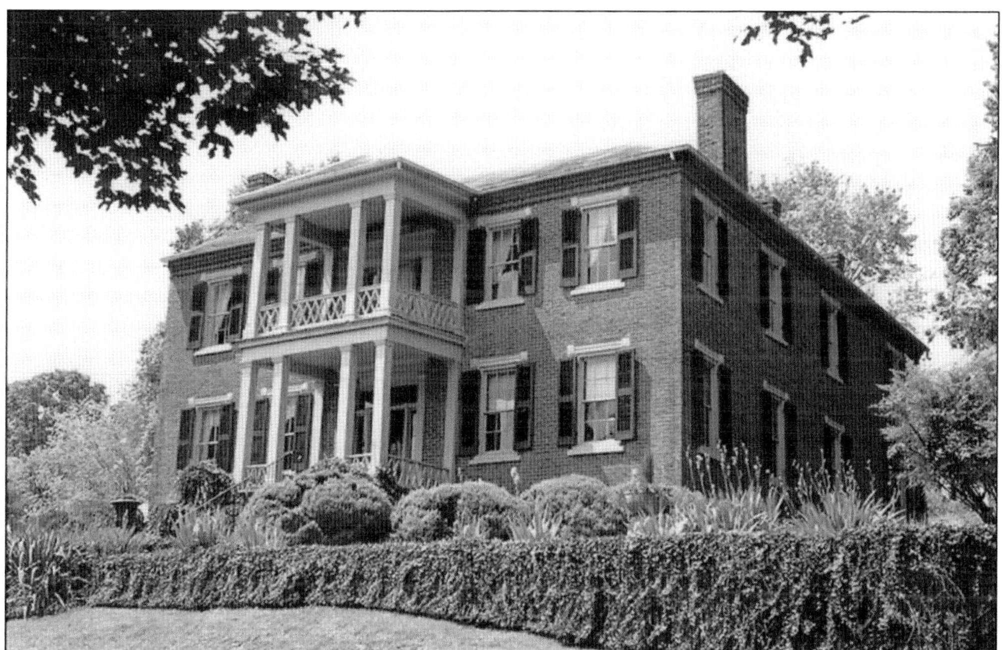

Hord House. The Hord House, also known as New Canton Plantation, was built prior to the Civil War in the Church Hill community. The home was likely built by slaves in 1840 for the prominent Eldridge Hord family. A gristmill was also built on the property. There was also a general store and blacksmiths shop. (Courtesy of Angela Birdsong.)

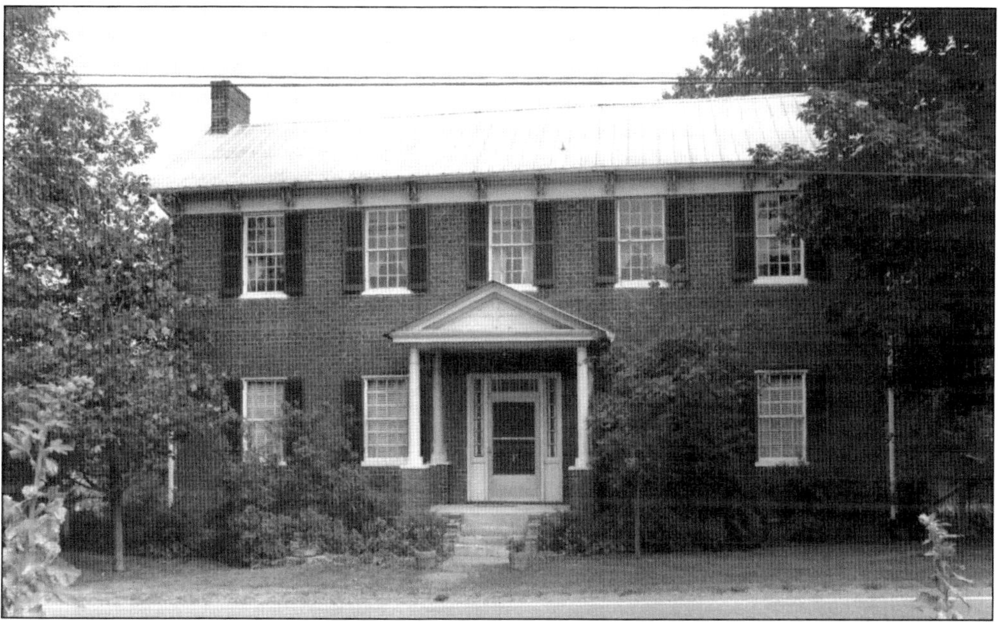

Fudge Farm. Fudge Farm, situated near Surgoinsville, was founded in 1852 by Conrad Fudge. The original farm has now been subdivided into a handful of farms. The main house, a two-story brick residence, was built in the 1850s. It includes an added front porch and a clapboard one-story addition. The farm also includes a log granary, barn, smokehouse, and an original slave quarters. (Courtesy of the Tennessee Historical Commission.)

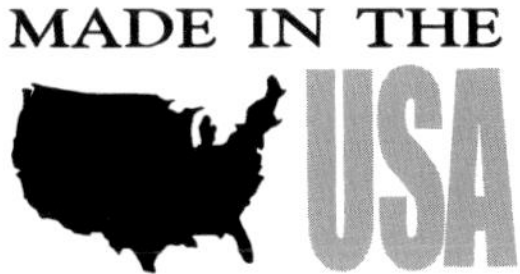

MADE IN THE
USA